DATE DUE

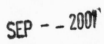
SEP - - 2001

The Evidence
Against Her

The Evidence Against Her

A NOVEL BY

Robb Forman Dew

Little, Brown and Company

BOSTON   NEW YORK   LONDON

First Edition

The characters and events in this book are fictitious.
Any similarity to real persons, living or dead,
is coincidental and not intended by the author.

For information on Time Warner Trade Publishing's
online publishing program, visit www.ipublish.com.

Library of Congress Cataloging-in-Publication Data

Dew, Robb Forman.
    The evidence against her : a novel / Robb Forman Dew. — 1st ed.
        p.   cm.
    ISBN 0-316-89019-7
    1. Ohio — Fiction.   2. Triangles (Interpersonal relations) — Fiction.   I. Title.

PS3554.E9288 E95 2001
813'.54 — dc21   2001029101

10 9 8 7 6 5 4 3 2 1

Book design by Robert G. Lowe

Q-FF

Printed in the United States of America

For Charles, always . . .

And in memory of
Bernice Martin Forman,
John Crowe Ransom,
and Robb Reavill Ransom

Part One

Chapter One

THERE ARE any number of villages, small towns, and even cities of some size to which no one ever goes except on purpose. There are only travelers on business of one sort or another, personal or professional, who arrive without any inclination to dally, or to dawdle, or to daydream. And yet, almost always in these obscure precincts there is a fine grassy park, a statue, perhaps, and benches placed under tall old spreading trees and planted around with unexceptional seasonal flowers, petunias or geraniums or chrysanthemums in all likelihood, or possibly no more than a tidy patch of English ivy. A good many visitors have sat on such benches for a moment or two, under no burden to take account of their surroundings, under no obligation to enjoy themselves. A stranger to such a place may settle for longer than intended, losing track of the time altogether — slouching a bit against the wooden slats, stretching an arm along the back of the bench, and enjoying the sun on a nice day, com-

fortably oblivious to passersby and unself-consciously relaxed —
without assuming the covertly alert, defensive, nearly apologetic
posture of a tourist.

By and large these towns are middling to small, and are never
on either coast or even any famous body of water, such as a
good-sized lake or major river. These are communities that lie
geographically and culturally in unremarkable locales: no towering mountains, no breathtaking sweep of deep valleys, no
overwhelming or catastrophic history particular only to that
place. In fact, with only a few exceptions, these unrenowned
districts are all villages, towns, or small cities exactly like Washburn, Ohio, about which people are incurious, requiring only
the information that it is approximately forty-five miles east of
Columbus.

As it happens, Monument Square in the town of Washburn
is not four sided but hexagonal and was a gift to the city from
the Washburn Ladies Monument Society, ceded to the town simultaneously at the unveiling and dedication of the Civil War
monument on July 4, 1877. The monument itself is a life-size
statue of a Union soldier at parade rest, gazing southward from
his perch atop a thirty foot fluted granite column, the pediment
of which is over twelve feet high. Altogether the monument
stands nearly fifty feet, and on its west face is the inscription:

OUR COUNTRY!
BY THAT DREAD NAME
WE WAVE THE SWORD ON HIGH,
AND SWEAR FOR HER TO LIVE
FOR HER TO DIE.
— *Campbell*

Within a year of the dedication ceremony the common idea among the citizens of Washburn was that the stonecutter — imported all the way from Philadelphia, hurrying the work, eager to catch the train, and possibly with a few too many glasses of beer under his belt — had chiseled into that smooth granite the mistake "dread name" as opposed to "dear name."

In the spring of 1882, Leo Scofield, soon after he and his brothers had cleared the woods and begun construction of their houses on the north side of the square, had written to Mrs. Dowd, who commissioned the statue but who had moved back to Philadelphia soon after its unveiling, to inquire if he might have the mistaken inscription altered at his own expense. He had attempted to cast his offer along the lines of being an act of gratitude for her generous gift, but Leo was only thirty-one years old then, a young man still, without much good sense. He was enormously pleased by the largesse of his idea — which had occurred to him one day out of the blue — and delighted that he finally had the wherewithal to make such an offer. A slightly self-congratulatory air tinged the tactlessly exuberant wording of his letter, and he was brought up short by her reply:

. . . furthermore, I shall arrange to have the statue removed piece by piece if need be, as it is I who pays out the money each year for its upkeep, should the inscription in any way be altered. I never shall believe in all the days left to me that the preservation of the Union was worth the price of the good life of my dear husband, Colonel Marcus Dowd, who left his post as President of Harcourt Lees College to head Company A. He died at Petersburg. The statue was undertaken at my instigation only as an honor to him. I shall live with nothing more than despair and contempt for this Union and Mr. Lincoln all the rest of my life. As my children do not share my sentiments in every respect, however, I have made arrangements to fund the maintenance of the monument and the fenced area of its surround. I have engaged a Mr. Olwin Grant who lives out Coshocton Road as a caretaker, and any further questions you may address to him. I implore you, Mr. Scofield, not to raise this matter to me again.

Leo spent several long evenings sitting in the square, contemplating that handsome statue, which towered over the young trees installed by the Marshal County Ladies Garden Club. It was his first inkling of the fickleness of legend, the ease with which one is misled by myth. He wrote a letter of deep and sincere apology but did not hear again from Mrs. Marcus Dowd, nor had he expected to.

He was young and perhaps still a little brash, but he was not an insensitive man, and he applied this glimpse of the possible effect of grief to his own circumstances, admonishing himself to take all the good fortune of his business and his marriage much less for granted. The spirit of expansiveness that had characterized his outlook up until the receipt of that letter was checked somewhat over the year that followed, and as his business ventures grew increasingly complicated, as his house took shape day by day, as his infatuation with his new wife inevitably grew more complex and profound, he became a man of a fairly solemn nature.

The three houses built just north of Monument Square in the early 1880s for Leo, John, and George Scofield fronted on a semicircular drive and shallow common ground that in the summer became a crescent of feathery grass that bent in bright green ripples across the lawn in the slightest breeze. In time the grass at the inner curve of the drive gave way to a golden velvet moss under the elms as the trees matured and produced heavy shade all summer long.

The houses were comfortable though not grand. They were well built and nicely spaced, one from the other, and for a number of years those three south-facing houses marked the northernmost edge of the town of Washburn, Ohio. During the several years the houses were under construction, and long after, the residential property of those three brothers was known all over town simply as Scofields, whereas the twenty-odd buildings comprising the flourishing engine-manufacturing business of Scofields & Company, begun as no more than a foundry in 1830 by Leo's grandfather, had for some time been referred to merely as the Company.

The second Sunday of September 1888, on either side of a muddy wagon track that led into the east yard of his new house, Leo Scofield, at age thirty-seven, planted eight pairs of cultivated catalpa saplings. Six days later, on Saturday the fifteenth, there occurred the unusual incident of the births — all within a twelve-hour span — of his first and his brother John's second child — a daughter and son respectively — and of the third child of Daniel Butler, a good friend and pastor of the Methodist church. John and Lillian Scofield's first child, Harold, born in 1883, had died before he was a year old, so the Scofields' compound had been childless for some time.

Some years earlier Leo had given up the idea that he and his wife, Audra, would have children. His wife was twenty-nine years old with this fourth pregnancy, and through the early months they both had dreaded and expected another miscarriage. They had been married for eight years when Lily was born. The planting of those young catalpa trees was only a co-incidence, of course; Leo hadn't intended any sort of commem-oration, but in spite of himself he developed a superstitious interest in the welfare of those trees. He had started them himself from seed six years earlier, and they were just barely established enough to transplant. Several days after his daughter's birth, when it was clear she and his wife and the other mothers and babies were thriving, his brother John and he walked the lane he had created, staking the saplings when necessary to guide them straight.

"And on the ides of the month, John," Leo said. "It's an amazing thing! All the Scofields are born on the ides of the month." Leo's birthday was March fifteenth, and his youngest brother George's was the fifteenth of October. John's birthday was February fifth, when he would turn thirty.

"Well, but this is September, Leo. The ides of the month was on Thursday. On the thirteenth, this month." But Leo wasn't paying close attention, and John himself, not born on the ides, was just as happy to be a little disburdened of "Scofieldness." He followed along, helping his brother. "But this is really some-thing, isn't it, Leo?" John said. "Here we are. Two *papas*. Only three days ago, Leo — three *days* ago! — we were . . . fancy-free. We were just *not* papas."

Leo glanced sharply at John but didn't reply for a moment. John was a tall, elegant figure among the little sloping trees, which were leaning this way and that. Leo himself was one of those men no more than average height who are somehow imposing because they possess an inherent certainty, a lack of hesitancy, an easy as-sumption of authority. "No, you're right about that, John. You're right about that. Three days ago we were only two *husbands.*"

John had squatted to secure the burlap around the spindly trunk of one of those young trees, and he aimed a considering look Leo's way and finally grinned, acknowledging the edge of chastisement in his brother's voice and feeling a genuine joyousness spike through him at all his sudden connection to the wide world. "Ah, Leo. Don't you think this'll make a good husband of me? Don't you imagine I get a clean slate now? The first baby . . . Leo, that nearly killed Lillian. And me, too." John's ebullience abruptly fell away. "But Lillian was just . . . It was like she had broken. That was it. That was what she must have been feeling," he mused. "But I was so stupid. I was just scared to death. I didn't know what it took . . . That poor little boy. Poor Harold! I couldn't *do* anything to help, though, Leo! It nearly drove me crazy to see Lillian so sad.

"But this one's so . . . he's so *lively,* Leo. Why, he hardly stays still a minute. Healthy as a horse! And I haven't even raised a glass to toast their health. I haven't touched a drop, Leo. And I won't. I won't." Then John fell back into his usual wry tone, which signified that it was at the listener's own peril to take him entirely seriously. "I'll start all over with the lovely Lillian. And I can, you know. Because at least *she* loves me more than you do," he said, but with a lilting, teasing cadence.

Leo watched John a moment as he stooped to hammer in a stake at an angle that would pull the rope tight, and he thought that even in so small a task his brother was graceful in the uncommon way with which he was at ease in his own body. "There isn't anyone in the world who doesn't love you, John. But that might not be such a good thing," he said, and he was quite serious.

"You're harder on me than anyone, Leo. Even Dan Butler's not so stern!" John straightened up and exhaled a short laugh, leaning his head back to take in the pale sky. "You'll have to go a little easy on me, you know. I've got to get used to it, still! It's wonderful that they're all healthy. As strong as can be. Lillian . . . and Audra and Martha Butler . . . everyone doing so well. *All* of them," he said. "I can hardly believe it!" They moved along, carefully wrapping the tender trunks before they looped and staked the guide ropes.

Leo had left the planting late because it had been an edgy summer and so dry that he had to haul water until the middle of November to irrigate that double row of saplings. The memory of June, July, and August merged into a blur of heat. The days had stretched out dry and hot, eventually falling into unsettling yellow green evenings preceding night after night of crackling thunder and hailstorms that lingered over the town with great bluster but produced very little measurable rainfall.

It had been a season that was not much good for planting, and a season that had produced a sort of communal unease, transforming the nearly simultaneous births in mid-September of Lillian Marshal Scofield, Warren Leonard Scofield, and Robert Crane Butler into an event that seemed less remarkable than inevitable. And the unwavering alliance of those three children took on the same quality of inevitability. Lily and Robert and Warren were rarely apart from one another during all the waking hours of their early youth.

But during the first months following his daughter's birth, when the heat finally loosened its grip and September led into one of those autumns of rare clarity in which everything seems to be in perfect balance, Leo made grand plans for his garden. In late November he stood in the wagon yard on a chilly but glorious day so dazzlingly clear that the air itself was charged with a blue translucent brilliance. He stood still and imagined the plot transformed. He became lost in the idea of abundant flowers, blooming bushes, towering trees.

The catalpas stood in fragile regulation, spare sticks once their leaves had dropped. They looked forlornly tenuous on the clear-cut acreage where the Scofield brothers had built their three houses. But by the time Lily was seven months old the following spring and those shoulder-high saplings finally budded and then leafed out, Leo privately exulted at their survival of the unusually brutal, snowless winter.

Leo Scofield was a good businessman, always a little skeptical, a trifle suspicious by nature. But he wasn't at all prone to melancholy; his brooding followed a more pragmatic course — he might fret persistently, for instance, about a minor innovation to a Scofield engine or an antiquated valve design. But it was quite in character, in late April of 1889, when he was a year closer to forty years old than to thirty-five, that the notion of the future flying toward him was only exhilarating. He wasn't at all troubled by the idea of his own mortality. He walked the rutted track between those newly planted trees and imagined his daughter's wedding procession making its way along a raked gravel avenue beneath the catalpas' eventual leafy canopy under an overarching clear blue sky.

And during the years of Lily's childhood it was a great pleasure for him on the hottest summer days to sit in his fledgling garden, stunned by the Ohio heat and the salty yellow scent of cut grass, with her light, fluting voice ringing out above her playmates' as she directed her cousin, Warren, and little Robert Butler in some game she had devised.

Leo was continually surprised by and enamored of the solace of the domesticity he had happened into, and in a span of twenty years he transformed that scrubby patch of land into his idea of a replica of an English garden made up entirely of plants native to Ohio. The catalpa trees, however, didn't mature exactly as he had hoped. In fact, he realized three years too late that he had intended to plant an avenue of yellow poplars — stately, flowering trees known locally as tulip trees. But when he had firmly fixed on the idea of his garden, had planned the east yard entrance, and had described the tree he had in mind, asking around town where he might find it, it was probably in the description of the tree's flowers that he had gone wrong. Leo never gave up the private notion, however, that the misinformation he had received was purposeful, that there might be someone in the world who was amused at his expense, and with solicitous pruning he coaxed the catalpas to assume a more elegant shape than was their unbridled inclination.

As the years passed, Leo came to like the pungency of a blooming catalpa, which was heavily sweet but elusive at a distance, drifting over the garden unexpectedly. He admired the tree's soft green, heart-shaped leaves, its abundantly frilled flowers, as showy as a flock of tropical birds in the rolling landscape of central Ohio. Daniel Butler, who had done missionary work in Brazil and Cuba, said that in midsummer, when the vining trumpet creeper overran the arbor, dripping with deep-throated red-orange blossoms, the entire garden took on a look of the tropics. Leo had nurtured that flowering vine from a single cutting he had taken from a plant growing on a pasture fence — just a slip of stem cut on the diagonal and wrapped in a handkerchief he had moistened in the ditch alongside the road. The afternoon he had rounded a bend and come upon the glorious trumpet vine cascading over an unpainted board fence, he had paused for a long time before he had stooped to dampen his clean handkerchief in the brackish water. He was careful of his dignity, and his fascination with and cultivation of his flower garden was the only frivolity he allowed himself.

Even though Leo had forced the sturdy trunks of the catalpas to extend straight up about nine feet before they branched, each tree assumed the self-contained shape of a softened, rounded obelisk. Their crowns didn't form the leafy vault he had hoped for — the branches didn't *arch,* didn't intermingle overhead, really, as he had envisioned. And each year, when the catalpas' fringed and ruffling flowers bloomed and produced their startlingly phallic, cigar-brown fruit, and when those flowers began to shed in stringy drifts of petals and oily pollen so that guests arrived showered with residue from the burgeoning branches, Audra would declare that the trees should be taken out.

"They're a nuisance, Leo. I always think that if you want a flowering tree you can't go wrong with a dogwood. Dogwoods won't get so tall, of course, but they are such beautiful trees. And more restrained when they're in bloom. Oh, and sometimes in the spring when the dogwoods bloom early, it looks to me like the whole tree has burst into white lace." But the catalpa trees remained, and Leo's garden and the wide yards of Scofields became the geographical context of the childhood of each of those three children born coincidentally on September 15, 1888.

Robert Butler was a ruddy, brown-haired child, and Warren Scofield, too, was sturdy and round limbed. They were little boys who seemed all of a piece, whereas Lily's pale, attenuated arms and legs, her fragile neck, her knobby wrists and ankles seemed flimsy, as if, in her always hectic activity, she might fly apart, although for a long time it was clearly Lily who was the center and star of that inseparable threesome. At four or five or six years old, Robert wouldn't have known how to articulate the impression that sometimes, in the blue or brassy light of any given day, a word Lily spoke — just the plain, flat sound of it — exploded cleanly into the moment, like a brilliant asterisk glinting through the atmosphere. Nor could he have explained that occasionally Lily's movements, a sweep of her arm, an abrupt turning of her head, would break through some ordinary instant with a flicker of blank white clarity.

And, of course, Robert had no way to know that his was a kind of perception lost to adults and older children. His mother was happier to see him only in Warren's company. Mrs. Butler didn't dislike Lily; it was only that it gave her a sense of satisfaction to see those two healthy boys absorbed entirely in the company of each other. Robert and Warren appeared to strike a natural balance between them that was disturbed when little Lily was with them, directing them to do this or that, dreaming up fantastic games with evolving rules that were played out for days at a time.

One summer afternoon Mrs. Butler was in the yard of the parsonage cutting flowers for a bouquet and inspecting the rosebushes for disease when the three children came tearing through the yard brandishing sticks, their heads wrapped turbanlike in white damask napkins, with Lily bringing up the rear, urging the boys on in her high-pitched voice. "Gallop, Warren! Gallop, Robert! We must not let them escape! We must run! We must run like the wind!"

Martha Butler's good mood was spoiled as she watched them race across the lawn and down the slope toward the creek. When she mentioned it to her husband that evening — mentioned that the two little boys never had a chance to play together without Lily — he wasn't interested, said he couldn't see what difference it made. And Martha herself couldn't puzzle out her objection, couldn't understand why their *threesomeness* disturbed her. "It isn't natural, somehow, Daniel," she said to her husband. "Three never works out. There's always someone left out. Though, I don't know, not with those three. . . . But it doesn't seem at all right . . . not *healthy* in some way. Well, I just don't know." And she let the subject drop.

But Robert's mother's censure emanating from the vicinity of the rosebushes that afternoon had overtaken and enveloped Lily as she herded their band onward, and she hesitated at the edge of the creek while the boys forged ahead. She was stricken for the first time in her life with self-consciousness. She unwrapped the napkin from around her head and was never again able to lose herself entirely in an imagined universe. She sometimes cringed in embarrassment when she remembered urging Robert and Warren to "run like the wind." She had only been eight years old, but for the rest of her life she could not forgive herself that moment of blatant melodrama.

Lily and Warren's uncle George returned from a business trip to New York one year with a remarkably fine set of marionette puppets for his niece and nephew's tenth birthday. George was an elusive and therefore romantic figure to the children and such a favorite of their parents because of his various endearing eccentricities that neither Leo and Audra nor Warren's parents, John and Lillian, let him know that such intricate toys were far too complicated for Lily and Warren. But as it turned out, the marionettes were immediately popular with Lily and Warren and Robert, too, and for the next five years or so they mounted numerous and increasingly elaborate shows. Robert wrote the plays, Warren took on the most difficult roles, and Lily kept everything organized and filled in wherever she was needed. All during their growing up, Lily relieved Robert and Warren of the effort of choreographing their own childhoods. Lily was forever keeping them from careening off on some tangent or another. It was clear to her that without her guidance they would not *progress.* And she loved Robert Butler always and thought of herself as one half of the whole of herself and her cousin Warren.

For Warren's part, his whole idea of himself until he was about eleven years old was as one third of this triumvirate. Answering Mrs. Butler's question, for instance, as to what the three of them had been up to all day, he knew instinctively to turn and weave all their disparate activities into a narrative that satisfied adults. Although he often interchanged the actions of any one of their threesome with those of another, he wasn't even aware of it; he was only reacting to some parent's slight uneasiness — only shifting the *details* of the truth to ensure serenity all around.

One afternoon when the three of them arrived at Robert's house dripping wet, Warren gave an enthusiastic account of his failed plan to build a fort and laboratory in the big low-branching cherry tree over the horse pond.

"A laboratory! Well, a laboratory. That's where so many of my canning jars have disappeared to, I guess!" Mrs. Butler said, but her initial alarm at the sight of them had softened. Later Robert reminded Warren that the whole thing had been Lily's idea. Robert was surprised that Warren had taken the credit, but Warren only looked at Robert, perplexed. Warren knew intuitively that Robert's mother would never have been pleased with the actual account of their afternoon's enterprise. Lily was their inspiration; Robert was their conscience; Warren was their ambassador to the outside world. So deeply was each child connected to the other two that each one's loyalty was unconsidered, their mutual devotion fundamental.

But as they grew older, and by the time they were putting on their puppet shows for children's birthdays and at the county fair, Robert himself was unable to recall or name the quicksilver charisma Lily possessed that had captured his sensibilities. As an adult, whenever he thought back about his childhood, he remembered Lily always in motion, full to the brim with ideas and energy, but he lost the ability to remember the incandescence with which she had imbued the long hours of his early days. And Warren, too, as he grew older, translated all the emotion of their passionate connection into a manageable version of nothing more than a warm childhood friendship. Only Lily, left behind at the age of twelve when the boys went off to boarding school, understood that it was she alone who was likely to lose the underpinnings of the pleasure of her life, and she was singleminded in her determination that nothing of the sort would happen.

Lillian Marshal Scofield and Robert Crane Butler were married in her father's garden in an extravagant ceremony on a very hot Saturday in the summer of 1913. In spite of the heat and a long dry spell that caused the broad catalpa leaves to lose their lazy flutter, to pucker and droop a bit; in spite of a succession of cloudless, dusty days that dulled the glisten of all the foliage in the garden, the wedding was as splendid as Leo Scofield had hoped it would be.

There is a way in which a town the size of Washburn, Ohio, with perhaps six thousand residents, comes to a collective judgment, and communally the town had become fond of Lily, who had been in residence all year round when she attended the Linus Gilchrest Institute for Girls. She was among them as she gradually lost her childhood look of frailty and took on a wiry athleticism. Nevertheless, even during her late adolescence, Lily was eclipsed by the celebrated beauty of her mother and aunt — the former Marshal sisters — and by her distinguished and handsome father, her two tall, striking uncles, and especially by her constant summer companions, Robert Butler and her astonishingly good-looking cousin Warren.

No one knew how or why Lily Scofield and Robert Butler decided, in December of 1912, that they would marry the following summer when he returned from New England, where he had gone to college. He had stayed on as an instructor at Harvard to continue his studies and to teach for several academic years. No one knew the details, but, on the other hand, no one was particularly surprised. Lily had gone east to college, too, to Mount Holyoke in western Massachusetts, but had been at home again for almost three years, courted by several hopeful suitors, and she was nearly twenty-five years old.

In fact, Robert had come home for a week that Christmas, and one morning he asked Lily to come along with him to Stradler's Men's Clothiers and help him select a gift for his father. He wanted to ask her advice about the right tack to take with a young woman he had seen a good deal of in Cambridge who was his good friend David Musgrave's sister. The weather was crisp but not cold for December, and Lily had on a dark green suit and a brimmed hat that dipped over her face so that Robert could only catch glimpses of her expression. She carried a small, sleek brown muff from which she withdrew one hand or the other to illustrate some point. The muff intrigued him, with Lily's pretty hands plunged into the brown fur, and then he caught sight of her wide orange-brown eyes under the hat brim and stopped still, putting his hand on her arm to make her hesitate. She turned back to glance at him, perplexed, peering out from under her dark, winged Scofield brows, which were so striking in contrast to the puff of bright blond Scofield hair beneath her hat. She was telling Robert all about her father and mother's recent trip to Chicago, where everything had gone amiss.

But Robert interrupted her. "Ah, well, Lily. Your father wouldn't care if he was stranded in the middle of a desert as long as your mother was with him. I've never known a man to admire his wife as much as your father admires your mother," Robert said. "With plenty of reason, of course," he added. "But I don't know when I've ever been in his company for very long without hearing him talk of those 'Marshal girls.' Of the day he first met your mother. Their 'blue gaze,' he calls it. I've always remembered that phrase."

Claire Musgrave had wide, sweet blue eyes. But as he gazed at Lily it suddenly seemed to him that there was no glance more engaging than Lily's warm, golden brown consideration. He was disconcerted for a moment thinking of himself and Claire Musgrave closed away together in a tall house somewhere in Cambridge or Boston while Lily carried on, both participating in and wryly observing the familiar life around her. He stood there with Lily and all at once found himself bereft at the idea of being always away from her.

"Why, Lily," he said, "Lily? I wonder if you'd ever think of marrying me?" Lily's expression was no longer vexed; she had assumed a placid look of waiting as she gave him her full attention. She wasn't exactly assessing him, but he saw that she was waiting to hear more. He was still catching up to what he had already said. He hadn't had any idea that he was going to ask Lily to marry him, although he didn't have a single qualm now that the words had been said. In fact, all the disparities and loose ends of his life suddenly seemed to cohere and his world to settle into its proper orbit.

"You're the smartest girl I know, Lily," he went on, in an attempt to explain. "It's not long before you realize that the world's full of pretty girls. Everyone I knew at school seemed to have a sister. A pretty cousin . . . but none with a mind like yours. Or your sense of . . . honor. In all the time I've known you — well, my whole life — I've never heard you say an unkind thing about a single person! You'd be surprised to hear a girl say terrible things about someone who's supposed to be her dearest friend." But Lily still stood quietly, looking at him with a mildly curious expression, so he tried to make it clear even to himself.

"There's no other girl I've ever met who I could ever care so much about. I must have always been in love with you." And though he was startled to hear himself say it he knew at once that it was the truth — so vigorous and absolute that suddenly the possibility of her refusal became dreadful. "I don't know that I'd ever be happy if I thought I'd go through my whole life and you wouldn't be with me. I think that all my life . . . Well, I can't imagine there would ever in the world be anyone else I would ask to marry me."

Lily continued to gaze at him in frank appraisal of his earnest brown head, his pleasant and familiar face. She tucked her arm through his and moved them along down Church Street toward Stradler's clothing store. "Of course I'll marry you, Robert. I've always thought I would."

In May of 1913, Robert returned from Boston, and, in late June, Warren traveled back from a branch office of Scofields &

Company in Pennsylvania to serve as Robert's best man. On the afternoon of Saturday, June 28, Warren stood next to the groom in the oppressive two o'clock heat of Leo Scofield's garden and looked on placidly with a polite air of expectation.

Lily's mother had arranged for the prelude and wedding music to be performed by a string quartet and a singer from the College of Music of Cincinnati, and although the strings were muted by the heat, the soprano's voice was vivid. Lily's five attendants and the two flower girls, sprinkling rose petals from a basket they carried between them, made their way along the shady aisle beneath those tall trees and emerged blinking in the sudden dazzle of sunlight in the garden, proceeding in traditional hesitation step along the freshly raked gravel path dividing the rows and rows of chairs set out upon the grass.

One by one they arranged themselves across from the groomsmen on the other side of the trellised arbor where huge, clumsy-seeming bumblebees drank from the throats of the trumpet flowers, causing a little uneasiness among the bridesmaids. Robert's father stood directly beneath the arbor, smiling solemnly, ignoring the bees, and waited to perform the marriage ceremony.

But when Lily emerged on Leo's arm from the shadows of the fervidly blooming catalpa trees, Warren startled visibly, lifting his hand and splaying his fingers across his chest. His gesture expressed not only surprise but dismay, and it appeared to a few of the onlookers that Warren hadn't believed until that moment that it was a *marriage* that was about to take place. It caught the attention of the assembled guests particularly, of course, because Warren was playing out a role that generally fell to the groom. It was Robert, though, who grasped Warren's arm to steady him. Nevertheless, just for a moment Warren's attitude was stripped bare of any pretense, as if he were a man who had lost any possibility of comfort in the world.

Lily saw nothing of that momentary drama. But Warren had been taken unawares by this clear bit of evidence that his youth was over. That he and Robert and Lily had become adults. It was the moment when he understood for the first time — grasped the clean, severe truth of the fact — that the three of them had become who they had become, and from now on the association of their youth would be relegated to nostalgic musings and remembrances. It was the first moment that Warren looked back at the years of his childhood and thought that they seemed to have flown by so fast.

Lily stepped from the filtered light into the blinding sunshine, her hand resting lightly on Leo Scofield's arm, so that she paused for a moment when he did while he waited to get his bearings in the bright day. For just an instant while she hesitated alongside her father she had a cursory glimpse of the waiting bridal party. She caught the gleam of her cousin Warren's fair hair in juxtaposition to Robert's darker head, and a hazy, amorphous happiness clarified itself in one swift thought before she stepped forward once again: Here we are together. The three of us. Here we are again at last. And then she remembered to move forward with care in order to accommodate her heavy satin train. She considered the next step and then the next, her mind fully concentrated on her progress. But in those few seconds, that fragmentary passage of time, she had satisfied herself that Robert Butler and Warren Scofield were both hers once again and ever after. And everyone looking on had seen — just during that tiny hesitation as she had stepped from the shadows into the sudden, shimmering, metallic illumination, in her pale dress and with her yellow hair — that Lily was as shocking and slender and brilliant with potential as the blade of a knife.

It was one of those singular moments that is seared into a collective sensibility. In that instant when simultaneously Lily stepped into the garden on her father's arm and Warren Scofield clutched his heart, there was a redefinition of Lily. That day in 1913, at just a little past two o'clock in the afternoon, on Saturday, June 28, Lily accumulated real consequence in the town of Washburn. Within the blink of an eye she acquired a reputation for possessing unparalleled charm and remarkable, if unconventional, beauty. It was the very same moment, of course, that Warren Scofield was privately acknowledged by many of the wedding guests to have suffered a broken heart.

Lily and Robert traveled east for their wedding trip. Lily wanted to go to the galleries and museums in New York, where she had missed the sensational opening of the Armory Show in February. Several of her friends who lived in New York had written her about it, and Robert had thought it was astonishing. They spent several days in South Hadley, Massachusetts, visiting friends and teachers of Lily's, and then they went on to Boston so Lily could meet some of Robert's friends she didn't yet know.

Robert's circle of Harvard friends, an educated but unknowingly provincial bunch, sitting around a table at Madson's in Cambridge, listening to Lily and watching her small, slender hands fly as she spoke, eagerly promised to visit Robert and Lily in Washburn once they were settled. Robert had been offered and had accepted a teaching position in the English department at Harcourt Lees college. Robert's friends — just like the girls who first encountered Lily at Mount Holyoke — were surprised to find themselves mesmerized by this glittery-bright girl from the middle of nowhere, and they inevitably concluded that Ohio must be a far more sophisticated and delightful place than they had imagined.

Three weeks after their departure, Robert and Lily wired Warren. They sent the telegram the morning of the day they took the Boston packet to Tenants Harbor, Maine. The family of Lily's maid of honor, Marjorie Hockett, who was Lily's dearest friend from college, had offered the newlyweds the use of their empty farmhouse through the end of August. The note Lily and Robert sent was a clever sort of message:

HAVE TOO MUCH FUN STOP YOU MUST USE SOME UP STOP
DO NOT HESITATE STOP WE ARE LOST STOP

It bore Lily's stamp of airy playfulness, and she later claimed that she had had her fill of culture and was sure that Robert would want more company than she was interested in providing to investigate the natural wonders of the Maine coast. Of course she didn't say — even to herself in any organized way — that she had been taken aback by Robert's passionate interest in her. She was flattered, and sometimes taken by surprise by simple physical pleasure, but by and large she found so much attention a little tedious, often absurd. It wasn't entirely unlike the one time at Mount Holyoke that Marjorie Hockett had leaned over — as they sat on Lily's bed studying — and kissed Lily lightly on the neck just behind her ear. A sizzling sort of thrill had shot through Lily, and she turned her head toward Marjorie, who kissed her lips very gently. But all of a sudden Lily had thought: What's this? For goodness sake! This is only *Marjorie!*

With Robert she often had to battle down the same notion, and she sometimes thought she would enjoy all of lovemaking much more if she were with an utter stranger. Familiarity bred in Lily a peculiar kind of self-consciousness. But she never let these thoughts coalesce; she never let them come into sharp focus. And she really did believe Robert would enjoy Warren's company. She thought it would be a good thing to have Warren among them. It would be a distraction, and Warren would love to go along with Robert for all the exploring he wanted to do. Also, Lily had great hopes of Warren and Marjorie getting to know each other even better. They had enjoyed each other's company during all the business of the wedding.

As she had explained to Robert's friends, and as she declared with slight variations when she and Robert returned to Ohio, "I love a game of golf, you know. Or tennis or croquet. Any sort of cards. Oh, I'll play just about anything. It doesn't matter to me if I'm any good at it. I like almost any sort of competition. But I don't think I possess a single *bit* of adventurousness," she said of herself ruefully.

"If it had been up to me I'd still be standing on my one wretched square foot of earth somewhere in England, struggling to subsist on whatever pitiful things I could coax from the kitchen garden. I've always liked the sound of that — a kitchen garden — and I'm going to be sure to have one of my own. Well! I probably already do. If there's a garden to be planted, I'm sure my father will have done it!" This bit was left out in her retelling back home in Washburn, but she had made great characters of her delightful parents in the little stories she spun out for her school friends and any of Robert's acquaintances who gathered around the couple during their stay in Boston.

When Lily and Robert and Warren returned to Washburn the first week of September, the three of them were filled with amusing anecdotes, sitting out in Leo's garden, where Lily and her mother had strung Japanese lanterns. Once back home, Lily merely turned the tables and with quick, clever verbal twists managed to portray even the least interesting of their East Coast friends as wonderful characters, full of endearing idiosyncrasies. Lily told a good tale, and Robert always sat looking on with a little smile of contentment.

She claimed to her family and friends in Ohio that she couldn't have endured alone so much *nature* as they encountered in Maine. She knew Robert would want company, she said, on his hikes and outings, but she wanted to enjoy the scenery — at least when Marjorie Hockett visited — from the comfort of a chair set out under the trees. The Hocketts lived nearby, in a handsome old house overlooking the village and harbor of Port Clyde, where Lily had visited them several times during her years at Mount Holyoke.

"Oh, no! I would never have made an explorer," she insisted when her Washburn friends protested that they didn't know anyone more likely than she to relish a hike through the wilderness, a chance to discover a mysterious cove, some out-of-the-way place. "I might have been quite shocking, say, insisting on playing polo — having a pony of my own." And the company in the garden laughed at the idea of tiny little Lily on some great horse, swinging a huge mallet about determinedly, with that peculiar air of insistence with which she went at any game.

"Or taking a turn at cricket," she added, to further laughter. "I can't ever resist trying something if there's any chance in the *world* that I might win. But I'd never have had the courage to venture into foreign territory. You know, I think it would be really frightening not to know the country. The customs and . . . well, it would be tedious, too. But anyway, I simply know I wouldn't have the patience or the forbearance or the courage. If I'd been born whenever the first Marshals emigrated I would have had to be orphaned. Staying behind and begging crusts of bread in the street. I wouldn't ever have set foot on any one of those little ships."

Lily was cheerfully self-deprecating. Everyone who knew her became fondly possessive of the shortcomings she found in herself, translated as they were into her own particular and amusing eccentricities, which she confided unabashedly and with charming chagrin. Everyone but her uncle John, who had never been fond of his brother's daughter. Who always said to his wife or to Warren that she reminded him of nothing so much as a scrawny hen that won't lay. "Pecking about and squawking, but not worth the feed it takes to keep her."

It was one of the few provocations that elicited a sharp rebuke from Lillian Scofield, whose namesake Lily was. "I won't have you say such a thing! Not another word!" Lillian never did realize that when she faced her husband down he backed off, just as he always did regarding his niece.

"Well, Lillian! Of the three of them . . . Even you've got to admit she's the runt of *that* litter, and . . ."

"I'll leave the room! I really will not hear another word of this, Mr. Scofield! You're speaking unkindly of someone very dear to me. . . . Why, John! She's my namesake! She's Audra's daughter. She might just as well be my *own* daughter!"

And Warren would notice that under the force of his mother's genuine pique his father would immediately become his most beguiling, his voice softening into a melodious wheedling. "Ah, my," he would sigh. "Well, Lillian. I suppose I ought to work harder at being a charitable man. But that girl is just slippery. . . . All right. All right. But my lack of . . . *gallantry* . . . well, it's truly your fault." And he would hunch his shoulders in a shrug of helplessness, hands spread wide apart and palms outward to illustrate the uselessness of any attempt to behave otherwise. "I do have to say that any woman has a hard time winning even a bit of my heart in comparison to you. You haven't changed since the day I met you. Won't you forgive me? Isn't there anyone in my own household who loves me just a little? Unkind — plain stupid — as I may be?"

Warren hated being in the company of his parents when his father's tone implied an extenuating and intimate connection between them. Lillian Scofield would soften and laugh a little, and Warren would be embarrassed for and even unreasonably angry at his mother, surprised each time at the evidence of her credulity. As an adult, Warren, too, objected to any criticism of Lily, but when he was a little boy it had been impossible for Warren not to be relieved to know his father favored him over his cousin.

Nor did Lily's lighthearted self-incrimination appeal to her mother-in-law, Martha Butler, who, pregnant and frighteningly seasick, had traveled with her husband to Brazil and then Cuba, where he had been entirely ineffective at the mission of founding Methodist schools for girls, but where she had given birth to Robert's two older siblings, both of whom were engaged in similarly unnerving work in South America. She believed — but couldn't pin the idea down enough even to mention it to her husband — that in some way Lily was tossing off her mother-in-law's own desperate housewifery in those hot and foreign places as an unnecessary — a foolish — sacrifice. She always thought that Lily was making an oblique disparagement, was indirectly — and, of course, unwittingly — belittling her.

"It's amazing to me that I could be even *distantly* related to someone who knowingly took a risk like that! Just sailing off to who knows where," Lily would carry on, and when the conversation got that far Martha Butler would look down at her hands folded in her lap and find herself restraining tears. "Leaving everything familiar behind. Well! And for that matter, someone who shouldered on even then — even after reaching land — to the wilds of Ohio!" Lily hadn't noticed her mother-in-law's dismay, but it was true that Lily had never forgiven Mrs. Butler for the subtle disapproval she had aimed Lily's way when Lily was just a little girl, unable to make a case for herself as a suitable companion for Mrs. Butler's last and favorite child.

It was Warren and Robert who were pressed about details of what became their most popular story, since Lily's role in it seemed so unlikely. The two men had come back from a day-long hike along the rocks, clear around Herring Gut Point to the lighthouse, where they got soaked by spray and had very nearly been trapped by the tide. They had returned to the farmhouse to discover that Lily and Marjorie had spread a cloth in the yard under the trees and set out a picnic of cold fried chicken and a miraculous lemon meringue pie. "Well, we were mighty glad to see that chicken," Robert said. "We were as sorry for ourselves and just as pitiful as two wet dogs."

Warren teasingly described the pie, the height of the meringue, its peaks of browned gloss, the unparalleled lightness and delicacy of the crust. "By then," he said, "we had blueberries coming out of our ears. There's not enough good that can be said for a fine, tart lemon pie." And Lily smiled indulgently.

"But Lily never wanted to cook anything in her life," her mother always interjected. "She was such a little tomboy. You mean to tell me Lily dressed that bird? Cut up and fried a chicken? You mean to tell me Lily made a pie?" her mother always asked, in a voice full of disbelief and a kind of tender musing.

The three of them described taking the little white mail boat to Monhegan Island, the beauty of the coast seen from the water. And to Lily's mother's horror, they described what they claimed were extraordinary meals prepared for them by the woman the Hocketts had found at Leo's behest to come in and clean and fix supper for the newlyweds and any guests they might have. Cod tongues and sounds and cheeks, Lily and Robert and Warren insisted, were delicacies indeed, although it made Audra Scofield shiver to hear about it. And finnan haddie. Why, it was wonderfully delicious, smoked over an alder fire under a hogshead. "I don't believe I ever knew there were as many things to do with fish," Robert declared, amused a little at his own landlocked bias.

"And thank goodness for that," his mother-in-law murmured.

One morning Marjorie had arrived in her father's big Regal auto with a picnic basket packed, but she and Lily ended up driving over muddy roads for miles, Lily said, while Warren and Robert devised a game of chess without a chessboard, drawing out and studying each successive move on a piece of paper. "The only time that afternoon I could persuade them to do a bit of sightseeing was when we all had to pile out while one or the other of them fixed a flat tire," Lily said with feigned disgust. "And I've never seen such roads. Why, we drove through small *lakes,* it seemed to me. But we went along the cove road and ate lunch at a spot where we could watch the beautiful sloops. Oh, they're sleek! They move like arrows through the water. We could see all the way to Matinicus!"

Everyone listened to these stories with real attention. At the heart of the abiding interest in every detail, of course, even among slight acquaintances, was the fact that Warren Scofield had joined the Butlers on their wedding trip, and that neither Robert nor Lily nor Warren ever satisfactorily explained the reason why. The people of Washburn silently pitied poor Warren Scofield, clearly so grieved by the loss of his cousin Lily — the love of his life — to the bed of his closest friend. And it was tacitly agreed that Robert and Lily Butler had pitied him, too, and had offered him the sad consolation of joining them for a visit after they had spent the first ardent weeks of their marriage alone. The situation was still fraught with the possibility of further developments. And trifling as they were, the stories the three of them told were incorporated in the town's communal, unrecorded history as a point of reference, to be reconsidered, if need be, in case anything else in the lives of those three became mysterious. Because Lily and Robert and Warren were young then, and anything might happen.

Chapter Two

ANGES CLAYTOR had just turned fourteen years old at the time of Lily Scofield and Robert Butler's marriage, and although her family had been guests at the wedding, it might be that her parents were the only two people in the area on whom nothing of the little drama of that ceremony registered, nor would they have been interested in the details of the wedding trip. And at age fourteen, neither had Agnes thought much one way or another about Lily Scofield's wedding.

Early on that hot June day of 1913, Agnes had been buttoned up in a long-waisted organdy dress not pastel but so gently colored that it was as though the cloth held only a suggestion of the color blue. At first she was delighted with the romance of the airy flounce of its skirt. When she had slipped the freshly ironed, still warm dress over her head, the roof of her mouth prickled with the clean, scorched smell of the starched, fragile fabric, and her mind's eye filled with a vision of herself as a graceful and delicate creature. But during the ceremony, when the dress wilted and drooped in the heat, making her uncomfortable with its damp scratchiness around her neck, that happy idea evaporated, and she lost interest in the whole affair.

She had turned to watch the procession as the bridesmaids and flower girls and finally Lily and her father came down the aisle, but Agnes hadn't noticed Warren Scofield's reaction. Certainly she had heard the incident recounted many times in the weeks following the wedding, but since it wasn't a story that anyone told to her directly — was simply one of those anecdotes that are loose in the air of a community — she had let any intricacy of detail just drift right by her.

A year later, though, by the time Agnes was fifteen and her friends at school began to be interested in everything about *any* wedding, what impressed Agnes most was when Lucille Drummond told her that Mr. Leo Scofield had imported forty-five dozen roses, that he had them shipped from New York in a special rail car just to be woven into the arbor under which Reverend Butler had performed the ceremony. "That would be five hundred and forty roses," Lucille pointed out, "just for that one day. But they wilted almost before the end of the ceremony. By the end of the day they were just as limp as string."

Agnes was also impressed when Lucille reminded her of the terrible heat of the week of the wedding. "So Mr. Scofield had sixteen full-grown trees dug up from out in the country — they were *huge,* and they all had to be just the same height! They had to match exactly!" Lucille said. "He had them planted in two rows so that his daughter wouldn't have to have that sun full on her in the hottest part of the day. Not on the bridesmaids, either, of course. And Lily Butler had *two* little flower girls. Well . . ." Lucille's voice became solemn. "She's Mr. Scofield's only child, so even if he *did* overdo it a little . . . It took more than twelve men working for three full days just to get everything ready on time!"

Lucille's family had only moved to town a few months before the wedding and hadn't really done more at that point than make the acquaintance of the Scofield family, but Lucille remembered that her father had sent a team and wagon over to Scofields on the Tuesday of the week of the wedding and hadn't gotten the return of them until Sunday, the day after the ceremony, although Lucille did say his mules had been well taken care of.

And, really, Lucille was not lying. Everything she described was as clear in her head as if she had seen it herself. The idea she had of the Scofield-Butler wedding was vivid and was made up of any number of bits of conversations, vague impressions, grand reinterpretations of various occasions. Lucille's sister Celia, for instance, had once told the tale of a friend of hers whose fiancé had arranged for a crate of oysters and three dozen roses to be shipped to her by train from Philadelphia. And Mr. Drummond *had* sent a team and wagon around Monument Square to help out when the Scofield wagon had become mired in mud one spring with its burden of a new piano for Audra Scofield, although Lucille had been in Columbus visiting her sister Grace at the time. Also, of course, Lucille had heard her sisters rehashing various accounts of Lily Butler's wedding: the bumblebees under the arbor, the overlong bridal procession as Lily and her father made their way beneath that avenue of trees while the guests sweltered in the garden.

It had never crossed Lucille's mind to imagine the impossibility of finding sixteen mature, matched catalpa trees growing randomly out in the country, much less the hopelessness of the task of transplanting them. But had anyone confronted her about her misrepresentation of the events surrounding Lily Butler's wedding, Lucille would have shrugged it off, discounted it, been sorry to have a grand story ruined, and Agnes would have been disappointed as well.

In Lucille's house it was in relation to her that her parents and sisters warned one another — sometimes with a slightly supercilious air — that little pitchers have big ears. And that was because even as a young child Lucille had been prone to repeat the most outlandish details she overheard, repeat them to utter strangers with a blunt and rather contentious insistence. She had been forced to make sense of fragments of whatever stories she happened to interrupt; she snatched up scraps of conversations here and there. As the youngest of four daughters, she was always faced with people ending sentences midway through when she appeared, or turning away and speaking in a hush, adopting cautious expressions of restraint and, Lucille thought, an air of smug superiority. It was maddening, but by necessity Lucille had developed a strong intuition and a remarkable imagination.

Agnes and Lucille had become good friends almost as soon as they met on their first day at the Linus Gilchrest Institute for Girls. Each one instinctively relied upon the other, because the world Lucille described to Agnes was so much more fraught with eventfulness than Agnes, as the oldest child in her family, ever discerned on her own. And for Lucille's part, she was nearly always eventually relieved when Agnes turned her pragmatic attention toward some notion of Lucille's that was getting dangerously out of hand and, in Agnes's oddly appealing, steely little voice, deflated Lucille's wildly spinning, free-floating fancy to the essential flat facts of its ordinariness. Agnes generally had difficulty recognizing drama even when she was in the middle of it, while Lucille had a tendency to invest the most everyday event with extravagant import, and they were useful to each other in managing between them to find a reasonable interpretation of the world.

The Claytors, Dwight and Catherine, and their four children, lived out Newark Road, where Dwight Claytor's grandparents had farmed comfortably, mainly growing corn but also running a good-size dairy. Dwight eventually joined his father's law practice in Zanesville, although he kept his grandparents' place and managed the dairy, which, by the time Agnes started school, was only about three miles or so north of Washburn, since the town had grown so much.

But even before Agnes was born, the majority of that vast, slightly rolling acreage had been given over strictly to the growing of corn for a mass commercial market. Her father had built a new house farther from the road under the shelter of a nice stand of walnut trees that shaded the southern-facing rooms in the summer. By the time Agnes left lower school and began to attend the Linus Gilchrest Institute for Girls, the Claytor farm was so extensive that the Claytors were never really thought of as farmers.

In fact, her father had hired a manager for the property and become deeply involved in state politics. He had been pressed to run for and had been elected to the state assembly on the Democratic ticket to represent Marshal County in 1913, and he had worked hard to ensure the reelection of Atlee Pomerene to the U.S. Senate in 1916. He was often in Columbus for weeks and sometimes more than a month without a visit home. And when he was at home, a great deal of time was taken up by people who came and went to discuss the business of politics with Dwight Claytor, who remained publicly courteous but who sometimes got closed-faced with anger — a tense flattening of expression — although perhaps only his children realized it. He kept his voice under tight control and even sustained a cordial tone, a flexibility of timbre that belied his displeasure. His children knew it well; their father rarely raised his voice, but they could always tell when he was disappointed or irritated or really angry.

Now and then his restraint drove his wife to distraction. "There's nothing *kind* about not saying what you mean!" she said to him. "It just leaves the children walking around feeling terrible. Not knowing what in the world they've done wrong." And this was true enough, although it surprised her children that she knew it. "My father always said . . . he *always* said that he would never trust a man who wore a beard or any man who never showed his temper. He said it was the sign of a stingy heart."

Her husband turned a cold eye on her for a long moment that was suddenly quiet with the caught attention of all four children. "I won't be insulted in my own home by my own wife, Catherine. *My* father always said to be careful what you wish for." And then the tension ebbed a little as he relaxed and drew his fingers over his jaw from cheek to chin. "Besides, I haven't ever worn a beard, Catherine," he said to her, his expression mildly amused, but she whirled around with her hands clenched at her sides, her face wide with contempt.

"Why, I just hope you can see that your father can be mean!" she said in the direction of her children, not speaking to Dwight directly. "Oh, I tell you, he can be mean as a snake! The things he says . . . the *way* he'll say things to a person . . ." Her voice rustled furiously, and the children distracted her, asked her questions, begged special favors. They drew her away from their father however they could; Catherine never would let go of an argument on her own.

As it happened, though, when Catherine had first met Dwight Claytor, what had originally caught her attention were the clean, round, unrancorous Midwestern vowels that shaped his voice as he politely defended some political position at dinner one evening. He had come to Natchez, where Catherine had lived all her life, to pay a visit to their mutual cousins, the Alcorns, and tidy up some family business, and he had become involved in an amiable debate with her father.

Catherine had listened as he maintained his support of prohibition against the subtle derisiveness of her father. She hadn't had an opinion about prohibition — hadn't thought about it one way or another. But she liked the seemingly innocent unassailability of Dwight Claytor's voice as it was pitched against the elegantly flat, sardonic questions and declarations her father put forth.

"Well, sir," Mr. Claytor said, "I'll tell you, there's a lot of industry in my section of the country. New enterprises springing up everywhere. And it certainly is true that industry, at any rate, has a large interest in the prohibition of *drunkenness*. It's not a bit good for productivity, as you can imagine. The Anti-Saloon League is a powerful political ally for any man with aspirations. I suppose it could reach a point where there's some danger in their intolerance."

"But I can see that you don't worry as I do, Mr. Claytor," her father replied, leaning back in his chair and pivoting slightly, crossing one leg over the other in an attitude that signified good temper and leisurely amusement, "that this whole thing might conspire against a man's pleasure. It doesn't seem to you to be the idea of preachers and unhappy women?"

This was meant as a bit of lazy teasing, but Dwight Claytor frowned in consideration. "I don't believe I know many of either," he answered pensively. "But speaking simply for myself — as to pleasure, anyway — I can say that prohibition would have no effect whatsoever." What he said was so straightforward it was clear that he was unaware of her father's assumption of a little ironic conspiracy between the two of them. Her father was taken aback, and Catherine was peculiarly satisfied.

Dwight Claytor had seemed to possess a placid sort of reasonableness. His tone never slid into the patronizing, slightly nasal, descending trill that she was so used to hearing in her father's voice in any conversation. Mr. Claytor was a handsome man, compact and dark, with wide-set brown eyes, but it was really little more than the sound of his voice that secured him such a sought-after bride. It was his agreeable, unflustered articulation of his own point of view that was exactly why Catherine Alcorn Edson married Dwight Albert Claytor in April of 1898, when she was twenty years old. It was the reason Catherine came to be established on the wide, rolling farmland in the middle of Ohio.

By 1916, though, Catherine had lost track of how she had arrived at where she was. She occupied a large new house with no idea of managing it, so that she was always surprised when each day she was confronted with the details of it, asked to make decisions about this or that. She had no idea of giving direction to Betsy Graves, the young woman her husband had hired to come in every morning to do domestic work — the two women stayed out of each other's way, each one uneasy, and nothing much ever did get done. And Catherine was the mother of four children whom she often yearned after with a terrible, lonely soul-sickness. They moved through the hours as though they inhabited time apart from the way she understood it. Their days seemed to hurtle along all ordered and precise so that even her children's everyday progression somehow excluded her. Sometimes she was mystified by the actuality of them and sometimes enraged.

By the time Catherine Claytor was in her thirties the ragged, cluttered corners of her mind were filled with the wheedling neediness of children, their boisterous games, their loud humor, their endless appetites and curiosity. It was constantly surprising that they required so much of her. Having settled some business or other with them, she was never, ever prepared for still another concern to crop up. She never grasped the fact that no matter what she did they would need something from her yet again. And all this — all the requests and demands and elation and dismay spilling out into the rooms of her house, spiraling out over the yard, overlaying the incessant drone of the news of the world as it was related and debated by visitors and remarked upon by her husband — it was bewildering. Catherine was often overwhelmed by the turmoil of her own life and desperate in the face of the publicly impassive, forbearing nature of her husband's attention.

After Atlee Pomerene's reelection to the U.S. Senate in 1916, the Claytor place became something of a political center. A good many men were pressing Dwight Claytor to consider a run for election to the U.S. House of Representatives in two years. They wanted him to challenge DeMott in the primary, in any case, with the hope of establishing a name for himself and winning the seat in 1920. Catherine no longer paid very much attention.

When her husband launched into a careful explanation of some business that troubled him, she settled back in her chair, her expression politely attentive. She gazed at him intently while her mind toyed with and turned over the seductive sounds of the exotic names she caught up out of his little discourse as though she were plucking threads out of her needlework — Carrizal, Chihuahua, Carranza, Pancho Villa.

She was equally detached when the talk turned to the war in Europe. So much impassioned rhetoric was cast into the atmosphere of her Ohio house that it affected her as if it were a sudden shift in weather: It brought on a constant, low throbbing in her head. She often lay in bed with the curtains drawn against the light late into the afternoon. By early 1917, the talk about the role the country should take in the war had gone on for months and months, had moved across the porch, invaded the sitting room, and resounded around her dining table. The idea of war had become so large on the horizon that it was no more urgent in her life than the idea of God, inevitable and unquestioned. The endless belaboring of the subject was tiresome to her and even baffling, and she often left the room without explanation, waving her hand in dismissal as the men began to rise from their seats when she stood to make an escape.

President Wilson called for a War Resolution before a joint session of Congress on April 2. By the time the Senate had approved it on April 4, and the House had concurred two days later, Catherine was beyond the reach even of the most simplistic patriotism. She let all the political agitation waft right by her, and she became so peculiarly vague and abstracted that it made Agnes uneasy, but it was probably the happiest season so far of Agnes's youngest brother's childhood. At first Edson was cautious, but he became emboldened and gregarious and a great favorite of all the company, some of whom visited with fair regularity.

When her mother's attention drifted and she failed to notice that some bit of hospitality was called for, Agnes often stepped in as a sort of hostess. She was regularly in the vicinity of the men who congregated on the long, shaded porch or in the parlor and eyed her not so covertly with an unsettling interest. "Why, that's a healthy-looking girl you have there, Dwight!" Her father never replied except with a vague nod, involved in a discussion about hog and wheat prices and the Lever Act.

But her mother would always find her later, Catherine's attention suddenly caught hard and apparently concentrated by intense disgust. "How can you let those men *gawk* at you like that? How can you *be* so vulgar? At least you could bind your breasts! You . . . you flounce around the table like some . . . You have all the delicacy of one of the dairy cows! Like someone *coarse!* You don't have any instinct . . . not an ounce of blood from my side of the family. No air of . . . subtlety. Refinement! And here we are in this *wilderness!*"

"Oh, Mama, please don't," Agnes would say softly. "Please don't say things like that about me." She could not bear to reveal that those furious images flung out into the air cut her to the quick and filled her with self-consciousness and mortifying shame of everything about herself. Instead Agnes would dredge up a teasing sort of jocularity.

"Now, Mama, you were exactly my age when you were presented at the Regimental Ball, weren't you? What was that like? I know all the men there wanted to dance with you! What was your dress like? Was that the dress with the green sash?" Agnes knew how to do this, but she was always abashed and peculiarly embarrassed and humiliated for her mother and for herself, too. Because almost at once her mother's fierce regard would lose its intensity; she would become reflective as Agnes's questions took hold, and she might settle down and begin to reminisce, or she might wander off in a reverie.

But sometimes Catherine couldn't be diverted, and any question only deflected her outrage. She would search out Edson and hector and badger him about one thing or another until he broke down, weeping and pleading with her to let him be. "Leave me alone, Mama! Leave me alone!" he would chant, his hands over his ears so that he could only hear his own voice as she lashed out at him — maddened somehow by any evidence of her children's successful engagement with the world — calling him a sycophantic little fool. He only knew how terrible that must be because of its hissing sibilance. Nothing could stop her once she swung full force into her fury — not even the objection of his two brothers and certainly not any word from Agnes.

Catherine's rage was less directed when her husband was at home, although all four children could sense it just simmering under the surface, manifesting itself in a sliding glance of scorn as she passed a bowl of mashed potatoes, or in a cautious, disdainful stiffening if a child brushed by too close. On days like those, her children sat at the table hoping that some other notion would distract their mother before they were — any one of them — alone in her company.

"Oh, you're so pleased with yourself!" she rasped at Edson, bending over him as he leaned away from her, bearing down on him as he dissolved in misery. "But I'll tell you, you're too pretty for my taste! Too *charming* altogether! Oh, exactly like, *exactly* like your granddaddy. Ahh! And so polite! 'Why, Mrs. Claytor, what a *good* little boy you have!'" she said in an enraged, high-pitched parody of some unctuous guest. "But I tell you what *I* think. You're too sweet by far! Too good by half! A little mama's boy! But not mine! Not mine! Not *this* mama. Sometimes I don't know where you come from! I can't imagine you're any child of mine!"

None of her children had any memory of a long stretch of time during which Catherine Claytor had been easy spirited or even content, but this new and sustained frenzy was baffling. All of their lives Agnes and her youngest brother, Edson, were most likely to try to smooth out any situation that might dismay their mother. And it was Agnes and Edson who were generally the primary targets of her arid rages, her thin, long-limbed flurry through the rooms. But there were other moments of their growing up when it was one of the two of them around whom she spun a cocoon of gentle intimacy, her long fingers unexpectedly intertwining with their own while she invented long, mesmerizing, magical stories all about the adventures of a character named Uncle Tidbit.

She had reeled those tales off her tongue like songs, so unlike the clotted sputtering of her invective. Leaning forward eagerly, widening her eyes as the story became comic or exciting, she would look at Agnes or Edson with a gleefully beseeching glance, entreating them to share her delight. She still wound out these stories for Edson, and he would sit transfixed by this woman whose head canted forward on her long neck in affectionate inclusion, whose every word and gesture indicated her deep and dreamy pleasure in his company.

Sometimes, too, in a less rarefied atmosphere, just on any day, she would search out one or the other of them to repeat some compliment. She was matter-of-fact but betrayed her pride in them by dwelling on some attribute in exacting detail. All the examples of the fact that Agnes was smart as a whip, that it had been no surprise to Catherine to hear from Miss Mc-

Crory that Agnes was the brightest girl in her class. Or she might remind Edson that his great-aunt had said that he certainly was a real Alcorn, already tall for his age, and so handsome. So clever. A real charmer through and through.

Now and then, out of nowhere, she confided startling intimacies to one or the other of them. She disclosed some triumph of her early life, a beau who had adored her, the trim of a hat she had designed and that had turned out to be exactly right, the astonishing beauty she had possessed — and on this point she was particularly adamant, determined that they believe her. Catherine would become urgent in her intensity, agitated as she insisted on the evidence of old photographs or urged them to study the large portrait of her hanging in the parlor. "You see?" she said. "See there?"

It was a dark, ominously glistening oil painting, larger than life-size, of a stiff-looking young woman with worrisomely pink skin, a very green dress, and hands that blurred into the folds of her skirt. It never dawned on any of her children that it was not at all a good painting and bore only a slight resemblance to their mother; they took Catherine at her word that it was a fair representation of herself as a handsome young girl. It never occurred to them not to believe wholeheartedly in her former beauty. But neither Catherine herself, as she stood before the mirror hastily pinning her hair in a loose knot, nor Agnes, nor either of the middle boys, as they glanced at their mother to gauge the temperature of her mood, thought much about what she looked like in the moment.

The two middle Claytor children, Richard and Howard, were such a united front — only thirteen months apart — that they managed pretty well to be sufficient unto themselves; they wanted nothing to do with their mother. They had grasped her unreliability as a safe harbor, and they were far more likely to count on each other in any case. But Agnes and Edson were weighed down with a sense of their mother's mysterious, inexorable, free-floating grief; they were unhappily aware of her fragility and vulnerability, and, therefore, their connection to her was a stickier business altogether. Agnes felt responsible for her mother, but in 1917, Edson, at ten years old, was too young not to be tantalized by the infrequent evidence of his mother as a woman to whom he was dear. He was heartbroken by and infatuated with what seemed to him the tragedy of his mother's life.

And also at age ten he was suddenly disenchanted with his sister, Agnes. Whenever his mother was driven into a rage at Agnes's flamboyance — at the attention she drew to herself when she served coffee to her father's guests, for example — Edson counted it against his sister, too. It seemed to him that she was forever bringing trouble down upon their heads. All three of her brothers thought Agnes was bossy. Their mother was often truly frightening, but Agnes just made them mad.

Agnes knew why those men loitering on the porch paid attention to her; she had discovered that she was at an age that attracted attention. But she wasn't sure if she was pretty or not, although she knew that neither of her parents thought so. If her mother was in one of her dark moods, she muttered over Agnes's hair, blaming Agnes for its coarse, dark, curly profusion, saying she didn't know how Agnes could bear to be seen in public with hair exactly like some gypsy or colored girl and skin the color of pea soup.

Her mother's disappointment in her only daughter's looks had been a theme in Agnes's life as far back as she could remember, and she had long ago accommodated her deep shame at her exuberant hair and the awful, yellowish cast of her skin. She bound her breasts with a length of muslin beneath her camisole in an effort to deflect attention, in a hopeless attempt to shape her figure into one of long-limbed, willowy elegance her mother would approve. She reminded herself to be guarded around the girls at school who seemed to admire her, because she knew that they must be insincere. Agnes knew that she would seem foolish if she ever appeared to believe in or rely on her own attractiveness. And she was grateful sometimes, in softer moments, when her mother was less direct and seemed to find Agnes's appearance tolerable.

She eventually discounted entirely the opinion of William Dameron, whose father managed the Claytor farm and who was two years older than she. They had been playmates outside of school all during their childhood; they had established a secret meeting place beneath the willows beside the creek, had spent hours constructing camouflaged hideouts where they could elude "the others" — William's older sister, Bernice, and all their younger brothers, none of whom was particularly interested in finding them. Agnes and William Dameron spent many concentrated hours of their young lives together, but William retreated to little more than a distant sort of cordiality when he reached his teens, and Agnes didn't think much about it because she had new involvements herself once she started school at the Linus Gilchrest Institute for Girls.

But William had sought her out the day before he left for Canada to join the RCAF in the summer of 1916 and found her outside sitting in the swing by the croquet court. She had visited the Damerons' house with her family a few days earlier to wish him good-bye and good luck. Mrs. Dameron had served cake, and the occasion had been fairly festive, but Agnes hadn't had a chance to speak to him alone, and she was glad to see him. They talked about his sister Bernice, who was at Oberlin College and hadn't been at home when the Claytors visited. William asked her about what she planned after her last year at school, and they just talked comfortably for a little while.

William lounged against the tree with his arms folded across his chest. "I hope you understand about my joining up," he said to her, and she looked back at him pleasantly enough; she didn't say that she hadn't given it much thought one way or another. "You know, it's not that I especially want to get into the war, Agnes, but America's going to be in it soon enough. It makes sense to me to sign up while I have a chance to get into flying. They'll take anyone who'll sign up. What I mean is, I don't have any experience, but it won't matter. I'm good with engines. I'll get the chance to train to be a pilot right off the bat! But it's not like these fellows who just want to get into the war because it seems like an adventure. Or that they . . . Well, I don't know what they're thinking, of course, but what I mean is that I don't have some grand idea about the whole thing. I didn't want you to think that. I didn't just decide out of the blue. It wasn't some sort of idea of being a hero. I do think it's important. I think it's the right thing to do. But now that I'm about to leave it's hard to know what will happen. It's hard to know when I'll see my family again. Or when I'll see you, either."

Agnes didn't comment. She thought he was being melodramatic in spite of himself, and she was embarrassed for him. "In fact, I expect you'll be married by the time I get back," he said, less like a statement than a question, although his tone didn't register on Agnes because she was so surprised. She didn't say anything for a moment; she just studied him to see if he was serious.

"William! Married! Oh, for goodness sake! You *know* I'm thinking about going on to Oberlin, too. . . . I don't know, though. . . . Mama thinks it's just a waste of time. . . ." Agnes lost track of their conversation for a moment, twisting the ropes of the swing as she turned in the direction of the house. But then she came back to the moment and let the swing come around again so that she was facing William. "Married!" She frowned in concentration as she looked up to see if she could read his expression — to see if he was teasing her. "I'm not likely to be getting married, William," she said with a little sarcasm, in case he was making fun of her, "since I don't even have a beau."

"That may be," William said, "but it's just because none of the girls at Gilchrest pay any attention to boys. Agnes, I don't think the war will be over very soon. It might be years." Even though they hadn't seen much of each other in the past few years day to day, Agnes still thought of William as her good friend, and he was so grave just now that he seemed to Agnes to be imitating a grown-up. He sounded suspiciously self-important. "Someone will snap you up in no time while I'm gone, I bet. You're the prettiest girl in your class at Gilchrest."

She pushed off gently with her foot so that the swing moved back and forth a few feet each way, and peered up at him with annoyance. "Oh, William, don't be silly! Please don't say anything like that." She waved her hand in a signal of dismissal. "I don't like to think about any of that. . . ." And she meant it absolutely — it made her uncomfortable since she knew that what he said couldn't be true. On the other hand, a little corner of her mind was curious to know who he thought was prettier than she in some *other* class at Linus Gilchrest Institute. "Anyway, I'm not a jar of *peaches,* you know. To be snapped up off a shelf or something."

And at that William finally fell right out of the earnest air of solemnity that had made Agnes a little scornful — it was absurd, somehow, in this friend of her childhood. He grinned widely. "Hah! Close enough. And a *lot* more tempting."

She wasn't flattered; she was shocked and also suspicious, and she stopped the swing abruptly and hopped off. She stood right in front of him, looking up at his face. He had a loose, smiling expression that she hadn't seen before, and she was angry at suddenly feeling uneasy. "Oh, William! *Please* don't talk like that." She watched as he glanced away, and she was interested to realize that he was nice looking. All the Damerons, she thought, were rangy and nice looking, with square, regular faces and sandy brown hair.

"Well, I was only teasing you," he said apologetically, and then he grinned. "I never even *liked* put-up peaches. I didn't mean to be rude," he said. "You know what, though, Agnes? This *is* just what I think makes sense for me to do. I'm not *sorry*. . . . But last night just sitting at the table eating dinner I realized how long it might be before I got back. I'm *ready* to go. . . . I can hardly wait to get into an airplane! I'll tell you that! But last night I wanted *not* to be going, too. I knew you'd be the only person I could tell that to. I don't know what I've gotten myself into." She was embarrassed now, herself, to see that he was moved by his own plight.

"Oh, William, you'll be fine," she said, surprising herself with the nervous sound of her enthusiasm. "If anyone can take care of himself it's you. You should hear Richard and Howie talk about you. They'd give anything to be doing what you're doing. Everyone is proud of you. Oh, everyone thinks it's brave of you!" That wasn't true; Agnes's father thought William was being reckless, thought he was foolish to hurry into action. "He'll have plenty of time to get killed for his *own* country," her father had said just the night before, without heat; in fact his voice had been subdued.

But Agnes was simply saying what seemed appropriate to the occasion while simultaneously taking account of what William had said about her, and her head filled up with new considerations and possibilities about herself as he saw her. She wanted time to turn this over in her mind, to go over every word, sift through every syllable. Agnes got so wrapped up in this new and tempting image of herself that William Dameron walked home across the fields just as horrified by the rash action he had taken as when he had set out to find her that afternoon. Any admiration of him on her part might have been reassuring, might have put a stop to the jangling onslaught of second thoughts. He went off to join the Royal Canadian Air Force, and eventually to fight in France, with no more than a cheerful good-bye and good wishes from Agnes.

When Agnes brought home the highest marks of anyone in her class, her father said to her that he was glad to see she was developing a good character, that she was becoming a sensible girl. He said that there was nothing more admirable in a young woman. "Even if you'll never be the beauty your mother was," he said, which didn't faze Agnes at just that moment when she was so gratified by a bit of praise, but which, curiously, caused her mother's temper to darken into fury. Catherine Claytor roamed the house in such a bleak state of undirected anger that her children scattered and stayed out of the way. "Not the *beauty!* Not the *beauty!*" Her mother lengthened and scorned every nuance of the word — "*bee-yew-tee*" — exulting in her own bitter articulation. "None of you have the slightest *idea* . . ." Their father, though, had his mind on other things, and Catherine's angry fluster blew all around him but left him untouched.

Agnes kept to herself the memory of the moment she had stood to recite at school and Miss McCrory had commented that Agnes was like nothing so much as a blossoming rose. Whenever she thought of it she reminded herself that the other girls in class had looked on amiably with no evidence of disagreement. Agnes knew she was fairly well liked, but this remarkable vision Miss McCrory had conjured up was a piece of evidence about herself that she tucked away to be examined later. She had made an effort not to give any sign of the deep pleasure she felt at the possibility of her own prettiness.

In fact, though, Agnes was not anything at all like a rose — at least nothing like the popular hybrid teas, so difficult to grow. She wasn't tall, nor was she elegant, nor in any way stately. At eighteen her figure was full-blown and so were her features — wide-set and large, with flaring eyebrows so that her round, dark eyes were startling. She was more like a peony, perhaps, uncommonly lush and vivid, although very few people would ever think to compare Agnes to a flower, because there was something about her appearance that was blunt and absolute and that negated the notion of fragility associated with anything floral. She didn't resemble anyone in her family, and sometimes when she studied herself in the mirror she thought she might be beautiful in a way that no one else recognized; other times she thought she was grotesque. The Claytor sensibility on the subject of physical beauty was shaped entirely by Catherine, and in her household there was short shrift given to any idea of a middle ground.

One Saturday in late September of 1917, Warren Scofield and Lily Butler visited the Claytor place and stayed on for some time, sitting in the front parlor. The two of them had ridden out on horseback, because Lily Butler loved to ride and needed an outing. Her husband was overseas, stationed in France, she said, at the field artillery training base in Saumur.

Lily was animated and chatty, but it wasn't really a social visit; Warren was particularly anxious to discuss the needs of Scofields & Company now that they were under incessant pressure from the War Department to increase production, and he also had business to discuss in his capacity as a representative of the Fuel Administration. He had come to raise the possibility of reopening the coalfields on land Dwight Claytor owned near Zanesville, where Warren's grandfather had worked as a young man in the 1830s, digging and hauling coal, in an enterprise that had eventually evolved into Scofields & Company. The Fuel Administration had pegged the price of coal at a high level, and Warren hoped to persuade Dwight Claytor that not only the price but the political capital gained by such an undertaking would make it worth the complicated and time-consuming logistics entailed.

Warren had been required by the War Department to remain in Washburn, Lily told them, in order to oversee the conversion of Scofields & Company to the exclusive manufacture of high-capacity presses to forge large guns and other war matériel. The fact that Lily herself was so familiar with the operation was enormously impressive to Agnes, who did think to slip out of the room for a moment to organize some refreshments.

The discussion had become technical and grave, though, and Agnes eventually grew tense and anxious on behalf of her mother, who had nothing to contribute to the conversation. Even with the furor everywhere over the war, it remained an abstraction to Catherine Claytor, and although she didn't seem bored, Agnes took note of her mother's placid expression, unanimated even by disdain. Agnes was pained at her mother's beige passiveness in the face of Lily Butler's startlingly clever blondness, and Agnes was also worried that her mother might perceive her own social ineptitude, as Lily's quick hands sketched neatly through the air illustrating whatever she said. In later years, whenever Agnes remembered that afternoon, she wondered how it was that Warren Scofield had not caught her attention when he was no farther away than across the room from her, and she generally put it down to Lily's nearly aggressive liveliness and intelligence.

Agnes had escaped the room as soon as she could without being rude, counting it a strike against herself that she was deserting her mother. She wandered outside and sat in the swing that hung from the big oak at the edge of the croquet court and watched her brothers set up the wickets under the cloud-streaked pale blue sky. She pushed the swing idly, just enough motion to flutter her skirt a bit. She was dreamily watching her own feet as she stepped them in patterns in the sparse grass beneath the swing.

"Agnes!" Edson was standing under an apple tree on the other side of the court. "If you won't play then it won't be any fun. We want to play partners."

"No, Eddie. I'm too lazy."

She continued to push the swing languidly, in slow circles, when she noticed that Howie and Richard were stuffing their pockets with fallen apples behind Edson's back. She stood and began to amble casually along her side of the croquet court, stooping now and then to gather a handful of small green apples herself. Out of the corner of her eye she watched the boys and at just the right moment wheeled and pelted Howard and Richard with perfect aim. Richard ducked behind a tree. They shouted in protest: Agnes could throw like a bullet, and apples came flying in her direction while she scrabbled for more ammunition, exclaiming and protesting.

"No fair! No fair!" she called. "It's three against one!" She ran back toward the house and slipped behind a tree herself, having managed to grab only four more apples before being bombarded. She glanced out at her brothers and leapt back as they took aim.

For the rest of her life Agnes could recall even the scent of those apples at the moment when she had turned and noticed Warren Scofield, perhaps twenty yards away, standing at an angle to her, saying good-bye to her parents. At a distance he was a sweep of yellow hair and dark brows as he briefly pivoted on the porch steps after shaking hands with her father. Before she gave it a second thought, Agnes drew her arm back and released a searing shot that caught him right between his shoulder blades.

Warren turned in surprise and stared at her, and then he bent and picked up that hard, green apple and inspected it before polishing it on his sleeve. He took a bite with a somber expression, and the working of his mouth and throat, for nearly a minute on that last Saturday of September in 1917, was the only motion in the world as far as Agnes knew.

Chapter Three

IN THE CLAYTOR HOUSEHOLD it had always been perfectly clear that Agnes was her father's daughter, that Richard and Howie were aligned more with each other than with either of their parents, and that Edson remained besotted with his mother. All the children had gone through a time of yearning after their mother, who had lavished affectionate attention on each one of them now and then, but Agnes's happiest idea of her childhood involved her father. By the time she was five or six years old, he had often taken her along with him to business or political meetings at the Eola Arms Hotel in Washburn. She was thrilled to be included and had no idea that her excited leave-taking had been perceived by her mother as a bewildering rejection of herself.

Dwight Claytor wasn't a sentimental or *doting* sort of father, but he solemnly held her dining chair for her — and all the other businessmen or politicians stood politely, looking on with real or feigned indulgence — until he assured himself that his daughter was comfortably seated. And Agnes was so careful in her best dress and uncomfortable dress-up shoes to be well-behaved, to keep her elbows off the table, to place her knife and fork exactly right on her plate when she was done, that the other men relievedly forgot about her and leaned forward on their elbows, jabbing at the air with an index finger — or a cigar streaming pale curls of smoke — to make a point.

In the middle of one heated conversation in the hotel dining room, silence fell over the table as coffee was served, and even at age six Agnes was aware of the tension in the pause during the general rustle of resettling. Finally Agnes felt compelled to speak up in that palpably hostile silence, "President Roosevelt never *will* reduce the tariffs or do anything about banking reform." And the men leaned back in their chairs with explosive and admiring laughter all around, all except her father, who nodded at her thoughtfully. The others looked at her earnest, round eyes in her serious six-year-old face surrounded by masses of curly black hair and peppered the two Claytors with murmurings of approval.

"Aha! Like father like daughter . . ."

". . . *should* get the vote . . ."

". . . cute as a bug and smart as a whip!"

Whenever Agnes rode alongside her father in the buggy or in his motorcar he discussed these things with her. He had laid out the need for a railroad-regulation bill. Her father was angry about what he felt was the president's failure to see the urgency of satisfying the Middle West's desire for more control of corporations, or to understand the region's need for direct election of senators. And on that issue, her father told her, Roosevelt really didn't grasp the mood of the Far West, either.

On those long rides her father also asked her about her own life. He wanted to know what she liked in school, and he listened with grave attention — he listened without one bit of condescension. Once, when she named the birds of Ohio that she had learned from a book at school, he pulled up on Newark Road and dexterously folded a bird out of a flat sheet of newspaper to illustrate to her how it achieved flight. And although Agnes failed to grasp the principle, she never, ever forgot the sight of her father loping along the dusty road with the paper bird raised above his head to show her how its wings would work as it lifted off the ground.

When she returned home with him from these outings, however, her mother would stalk and find her alone somewhere. Catherine would be beside herself. "He only takes you along because it makes a good impression. It's only that it *amuses* people now. It hasn't got a thing to do with *you*. He doesn't take you with him because he cares one bit about how you feel. You ought to know that. You'll find that out soon enough!"

"Don't say that, Mama!" Agnes would plead. "Don't say that!" But even though her mother never recanted, Agnes didn't entirely believe her. When she had been Edson's age — even younger than that, in fact — Agnes would watch for her father from her window in the afternoons when she knew he was due home. He would heave shut the barn door and then take a moment to adjust his coat, straighten his collar, carefully adjust his hat — make himself ready to face his own life. He would cross the yard deliberately, keeping to the path, and he would cough exactly two times midway to the door. Agnes would race down the back stairs to meet him, because he seemed to her somehow so sadly solitary. It had been impossible, too, for her not to court the one of her parents who seemed to like her best. But she spent long, agonized hours at night, awake in her bed, longing for her mother. Recounting any instance that might be interpreted as evidence that her mother loved her or at least approved of something about her.

The day after Lily Butler and Warren Scofield's visit, Dwight Claytor left early for Columbus, where he kept rooms at the Curtis Hotel while the legislature was in session, and Catherine Claytor grew restless in the waning hours of that Sunday afternoon in September. Edson followed worriedly in her wake as she drifted from room to room through the tail end of the day. At supper, when she was lost in some remote musing all her own, he became overly animated in anxiety, and when he knocked his water glass off the table, Agnes and the other two simply kept their heads down, but Catherine didn't take much notice. "Just leave it, Edson. Don't cut yourself. Mrs. Longacre will get Betsy to take care of it in the morning," she said, and her older three children were — each one separately — ashamed to have felt a clutch of panic when the glass had shattered on the carpet in a series of subtly ringing, fragile little chinks.

And, in fact, Agnes swept it up after she cleared the table, because she knew that Mrs. Longacre didn't like any of the Claytors much except her father and perhaps Edson. Agnes never let herself browse for long in that particular region of her own deep shame. It had been she, when she was nearly ten years old, who had been so inept at taking care of Edson that when her father arrived home earlier than usual late one afternoon he had come into the house looking for his wife and had found Agnes desperately trying to quiet the baby. Agnes had been trying to coax Edson quiet through the bars of his crib, sitting back on her haunches to be at his level, holding up offerings of toys, but he had only turned his head back and forth frantically, with loud whoops of angry despair. Finally she had climbed into the crib with him, meaning only to rock him, because she wasn't tall enough to lift him over its high sides, but she had resorted to a desperate jostling as his crying crescendoed in direct proportion to her efforts to calm him.

She hadn't even heard her father come up the stairs and had let out a shriek herself as he had clasped her by her upper arms, lifted her straight up over the railings, and set her on the floor. He had leaned down close to her face. "What are you doing to the baby, Agnes? What in the world are you doing? Where's your mother?"

Agnes didn't know why she had been taking care of Edson at that moment or where her mother had been. She only remembered that her father had scooped the baby out of the crib, holding him with one arm, and taken hold of her own arm once more just above the elbow so that she straggled along with him down the stairs and out the front door. They went along the fraily established dirt path across the yard, catty-cornered over the field and through the vegetable garden of their old house, where the farm manager, Jerome Dameron, lived with his family, which included his mother-in-law, Mrs. Longacre. She was alone in the kitchen snapping peas when Dwight Claytor rapped at the back door.

"We need some help up at our house, Mrs. Longacre," her father said. That's all Agnes remembered: the precision of each word as her father spoke in a soft, courteous, but chillingly brisk voice, and she never forgot Mrs. Longacre's lengthy, inquiring, pursed-mouth scrutiny as she took a long look at Agnes and the baby.

It was Mrs. Longacre who taught Agnes, and her brothers, too, when they were a little older, just the right way to make their beds so that the sheet didn't come loose in the middle of the night. And it was she who tore all the bedclothes off any child's bed left unmade and dropped them for that child to find in a tumbled heap on the floor as she made her morning rounds through their rooms, straightening up and putting away the ironing that Betsy Graves left each evening in the pantry. It was Mrs. Longacre who was appalled when the Claytor children came trundling into the front hall with their shoes still muddy, and it was she who, Monday through Friday, imposed as much regulation as was possible on Mr. Claytor's household.

It was also Mrs. Longacre's sudden presence in the household that seemed to quell any possibility of joy Catherine Claytor still harbored. She was sullen and broody in the company of this other woman, insisting to her husband and her children that Mrs. Longacre was robbing them blind, that she had made off with two of Catherine's grandmother's silver spoons.

"Catherine!" their father had exploded one evening, as she fell once again into this litany, and the children froze at his tone. It was in the first year Mrs. Longacre had taken over the running of the house. "What on earth can you be thinking? She has no use in the world for your silver spoons! She has *plenty* of silver spoons in her own house! And if you don't understand that you must treat her with courtesy . . . She's agreed to run this house, Catherine. I don't know what we'll do if she decides to leave! Her family are fine people. . . ." He sounded helpless for a moment, impatient, and dangerous with frustration. "You don't seem to understand that it took some persuading. . . . She *agreed* to work for us, Catherine, but Mrs. Longacre *is not your servant!*"

Catherine turned her head away, her eyes shocked, her mouth trembling, and the children — who just moments earlier had been hating the sound of their mother's every word — at once turned mutinous against their father. Not one of them said anything, but they had all aimed stunned and reproachful faces his way — even the baby had looked up at him somberly in a dark surveillance. Dwight Claytor took them all in at a glance and slammed out the front door.

However they felt about her one moment to the next, Catherine's children did all understand early on that their mother was a victim of circumstance. Howie and Richard certainly believed her when she apologized for and tried to explain some injustice she had visited upon them. She would approach them somberly, bending her serious face to theirs, and wave her arm in a vague gesture and murmur on about this place, this wretched countryside.

But neither Richard nor Howie remembered a time when he was not primarily connected to the other as an ally or an enemy. Both Agnes and Edson, however, had spent several years as tourists in their own family, isolated simply by their own childhoods, and they had a keener understanding of the fact that their mother resided in a foreign country. And all four of those children had learned from their mother that every square inch of the godforsaken state of Ohio was loathsome. There was simply nothing good that could be said about it.

"This whole place," Catherine once said to Agnes with ferocity when Agnes was just a little girl, "is just exactly as skinned looking as a peeled grape. It's just a hateful place. All bare. The fields . . ." She had gestured widely outward to indicate the land rolling away beyond the yard. "Corn and corn and corn, and the trees as naked as jaybirds! It's no surprise to me to meet the people who live here. It's no surprise at all. *Flat*-minded people. No idea of graciousness in the world. Just to think of the sort of people — any people who would live with such weather . . ."

Her mother had spoken to her conspiratorially, inclusively, but nevertheless, it had been an injury of a sort to Agnes, even then, and as she got older she understood it as one more indictment of her own personality. Because, of course, Agnes *was* a person who lived here, and Agnes suspected that her own thoughts and motives were very likely as insufficiently complicated — as flat and direct — as those of all the other Midwesterners at whom Catherine scoffed.

Agnes did her best to honor her mother's desperate grudge against the vast, blank idea of the region, but each year as the seasons changed, she was overtaken time and again by the drama of all the extraordinary Midwestern contrasts of hot and cold. The first morning each year when Agnes looked from her upstairs window at the bare, intricate, curly black branches of the old trees traced with snow that had accrued overnight without her knowledge, it astonished her.

But Catherine Claytor hated the snow, and she would mutter through the house, personally affronted, so Agnes kept quiet. Nevertheless, and in spite of herself, Agnes never failed to be elated to find she had gone to sleep when the earth was camouflaged in subtle shades of gold and beige and brown, and had awakened in a world that shimmered silver. Agnes would stand and gaze out of her window as long as possible while the sun rose and the temperature warmed enough to liberate the snow-burdened evergreen branches, so that all around the yard they sprang free one by one, sending glistening sprays of snow dazzling across the air.

It never occurred to Agnes to dislike one season or another. She didn't mind the deep and treacherous mud of early spring, miring machinery in the fields, sucking at the heels of her sturdy boots. And unlike poor Catherine, Agnes never dreaded the summer onslaught of brutal weather. She was stirred by the first peppery scent of an oncoming storm; she even relished the storm itself, coming in so fast that once she had had to dismount her horse and flatten herself in a ditch as lightning struck all around her. She had lain facedown with her hands clasped over the back of her skull, her elbows cradling her temples as though she were waiting out enemy bombardment. She had been terrified, her mind filled with nothing else but one long plea — Dear God Please Dear God Please Dear God — as she felt the concussion of thunder and closed her eyes against lightning so pervasive that it was a constant, flickering white illumination. But later, dripping wet, traipsing after her horse, her hair and skirt trailing weedy grasses, and still shuddering from shock, she had also been deeply thrilled.

By the time she was fourteen, Agnes had sometimes been so unhappy that there had been moments she had wished that she did not exist at all. Sometimes she had been sad enough to let her thoughts wander tentatively over the possibility of giving up altogether, but also by the time she was fourteen and fifteen she had become fairly fascinated by the drama of her own self. And, too, she had invested a good part of herself in the world beyond her own household, so by and large she was glad to draw another breath. If she had considered it one way or another, she would have conceded that even at the worst of times she would

choose to continue to occupy a place on the earth. And therefore she was necessarily devoted to the place where she lived. It
was where she was as she shaped her expectations of the world,
and it was a landscape she embraced because it inescapably defined and contained her, heart and soul.

None of the Claytor children, however, was entirely im-
mune to Catherine's contempt for Washburn, Ohio — a contempt that in some way conferred upon her children a little
superiority. Agnes sometimes said to her friends, unaware that
she had taken on a certain air of condescension, that it was too
bad to be stuck in a place of so little distinction. A town as little
known as Washburn. And then it was her good friends who
brooded privately over such an insult to the place their families
had chosen, for whatever reason, to live. To the place where
they were becoming who they were to become. And then any
one of those friends — Lucille Drummond, say, or Sally Trenholm — at home and vexed by some request denied or desire
made light of, might blurt out some remark to her own parents.
Sally or Lucille might say something along the lines of how
could her parents possibly understand the need for something
finer than plain cotton serge for a new dress, given that — as
Agnes Claytor said — they lived in such a backwater.

But by 1917, Agnes was old enough to be healthily self-
involved, and Howie and Richard had each other as a protective
frame of reference. It was only ten-year-old Edson Claytor who
occasionally glanced darkly out at the unforgivable everlasting-
ness of the rolling fields of Ohio with dismay, a bitter sorrow
overtaking him when he considered that his mother had to bear
up under conditions so unlike the soft, kind climate, the amiable
environment, of her childhood home in Natchez, Mississippi.

It was quite a ripple that Catherine's stone had made when

she tossed it unthinkingly into the clear water of her young children's sensibilities. It was quite a ripple, and in such a small pond that eventually it broke against her own shore. Catherine Claytor was held in great suspicion among the parents of her children's friends and never was able to form any easy alliances. But her children understood that this landscape where she was so hard-pressed to eke out a single satisfactory hour was infinitely inferior to her own territory. And that territory was a place they believed they had never been. They had yet to make the connection between the actual geography of Natchez, Mississippi, and that wondrous place their mother always referred to as home.

Three times in her life Agnes had visited Natchez with the rest of her family. She remembered the trips a little bit, although often if she mentioned some particular detail she was told by one or the other of her parents that it never had happened or that what she thought she had seen did not, in fact, exist. It had been hot forever, Agnes said, in the backseat of the car with Howie and Richard pressed against her. No, her father said, it had been chilly, and the three of them had been wrapped in an old feather quilt.

It had frightened her to watch their automobile float away across a river on a raft that seemed to evaporate. Agnes remembered that she had thought the car was proceeding across the water all on its own, growing smaller as it moved away. Yes, indeed, her mother said, it had not been a good idea at all to take that crossing. No, her father said, it had only been a creek, no matter of any consequence, and they had remained in the car as the ferryman hauled them across by rope, hand over hand.

Her cousins had not liked her, Agnes thought. And her

mother said it wasn't true at all, it was just that Agnes seemed strange to them. "It was only your accent," she said. "They think you're a little Yankee." Celeste and Peggy Alcorn were older than Agnes by several years, and she remembered that they had given her a piece of chocolate candy she had bitten into only to discover that it was a flat patty they had fashioned out of mud. But she didn't mention this to either one of her parents because it was not so out of line with the general perils of childhood. She hadn't ever, but might have considered pulling such a trick on one of her brothers. It wasn't entirely beyond the realm of possibility. She remembered the wide porch where she sat and cut pictures out of a magazine her grandmother Edson gave to her, and she remembered that Celeste had helped her and that they had had fun until Peggy turned up.

Agnes hadn't been back since they had gone to Mississippi after her grandmother died, just a little while after Edson was born. Her mother and Edson had traveled by train to Natchez when he was four, but Agnes and the other two were in school and had stayed in Washburn under Mrs. Longacre's care. Peggy Alcorn had traveled back to Ohio with Catherine Claytor and Edson, but Agnes had the hardest time really believing that the tall, pale, weak-chinned girl who drifted around the Claytor house could possibly be the same person who had instilled such dread in her only four years earlier. Peggy had stayed with them for two months, sharing Agnes's room, and Agnes couldn't, during all that time, form any fixed impression of her. She seemed to Agnes not to have much personality at all, although her mother said Peggy had beautifully cultivated manners.

Whatever Catherine Claytor did or didn't understand about the delicate agreement with Mrs. Longacre, it was when she had consented to take over as the Claytors' general housekeeper that the older three children, even at their young ages, began the complicated business of leading a multilayered life. They became duplicitous by default. It had nothing to do with how they felt about Mrs. Longacre; they liked her well enough but kept their minds open to doubt out of loyalty to their mother. They couldn't possibly have sorted out all the complexities of their new arrangement. For one thing, Mrs. Longacre's grandchildren were their playmates, and her oldest grandchild, Bernice, had been three years ahead of Agnes at school.

The Claytor children, though, deduced some sort of unspoken but deep embarrassment on the part of both their parents, and, too, those children had a certain, inherent sense of propriety and an easily tapped reservoir of shame. The older Claytor children were filled with unnatural cheer and goodwill toward Mrs. Longacre. They behaved with astonishing decorum under her rather brusque supervision and often took it out on one another in her absence. After all, a united front doesn't hang together very well in the absence of the enemy.

Edson alone — clearly Mrs. Longacre's favorite of the Claytor clan — maintained a scrupulously polite but distinctly restrained manner toward her. He never told her jokes, as Howie or Richard often did, sometimes earning a stiff smile. Edson never asked for her advice or told her stories of his day at school. He never begged a special treat or enthused over the plates of cookies or a cake she sometimes prepared. He always thanked her solemnly, but he saved all his secrets — any newly discovered ardor about one thing or another — to tell his mother, to seduce his mother's elusive attention. Mrs. Longacre was merely dependable; his mother, in those moments when her concentration was caught and aimed his way . . . well, his mother was magical.

By 1917, Mrs. Longacre was a fixture in the life of the Claytor household, and the Claytor children were no longer even aware of the careful fusion of all the layers of their lives. There were so many separate, secret, unadmitted elements to the one instinctive, collective presentation of their adherence as a family that it would have required a sort of emotional archaeology to bring them all to light. By that Sunday evening in September when Agnes was carefully picking bits of glass from the dining-room carpet, it was more reassuring than not that Mrs. Longacre would be arriving at eight o'clock the next morning.

Agnes woke up off and on during the night to the sounds of doors opening and closing, of her mother's steps, sometimes stealthy, sometimes clattering on the front stairs, of a general stirring about within the house. The whole of Agnes's night had a nervous, streaky quality; she endured a shivery, pale restlessness and never had the satisfaction of falling away into the deep blue-black of heavy sleep. Edson woke her, though, from a state of near unconsciousness so early in the morning that only a barely discernible lightening of the sky seeped around the edges of her window shade.

"I don't know what Mama's doing, Agnes. I don't know what she's doing." He was bending over, shaking her shoulder, his hair still spiked from his pillow and his face shiny and luminous in the dark room, his eyes silvery with restrained tears.

Agnes only looked at him a moment, coming into wakefulness and bunching her pillow under her head to prop it up a bit. "What do you mean? I don't know what you mean. Where is she, Edson?"

"She's in the pantry. But I don't know what she's doing! She's cutting up all her dresses. She's got piles and piles of clothes. For the poor, she says. She says we're not to think of her at all. That what happens to her, as old as she is, just doesn't matter. That it's her birthday, after all, and that she's too old for all those bright dresses." Edson implied his mother's speech — the emphasis, the strained timbre infused with desperation — in his own despairing boy's voice.

"Oh, no, Edson! Her birthday! Is it? What's today? Oh, Eddie, it is! It's the first of October. Oh, no! Oh, and Papa didn't remember. You know he didn't." Agnes threw off the blankets and got out of bed, cinching her tangled hair away from her face with her hands. "Go get dressed, Edson. Get dressed for school, and we'll go down together. Where're Howie and Richard? Go wake them up and tell them I said to wash up and get ready for school. Tell them it's Mama's birthday and that I said for them to get up right now. Tell them I *mean* right now! And you be sure to comb your hair, Eddie. Get it really wet first. I don't have time to help you with it."

Agnes was the first dressed, pulling on her white stockings while hopping first on one foot and then the other, wrenching on her skirt and middy blouse, scraping her brush mercilessly through her mass of wiry hair, which she fastened tightly in a tortoiseshell clip with a slightly wilted navy blue bow attached. She scarcely took time to observe the effect — even the bow was school regulation — she only checked to be sure she was all straight, and then she hurried down the stairs in a rush to find her mother before Mrs. Longacre arrived. But she slowed to a saunter as she crossed the kitchen.

The sight of her mother was alarming. Catherine's hair had come loose on one side and fell against her cheek as she stood with her bare feet slipped into her nice black buckled shoes, but otherwise she was dressed only in her wrapper and poised over a jumble of clothes — dresses, blouses, petticoats, hats, gloves, strewn everywhere — wielding her pair of long seamstress's shears.

"Mama, what are you doing up so early? What are you doing awake before the sun's even up? And on your birthday? The boys and I were going to surprise you with breakfast before Mrs. Longacre got here." Agnes's voice was artificial and tense with feigned cheer, but Catherine cast a disinterested glance at her daughter and bent and snipped, bent and snipped, curiously birdlike.

"Mama, what are you doing? You aren't dressed yet. Aren't you too cold?"

Catherine worked steadily for a moment more on a blouse whose sleeves hung forlornly to the floor as she held the bodice draped over one hand, and then she cast it aside and turned to Agnes, displaying a handful of buttons she had cut away, beautiful, intricate pierced bone, some of them, others of filigreed silver, of shiny brass, and some only plain shell. She was triumphant. "Now won't your father see how thrifty I can be," she said, elated. "He'll be awfully pleased, you know. Why, *he* has no idea how a household can work!"

"But Mama! All your clothes . . . Won't he be upset? What about your clothes?"

"Oh, these are all for a *young* woman. A girl! For a girl, I think. I'm sending them to the church, but I've saved the buttons, you see. And some of this trim, so when Cleo comes to do your hems she can start cutting my dresses, and I'll have all the buttons she needs. And this nice lace collar. Hat trims. Ribbons, you see. I *refuse* to be foolish! I *won't* be thought of as a woman who doesn't even know any better than to dress her age. Oh, not for a minute! Not on any account will I be one of those awful, foolish old women!"

Foolish, foolish, was all Agnes could think as she looked at the ruin of her mother's wardrobe — Catherine had cut away lace cuffs, had unseamed sleeves, had removed tulle insets — and Edson stood beside Agnes, stricken. "But Mama. Your dresses are so pretty," he said. "Can't Cleo put the buttons back? Can't you fix them back?" Both he and Agnes knew that this was one of those acts on their mother's part that might enrage their father.

Although they never spoke of it to one another, none of Dwight's children was ever entirely surprised late in the night to come awake to a distant bark of anger somewhere in the dark interior of the house. They had all four awakened separately some weeks before on a stifling hot night when the windows of the house were open to catch any shift of damp, warm air. They had awakened to their father's voice, in the dark yard, raised in hollow, nasal, high-pitched, prolonged fury that flattened without resonance in the humid air, overriding the plaintive upward climb of some complaint their mother, who must have followed him outside, made.

". . . and you can't . . . if you leave me here again," she was saying, "all alone I won't . . ." But her words were drowned out by a simultaneous and furious declaration of their father's, unintelligible to them word by word but terrifying in the clarity of its fury:

"— are the *ruin,* are the *ruin,* the total ruin of my life, my whole life, of everything I know! *Wrecked!* All a shambled *wreck! Wrecked!*"

"Stop . . . Dwight . . . stop . . ."

". . . *never* helped me, *never* listen to what I *tell* you!"

And each emphasis was accompanied by the unmistakable smack of a blow.

"Stop it . . . don't don't don't . . ." Their mother's voice muffled finally, and there was the soft falling-to of the kitchen screen, the door slamming as she retreated indoors followed by the clunk of the bolt being thrown and — in a little bit — the rasp of the barn door heaved open. Each child stayed still in bed, frozen with dread, until their father's automobile sputtered to life and finally couldn't be heard any longer after it rounded the bend on Newark Road. They found their mother folded angularly into a kitchen chair, with her hair loose and falling forward over her face, which she had lowered into her cupped hands on the table, and they huddled around her, trying to get her back to her bedroom.

"You see . . ." She exhaled in a long, hissing sigh, raising her head like a wraith in her flowing white nightgown. "Just see what kind of husband I have. . . . Look what he does." She lowered her head again gently into the palms of her hands and wept in long sweeps of expended air and shuddering gasps in an effort to catch her breath, her mouth dark in her pale, shocked face.

Agnes and Howie and Richard and Edson couldn't help but look; they couldn't help but see. They were overcome with desperation and embarrassed sorrow and pity, and they were overwhelmed with unspecified shame, as well. But the older children hated their mother a little, too, for her terrible baffled sadness. Only Edson moved forward and attempted to embrace her. "Oh, Mama! Mama! Mama!" he said as he patted her head awkwardly.

Agnes and Howie and Richard hated her in the days that followed for the dark bruises that appeared on her cheek and along her arm where it was exposed beneath her sleeve. In spite of themselves they held her misery against her; it was such thoroughly irrefutable evidence of failure on all their parts, somehow. "Look at this," their mother would say in apparent bewilderment, raising and turning her arm in surprise. "How could this happen? How could this happen to me?" she would ask her children when she came across them as she wandered though the house after Mrs. Longacre had gone. "Why, look at what your father's done," she would say mildly, perplexed herself. The older three would glance away, would refuse to contemplate her lament, but Edson would study his mother in despair and take himself off to his own room, where he flung himself out flat on his bed and wept silently with fury and sadness. Their father was gone for days and days, and Agnes heard Mrs. Longacre say to Edson that sometimes people were bound to get what they deserved.

On the morning of her birthday, though, Catherine was positively jaunty, straightening up, pushing her hair behind her ear. "Oh, I think your father can afford to buy me a few sober dresses . . . a hat with a plain brown velvet band, I think . . . ," she said in a dreamy, thoughtful voice, putting the shears down on the bench where most of the clothes lay in disarray. "I think that won't be too much to spend on his old wife. *This* old lady needs some new clothes for her birthday!" And she seemed triumphant, as though she had put one over on somebody. But Edson shivered in misery beside Agnes, and Howie and Richard were behind them looking on.

"Well, don't you four look like death warmed over?" their mother said, reaching up with both hands to fasten her hair securely, although her wrapper fell open as she raised her arms, revealing the sharp wings of her collarbone, the shadowed hollows of her breastbone, and the tops of her slack breasts. Agnes moved in closer to block her from view, though Catherine took no notice. "But you can just wipe off those gloomy faces. We're going to have a *wonderful* day! We're going to have a picnic. Anything we like we'll take along and nothing, *nothing* we don't long for with all our hearts! We're going to make ice cream, too, when we get home.

"Oh, that's what we always did back home for my birthday! I always asked Ida to make fried chicken and my daddy made his famous ginger ice cream. Mama couldn't cook to save her life, of course, but she always was just so much fun! We'd go out the Trace to the Indian mounds, and Mama would bring along big sheets of cardboard. We'd use them like sleds. We'd go flying down from the top of those mounds. Just flying down. And they seemed so high to me, but they weren't at all, you know. She'd settle everyone under the trees, and they always made me take a nap before we had dinner. It almost killed me! Lying there with my eyes closed, listening to everyone laughing and talking." She was a little brittle with excitement, hurtling through the words and beaming, but then she slowed down and fixed them with a look of mock reproach. "In Natchez, you see, I didn't have to deal with such a bunch of spoilsports and sourpusses."

"Mama, you'd better go get dressed," Agnes said to her mother with discouraging deliberation, and her mother's expression began to lose its animation. "Mrs. Longacre will be here any minute. We have to get to school, Mama. We can't go on a picnic today. But we can have fried chicken for dinner if you'll just tell Mrs. Longacre. And we can make ice cream, too.

Hadn't you better go get dressed?" She spoke kindly enough, but she was no longer cajoling. Her mother made a childish, bitter face at her.

"Hah! Mrs. Longacre makes fried chicken I wouldn't even feed to a bunch of Yankee soldiers! *Boils* it first! It truly does amaze me! Honestly, it does! These people have no idea how to cook. I tell you, I've seen Ida take a couple of handfuls of dandelion greens and a little bacon fat and turn it into the finest . . . oh, well, the most delicate salad you can imagine. But in *this* godforsaken place . . . Ugh! Disgusting!" Then her voice slipped into a tone of supplication. "But you can stay home from school today. You all have my permission. It's just one day. Just one day."

"Mama, you know we can't do that. We'll miss enough being sick. It's too hard to catch up. I'll fix griddle cakes and we have cane syrup, too, that Peggy sent from New Orleans. You get dressed and we'll have a celebration."

But as they walked along to school in the crisp air, Edson lagged behind his two older brothers, and Agnes was yards behind him, having stayed on to speak to Mrs. Longacre. Richard and Howie joked with and elbowed each other, walking for a while with each one trying to push the other into the ditch alongside the road while the other strained mightily to keep his balance. The rule between them was that you could try to unbalance the other in any way except tripping or using your hands.

"You two stop it right now," Agnes called ahead to them, over Edson's head. "You'll get wet and have to wear those shoes all day."

Howie turned around and walked backward for a little while, miming someone about to lose his balance, arms flailing wildly, fingers splayed, pretending to teeter along. "Well, Agnes, if I fall in, maybe I couldn't go to school at all. Like Mama said. I have her *permission!* Why, I could just go right home and go on Mama's picnic!"

He stopped still and struck a pose with one hand on his canted hip in ridiculous exaggeration and gestured to Richard with a sweep of his arm, adopting a silly falsetto voice and copying his mother's Southern accent, the words sliding away before they ended: "Now you just go grab a handful of those cattails and a bucket of lard, and I tell you, Ida'll make you the daintiest dish you ever *did* see! Don't you know, Ida could fry up a batch of chicken, and we could all run out and slide down the Indian mounds. Just *fly* down those hills," he mimicked. "Oh, my, they're so *tall!* And if I have to take a nap before dinner, why, I'll just *die!*"

But then he let his voice fall back into its own pitch. "And I think Mama was just about to celebrate her birthday in her birthday *suit!*" And this just knocked them out, he and Richard, it was so scandalous a thing to say — to imagine. They fell against each other in delighted embarrassment and illicit glee. Agnes didn't reprove them, and Edson studied the ground as he walked, not looking at them but flushed red with repressed laughter and overwhelmed with an ache like homesickness. They were mean, all so mean, to their mother.

Of Catherine's four children, only Edson, at age ten, still carried in his head on the morning of his mother's fortieth birthday an image of her remarkable face, the high, wide, rounded brow and long straight nose of a great beauty. He had no idea of comparisons, of judging her against any other person at all. In fact, he didn't even know that what she looked like had any bearing on his sorrowful recollection of her face. The consequence of apprehending beauty, however, is truly mysterious, and Catherine Claytor was not merely attractive, not just pretty, but powerfully lovely. In the same way that — regardless of circumstance — horses are beautiful and camels not, she possessed beauty out of context.

When she turned her wide, pale, down-slanting eyes on him, or whenever he recalled her happiness and then her eventual closed-down look of resignation — her inevitable surrender to a kind of hopelessness — he forgave her anything and was filled with a powerless protective pity for her. In spite of the moody fury that increasingly *was* the context of his mother's life, in spite of the terrifying rage she sometimes directed his way, her periods of endearing, heartbreaking optimism, along with beauty of the high order that she possessed, remained for him an extenuating circumstance. The rest of her children had lost faith, lost the ability to see her at all separate from whatever demons had overtaken her.

In good weather the Claytor children walked to school, and the first of October, 1917, in Washburn, Ohio, was a glorious day. Edson was still young enough that it didn't cross his mind to weigh whatever the weather happened to be compared to what it had been the day before, and his brothers didn't take much note of the weather either, except in connection to some other event in their lives — outdoor recess, for instance. But Agnes's spirits lifted in the sparkling day as she rounded the bend and approached the grove of trees beyond which the Claytor place could no longer be seen from the vantage point of Newark Road.

At first just the rhythm of her body moving easily along the familiar road lulled her out of her worry over the marshy quagmire of life at home into a determined musing on the affairs at school, ideas she had for the class book, the news about Lily Butler and Warren Scofield's visit she was eager to tell Lucille, and a host of questions to ask her in private. She brought the memory of Lily's quick mind and delighted curiosity firmly into focus, and she realized that the notion of Warren had never been out of her head at all. She allowed herself to see him standing with that apple in his hand, slowly bringing it to his mouth and biting into it.

But she wasn't far enough away from home yet to be completely free of a little catch of anxiety at the edge of her thoughts. It made her uneasy to think about her mother alone all day with Mrs. Longacre. Agnes no longer assumed that her mother would know to come up with a plausible explanation for her behavior. Agnes wasn't even sure anymore that her mother realized, as she once had, when her behavior was out of the ordinary. When Agnes had watched from the window for Mrs. Longacre's approach and contrived to meet her at the door just as they each were passing through, Agnes had pretended that the request she made was a sudden whim, a spur-of-the-moment idea. She had moved across the threshold past Mrs. Longacre and then turned back.

"Oh, Mrs. Longacre? I just thought! Do you think you might have any time at all today . . . Well, it's my mother's birthday, you know. Of course we won't celebrate or anything until my father's home on Saturday." She infused her voice with the casual, confident certainty of a person aware that she is only politely restating an already known or assumed fact. "But the boys wanted — oh, well, I should say, actually, that *Edson* especially wanted to give Mama the present he bought for her tonight. It's so hard for him to wait," she added fondly. "You know how excited he can get! I thought maybe we could do something especially nice, and I was going to make a cake this afternoon. But," she sighed, "I have to stay late to work on the senior pageant." She assumed a wide-eyed look of resignation at the unforeseen responsibilities of her own life.

Mrs. Longacre's granddaughter had been editor of the yearbook when she was a junior at the Linus Gilchrest Institute for Girls, and editor of the class book her senior year. The girls at school still talked about Bernice Dameron with admiration, and Mrs. Longacre looked back at Agnes with a succinct little nod of acknowledgment. Agnes pressed on. "I wonder if you might possibly have the time to make a cake? Oh, just any kind that's easiest. Not even any frosting. It's such trouble, I know. I'll just sift some sugar over the top. I should have done it last night, but I was determined to help my mother get her clothes sorted out before Cleo Rutledge comes to let down my hems. And, my goodness! We certainly didn't finish. Please don't bother about all the things we've got spread all over the place in the pantry," she said in a sort of breathless, dismissive rush. "But it would be awfully nice to have a cake to cut after supper tonight. Do you think . . ."

"Oh, yes, yes," Mrs. Longacre said, to hurry her on, standing turned to listen while she impatiently removed her gloves and coat and hat. "I don't see why I can't do that." And Agnes beamed at her.

"It's awfully nice of you, Mrs. Longacre. Edson will be so glad! We'll *all* be glad! But Edson was so disappointed."

Agnes decided she had done all she could, and as she walked along Newark Road, farther and farther from home, she fell into a pleasant anticipation of where she was going as opposed to where she was coming from. But she felt traitorous, too, in her slow accretion of pleasure and her metamorphosis, during that forty-five-minute walk to school, into a seemingly untroubled, assured, and capable young woman who was, as it happened, one of the stars of the Linus Gilchrest Institute for Girls, class of 1918. Nevertheless, she walked along growing increasingly happy on this particular morning as the billowing pure white clouds moved fast through the bright sky, casting flying shadows over the tall grass in the meadows soon to be mown for hay.

Chapter Four

EVERYONE IN WASHBURN KNEW that Warren Scofield had been in love with his first cousin, Lily, all his life. It was simply understood that he had been in love with her probably since the moment he was born, placed in a hastily retrieved bassinet next to hers in the nursery at his uncle Leo's house. His mother, Lillian Marshal Scofield, had been visiting her sister, Audra Scofield — had just had a glass of lemonade, in fact — when Audra noticed that Lillian looked peculiar. Audra had glanced up to discover that Lillian's chin was tucked down in concentration and that she was clutching the frame and fabric of her needlework while also gripping the arm of her chair. Audra only noticed because she happened to look up from her own needlework: The two of them were embroidering a set of chair covers just to keep themselves busy during the last months of their pregnancies.

"Oh, Audra!" Lillian had said, "I think I shouldn't have drunk that cold lemonade so fast." But Audra heard the tamped-down quality of her sister's voice and got Lillian upstairs and into bed. Ever after, Audra Scofield wondered how she had known so surely that her sister had gone into labor when she had not recognized the symptoms in herself, had confused the oddly clenched tightening of the whole middle of herself — which seemed to be separate from the rest of her entirely — as being only an increased aggressiveness of the baby's movements. As it happened, though, Audra gave birth just three hours after the doctor arrived to attend Lillian. Lillian's labor waxed and waned through the day, whereas Audra felt as though she had been knocked flat by a train, without time even to take stock of exactly what was happening to her.

By the time Lillian gave birth to her son, there was his mother's namesake. Audra's daughter had already been born. She had gotten there before him, and by the time he arrived, she was already nicknamed Lily and was already far more worldly-wise than he. By the time Warren made his way into the world, little Lily had learned the terror of being unencompassed, the comfort of being cosseted, and discovered the exquisite satisfaction of slaking thirst and assuaging hunger. She had arrived a little more than eight hours ahead of him into the vast daylight — not so much time, perhaps, and yet the only world he was ever in already contained her.

At least, that's the way Lucille Drummond told the story to Agnes Claytor at school on the Monday afternoon following the Saturday visit to the Claytor place of Warren Scofield and Lily Scofield Butler:

"*Warren* Scofield was the last of those three babies to be born that day," Lucille told her, "eight hours after *Lily* Scofield. And she's been his heart's desire since that exact moment. It was *meant* to be, even though it's just tragic for poor Warren Scofield. But when the three of them were born, it was like a spell had broken. Until then that year had been simply terrible! In the afternoons the clouds came up every single day in the west. Like walls! So dark they were almost black. Storm clouds, I mean. Men would sit out on the roof at the railway station, where they could see all the way out to the edge of town. They would make bets on how many funnel clouds they could count."

"Lucille . . . ," Agnes tried to interrupt, wanting to bring Lucille back to the subject of the current status of the connection between Warren Scofield and Lily and Robert Butler, but Lucille overrode her.

"No, *everyone* knows that's true, Agnes." There was a leftover note in her voice of argument and injury from the previous Friday, when Agnes had scoffed at one of Lucille's ideas for the senior pageant. "You're not even trying to *imagine* the day those children were born — probably the most *unusual* thing that's ever happened in Washburn! The doctor had to have a horse saddled at Scofields and just *race* back and forth to take care of Mrs. Butler at the parsonage. I'm not sure why, exactly," Lucille said, as though she were talking to herself, falling into uncharacteristic uncertainty, "since the parsonage is just next over from Scofields. I don't know why he couldn't just *walk*. I imagine there was some sort of *terrible* . . . There must have been some kind of awful, *desperate* complication! I don't know why else . . . because Robert Butler was already born by then. Nearly two hours before Lily Scofield . . ." Lucille paused for a minute, still working out this little mystery, but then she recovered herself.

"Why, it was like the end of a *plague!* It was like a miracle!" she exclaimed. "But honestly, Agnes, I think you're a little vain. I don't think you realize how *proud* you are of what you think of as your 'common sense.' It isn't at all attractive. And to tell you the truth, it isn't a bit feminine. You're so stubborn about always being the *only* one who's sensible."

The debate about the practicality of Agnes's nature had been brewing since the beginning of Agnes's and Lucille's last year at the Linus Gilchrest Institute for Girls, where the two of them, along with Sally Trenholm and Edith Fisk, had been charged with writing the script for the senior pageant. It was an honor, and an honor that Agnes had secured with a good deal of complex political maneuvering, but it was a job that was proving to take up a great amount of time, and Agnes was feeling pressed, because she and Edith had also been chosen as coeditors of the class book.

Traditionally, the senior pageant was something of a morality play performed by a group of senior girls elected by the student body. All nineteen girls in the senior class would be incorporated into the performance, but only four girls were elected to portray one of the roles of the cardinal virtues: justice, prudence, temperance, and fortitude. Just three others would be chosen to play one of the theological virtues: faith, hope, and charity. And the whole production had to be tied in, one way or another, with the gratitude, devotion, and loyalty of the class of 1918 to one another and especially to the school.

Not only was the whole enterprise time-consuming, it was a passionate endeavor. Some part of Agnes's thoughts was always turned to the problems of the play, the vanities and difficulties of the personalities of the three friends she had to work with. Edith Fisk and Agnes had hoped to do something a little whimsical, tying the play into their idea for the class book, but Sally, and especially Lucille, had been adamant about keeping the drama conventionally somber and reverential.

Agnes had been unwise during the previous Friday's meeting. "Lucille! I wish you wouldn't be so pigheaded! Sally is just going along with you not to hurt your feelings. Last year the pageant wasn't any fun. It was so high-minded — and it was so *long!* We were all bored to death. And you know it! I think we ought to do something with a little humor. We could have each virtue also be one of the teachers, say. *Only* in the *nicest* way . . ." She held her hand up flat, palm outward, in a gesture forestalling Lucille's disagreement.

"The way Miss McCrory is so pretty — and she's so kind — we could do a sketch on how we have learned to ignore vanity, or not to wish for beauty. That her 'stern face, and strict nature' . . . something along those lines. Or since Miss Fogelman is clever . . . her puns . . . you know, all that sort of thing. We could say how we learned from *her* to . . . oh . . . avoid hilarity, or 'keep an earnest heart.' The *opposite,* you see, of what everyone admires them for. We could go about it in a sort of overblown way. Flowery and serious. It would be at least a little bit more fun. . . ."

But even as Agnes was speaking, Lucille had tucked in the corners of her mouth and sighed in resigned disapproval, and Agnes snapped at her. "Lucille, you never listen to anyone else! You always are so *stubborn* about everything. . . ." She stopped herself too late; she realized she had hurt Lucille's feelings. Lucille was insulted and Agnes exasperated.

Their disagreement had reached its height when Lucille presented her sketch for the section of the little drama that was to illustrate the idea of the legacy each girl took away from the school. Lucille's sister Grace had been visiting from Columbus with her two little boys and her baby daughter, and Grace and Celia had gotten quite caught up in their youngest sister's project. Together the three of them had worked out a rather long piece at the end of which Faith, Hope, and Charity would come together at front center stage, each with her right hand over her heart and her left arm stretched forth in entreaty — Lucille stood gracefully to demonstrate and recite, her long, pretty, melancholy face sweetly sheeplike:

> As the saffron bag that hath been full of saffron,
> or hath had saffron in it, doth ever after savor
> and smell of the sweet saffron that it contained,
> so our Blessed Lady, which conceived and bare Christ
> in her womb, did ever after resemble the manners and
> virtues of that precious babe that she bare.

Agnes had been astonished and embarrassed for Lucille, and had let out a startled laugh. "You can't have that in the pageant, Lucille!" Agnes had protested. "For goodness sake! Use your head! It would just look foolish. And they can't say anything like that. Just do something like . . . oh . . . if you want something earnest — sort of dramatic and *preachy* like that . . ." She bent her head and began writing out phrases. "Umm . . . no," she said, scratching through whatever she had written, pondering it for a moment and starting again. "Well . . . maybe something like this. If that's the tone . . . if that formal kind of high-minded tone is the sort of thing . . . How about this? Something like this? 'As you shall embody and represent all that is the character of the Linus Gilchrest Institute for Girls, so will you all your life carry with you . . .' No. Let's see . . . 'So will you be infused with the sense of virtue and charity . . .' Oh, no, that's pretty awful."

Agnes had sat at their crowded table scribbling out possibilities and thinking out loud. She was so intent on what she was doing that she hadn't noticed that Lucille was looking away from the three of them with her face frozen in an attempt not to cry at the surprise of being so succinctly and arbitrarily crossed by her best friend.

"But if we could reverse it . . . ," Agnes muttered, "put it the other way round. 'As the spirit of the Linus Gilchrest Institute for Girls is imparted to you as you pass through its . . .' Uhmm . . . I don't know . . . 'Through its echoing halls . . .' No, that won't do. That's not quite right. . . . 'Through its *vaulted portals!* . . . so shall you represent and embody all that is fine in its character, and ever after *be its daughter!*'"

Sally and Edith had been delighted and relieved and especially impressed with Agnes's having worked in the idea of being forever after a daughter of the school. Lucille had collected herself, but she was as scornful of Agnes's effort as Agnes had been of hers. "The *portals* are hardly *vaulted,* Agnes."

Sally and Edith, and Agnes, too, turned to look at her in surprise, so carried away had they been with getting the sketch sorted out. At the sight of Lucille's gentle features sternly drawn in an expression of reprimand they all three remembered the imposing but relentlessly squared off entrances to the assortment of buildings that made up the Linus Gilchrest Institute for Girls.

"Oh, that's true," said Agnes, relaxing back in her chair and dropping her unwittingly urgent note of insistence. "But I was trying to get at the tone you want . . . and there *is* the arch of the west entrance to the old chapel . . . ," Agnes offered, but Lucille was not so easily appeased and argued the merits of her idea until finally Agnes had become cross again.

"You don't have an ounce of common sense, Lucille! What can you be thinking?" she had said. "You can't talk about the Blessed Lady bearing Christ in her womb! Imagine the fuss that would cause! They'd never let us, and it's too . . . *imaginable,* anyway. It would seem vulgar. And besides, no one will understand what you're getting at. That the students pass through the school the same way Christ was born of Mary — or, *actually,* Lucille, I think your piece implies that *Mary* is like the baby she gave birth to. So that wouldn't even make sense. You'd be saying that the *school* becomes like the students who leave it!"

Lucille objected stoutly. "Well, you didn't let me finish the whole thing! So how can any of you have even the *slightest* idea what I was saying?" Lucille's voice trembled. She was astounded at Agnes's treachery.

This was all quite serious to these girls, not at all silly or frivolous. Agnes, for instance, weeks earlier, had tried out her notion for the class book on Howie and Richard, who sat listening to her reluctantly one afternoon when she insisted they give her an opinion.

"I'll give you a whole hour to practice hitting," she said. "You can take turns pitching and I'll field for you as soon as you tell me what you think of this. Edith and I've been working on it off and on for two weeks now. It'll only take a minute."

They sat back resignedly. Only Richard, when he first started school following his sister, who was three years ahead of him, had tried to evade Agnes's authority. "Leave me alone,

Agnes!" he had said. "You're not in charge of me," he had objected the first school day he came home with work to be completed for the next day. He had looked to his mother for reinforcement — she had been waiting for him to get home and had urged him to come see what she and Howie had discovered down by the creek during the day. But Catherine Claytor went vague in the face of Agnes's direction, even though Agnes was only nine years old at the time.

"You can play with Mama and Howie just as soon as you do your alphabet animals," Agnes said. Their mother made no objection, and so the Claytor boys discovered that in many instances Agnes *was* in charge of them. By the time Agnes was eighteen and Richard and Howie were fifteen and fourteen respectively, it didn't even cross their minds to object to this relatively minor irritation.

"Now, look here!" She handed them the mock-up she and Edith had done for the cover of the class book, and she read aloud from the little bit of the introduction they had worked out. It was only a rough draft; she and Edith had made a stab at getting the general tone they wanted:

THE LINUS GILCHREST INSTITUTION FOR THE INSANE
REPORT FOR 1918
DESCRIPTIVE SKETCH OF THE INSTITUTION

The grounds of the Linus Gilchrest Institution for the Insane occupy over four acres of land in the center of the bustling city of Washburn, Ohio, and are covered with grass which may not be walked upon; with shrubs and trees which may not be handled; with any number of native plants and flowers which may not be harvested even to be used as gifts from the patients to the presiding physicians of the Institution. The site supports four white clapboard buildings and a fine stone structure where a few of the patients are hospitalized and where all are treated to afford a general improvement of their mental condition.

Her father had wandered into the parlor to read the newspapers he had brought from town, and he had asked to have a look at what she was doing, but he had passed it back to her after only a cursory glance.

"Agnes, this is a silly business. I'm surprised you would waste your time on this kind of foolishness. I thought you were such a sensible girl. You have a good mind. *This* sort of foolishness is a waste of your time. This . . . I thought you would be doing some sort of work that's worthwhile. With the war . . . people near starvation in Europe and the wheat blight here . . ."

Agnes had quite docilely taken back her papers as he held them out to her, but she had been dumbfounded by the severity of her hurt feelings when he spoke with such casual dismissiveness to her. She worked hard to earn her father's approval, and she had always secretly thought that he prized her in the same way Lucille's father simply doted on his four daughters. Agnes thought that her own father would never be so undignified as Mr. Drummond — Dwight Claytor would never be so foolishly smitten with anything. But she had tucked away and cherished every compliment, every kind word her father ever said to her.

When the Claytor children started school — especially the two middle boys — Catherine Claytor had seemed baffled at such a turn of events. She seemed to think of the whole endeavor as a sort of unexpected rivalry for their affection and attention, and for the first few months of each child's first-grade year the contest entirely captured her attention.

Catherine spent those very early school days brooding through the mornings, anxious on behalf of the unhappy child who had just been dispatched to his first day of school and planning wonderful games and surprises to console him when he was finally set free and sent back to her. She would range around the property, discovering a copse of trees where a new fort could be built; she would browse through *The Burgess Book of Games of Fun* and come up with all sorts of ideas and even new card games: high tide, round the town. Or she would rustle through the boxes of books she had brought from Natchez from her own childhood and find a splendid old favorite to read aloud. But Agnes was always quick to step in.

And Agnes stepped in because she herself had been seduced by her mother's delighted greetings when she came home every afternoon in the first few months of the first grade. Agnes would come into the house after the long walk home to sit in thrall to her mother's enthusiastic distraction from and dismissal of the drudgery of homework.

"So *silly*, Agnes," she had assured her daughter. "Why, being who you are, the *last* thing you need to worry about is doing all this make-work. Let's play one more game of king's cross!"

But when Agnes had failed to receive a gold star beside her name on the class graph posted in the schoolroom — failed to receive one in several categories, including Diligence in Work Completion — she had closed her ears to the siren call of her mother's afternoon enchantments, and Catherine had been terribly put out and her feelings deeply hurt. She was mystified, because clearly her daughter was learning everything she needed to know. She was well ahead of her class in almost every subject.

"Why, Agnes, you just want to be a little teacher's pet!"

And when Agnes was adamant that her brothers do the same, Catherine was disdainful. "Oh, Agnes, you're already a twelve-year-old *old maid,*" her mother sulked, and Howie or Richard and even Edson would glare at their sister disgustedly, but they all did what she said. Even Mrs. Longacre didn't interfere, although at home she said to her grandson William, "*That* one's a bossy little puss! I wouldn't want to tie up with her."

But all four of the Claytor children were exceptional students and leaders of their classes. Any teacher at the grammar school who looked at her class list was delighted to find a Claytor enrolled for the following year. And that's what Agnes had figured out was necessary the moment she took account of that large graph posted for all the world to see and found herself unstarred. She had understood at that instant that school was essentially a competition, and that it was absolutely necessary for her sake and the sake of her whole family that she and her brothers excel.

Her father had always expressed enthusiastic approval of his children's stellar academic performance. Agnes had even heard him speak of their achievements with pleasure and satisfaction to his constituents who came by the house — the businessmen and farmers who gathered in the parlor or sat out on the porch discussing politics. It enhanced his reputation to be the father of such exemplary students, she thought. It seemed to Agnes that his children's respectable behavior bestowed upon her father and their family an element of admirable conformity.

Agnes courted her father's approval and reinterpreted or shut out any evidence against him. Occasionally she descended to a level of obsequiousness when she was around him that sent her mother into a raging despair. Agnes was desperate for his approbation. But the afternoon he was derisive of her efforts when he glanced over the little sketch of the introduction Edith and she had worked out so arduously, she made no effort at all to explain herself, to persuade him into admiration, to appease him, to court his favor. She only looked straight into his face with her expression drawn in, unyielding.

He looked at her a moment but not quite long enough to register her uncharacteristic hostility, and he settled peacefully into his reading. Agnes swept off upstairs to her room, and Howie and Richard had caught enough of her expression — Agnes's "round-eyed look" — not to press their luck. They didn't pursue her; they practiced their hitting, but they fielded for themselves. She retreated to the privacy of her room near tears, astounded by her father's failure to congratulate her on her cleverness. It amazed her that he didn't understand that she had achieved quite a social victory in her life away from home.

The Claytor children had no idea — nor did their parents — that the community as a whole admired Agnes, liked Howie and Richard, and cherished Edson to such a degree that the townspeople brushed aside gossip and speculation and even genuine concern, accepting the family's presentation of itself at face value. For the most part, the Claytor family was granted the concession of concocting its own legend.

Agnes didn't know, though, that Mr. and Mrs. Drummond often worried over her to each other, or that Mrs. Longacre had for years, and with a flinty affection, referred to Edson as "that poor little boy." The Claytor children tried with all their might to maintain a benign myth of family serenity, to offer a single, auspicious idea of their household to the community.

Certainly Agnes and her brothers were not miserable all the time, but underlying any fun they had was the dreary anticipation of unhappy endings. The older three had come to distrust almost any single moment of pleasure. All during any day at home, for instance, especially any sort of celebration, there lurked chaos in the very next moment, and so day after day Agnes leaned in full force to her time at school, as did her brothers.

By the time she had reached her senior year at Linus Gilchrest, Agnes could walk out her front door, shuffling her arms into her coat with her mother's fury flying at her back, or she could leave her house with contempt strung out between her parents like the tension of an ice-laden wire, and arrive forty-five minutes later at school to become instantly absorbed in the issue of the day. She had learned to take up the daily and serious drama of her public life all the while knowing that as soon as she set foot on the walk home she would have to begin the heavy work of keeping her head above despair.

It was school itself that was the work of Agnes's life thus far, and it was a realm in which she and her friends possessed some measure of power, the only sphere open to them in which they could lay claim to some degree of authority. As it happened, Agnes, Lucille, Sally, and Edith, those four girls, all of them, had proved to be especially good at going to school, good at the business of surviving it.

It's an enormous endeavor, getting through school. And for those four girls the academic work itself was the least of it: accommodating new ideas, committing great chunks of information to rote memory, mastering complex mathematics. There it was, all that knowledge, laid out and presented in sequence, so that it was for them a relatively simple matter to master one thing in order to understand the next bit coming along. Naturally it required effort and concentration, but there was nothing ambiguous about the process.

As a matter of fact, to those four bright girls, the pure, clean intellectual stretch to grasp some new concept, or even the hours of deadly memorization required for Latin or French, had a pristine aura as opposed to the murky and demanding challenge of being popular, of being perceived as admirable, of all the slippery subtleties of social success to be deciphered.

Now, with only Saturday and Sunday having intervened since Friday's discordant meeting of the senior playwrights, Lucille had arrived at school reinforced by her sisters' continued enthusiasm for the piece they had worked out and by their concurring indignation at Agnes's blunt and public disapproval. "Why, I'm amazed that Agnes would say such a thing to you!" Celia had exclaimed. "I'm surprised that Agnes would ever be so rude to *anyone,* but the two of you have been such friends now for years and years. She's almost one of the family. But who knows, of course. All the problems . . . well, her mother. And then, too, she has to worry about her little brother. . . . Don't let it worry you, Lucille. After all, she counts on you almost as family."

And it was true that the Drummonds thought of Agnes as being a sort of cousin, because she stayed in town at their house often during the long school year if the weather was bad, or if there was a school event in the late afternoon or evening. There were always several girls from outlying districts boarding at the Gilchrest Institute, and Lucille's family were an exuberant, extroverted lot who each year insisted that those girls, too, feel free to come and go as they pleased in the Drummonds' big three-story house on the south side of Monument Square. It was one of the few places where Agnes was completely at ease, and generally she would have realized over the weekend that she needed to make amends to Lucille. She would have been ashamed of herself and known that what she had said to Lucille would have been uncommonly hurtful in light of the special and reciprocated loyalty between herself and Lucille, and the whole Drummond family.

But in those same two days, just in that bit of time that had elapsed during the last weekend of September, Agnes had developed an indifference to the whole business of the senior pageant. Lucille had spent Saturday and Sunday fretting over and readying the case she wanted to make for her own idea, but that Monday afternoon when the two of them were the first to arrive at the playwrights' meeting, she found she was disappointed when Agnes said it really didn't matter to her. Whatever Lucille wanted to do would be fine. Agnes said she *did* still wish the whole thing could be a more lighthearted affair, but that she would go along with Lucille and Sally and Edith's decision. And it was while Lucille and Agnes were waiting for the other two that Agnes initially brought up the subject of the Scofields.

"Well, and, say, speaking of the Scofields," she said, after Lucille had answered Agnes's question of what were the facts behind all the rumors of those coincidental births, "Lily Scofield Butler and her cousin came out to the house Saturday afternoon. Mr. Scofield wanted to talk over some business about fuel — something about the war — with my father," Agnes said, just as a matter of fact, since she had killed off any further discussion about the pageant, at least for the time being. But Lucille didn't comment one way or another.

"My mother thinks," Agnes finally remarked, "that *all* that business about those Scofield children and Robert Butler being born on the same day is nonsense. Just foolishness. She thinks it's only a tempest in a teapot. People don't have anything else interesting to talk about in a town like this, she says. And I guess I would have to agree that she's right. I imagine it's just a way to make things seem more important than they are," Agnes maintained, sounding almost accusatory, even a little petulant, as if she didn't believe Lucille had told her all she might.

"Oh, well! If you don't believe me you should ask my father about that year before those babies were all born!" Lucille said. "And then you would understand how terrible it was. And it was the year just after the locusts had eaten everything above ground!"

"But Lucille," Agnes was almost plaintive in her simultaneous need to know whatever she could about Warren Scofield and Lily and Robert Butler and her reluctance ever to let someone get away with such a flight of fancy, "your family didn't even move here until more than twenty years *after* that." Agnes made her voice solicitous, a wheedling plea for reason, but Lucille was affronted nevertheless.

"Oh, Agnes! That doesn't have anything to do with knowing what happened! My father has heard everyone talk about it. You have no . . . I don't know why you bother to ask me anything at all, since you never believe me or approve of anything I do. You always think I exaggerate too much. But you're like a . . . like some *stone!* Sometimes I think you don't have a whit of imagination! And to tell you the truth, Agnes, I think you would . . . *understand* more if you *would* use your imagination now and then! You're too logical about everything."

"I don't know if anyone *can* be too logical," Agnes put in mildly.

"That's just exactly what someone who *is* too logical . . . too *scientific* about everything . . . so literal minded . . . would say. Agnes, you don't have a romantic bone in your body!" Lucille had heard her sister Grace say this once about their mother.

"Well, *you* certainly have —"

"But after those three babies were born — Robert Butler was the first one, and you can tell it, too, just by the way he is. My sister says he has a natural dignity. But it wasn't till after that day they were all born that those terrible hailstorms stopped. Lightning and hail, but the ground was as hard as a rock. Finally, after that, the town got some rain, and farmers could put their crops in. My father says it's uncanny. That it's even in Shakespeare. 'Beware the ides of March!' That's the day they were born, you know. Until then, though, not a single thing would grow."

"March! Lucille! What in the world *would* be growing before March?"

Lucille looked away from Agnes and considered for a moment. "It might be May," Lucille said. "Beware the ides of May," she tried out. "But that's not what's important, anyway. The thing is, it's not what my father says. It's what everyone says. *Everyone* says that everything changed after those three children were born all on the same day."

"I haven't ever met Robert Butler," Agnes said, letting the argument drop, "but Lily Butler and Mr. Scofield stayed almost four hours Saturday afternoon. There's a lot of pressure on Scofields and Company from the War Department. That's why Warren Scofield had to stay at the Company and couldn't enlist.

My father said that old Mr. Scofield — Mr. *Leo* Scofield — is worn out with all this, and that his youngest brother, George Scofield, has never really been involved in the *management* of the business. And he says that Mr. Scofield's other brother — that's Warren Scofield's father, John — ought to be the one in charge but that he was out of town so much. In charge of the sales division, my father said."

What Dwight Claytor had, in fact, said was that John Scofield stayed out of town as much as possible or in some tavern or other filling the workmen's heads with all sorts of dangerous ideas. But Agnes knew not to repeat that in public. "Anyway," she went on, "my father said it sounded to him as if Warren Scofield was pretty much overseeing the conversion of the Scofield company to munitions production."

Agnes looked at Lucille across the table in the little room eked out of a storage space and given over to the editors of the 1918 class book and the senior playwrights, and saw that Lucille was annoyed and not really paying attention. She was absorbed in sketching a border of flowers around the edges of a piece of paper. Sally and Edith had still not arrived, so Lucille and Agnes were just idling away the time.

Agnes hadn't meant even to mention Warren Scofield, although she could scarcely force the thought of him out of her mind, and the saying of his name worked on her like a spell once she had allowed herself to utter it. She kept circling back to form the sound once more until at last she forced herself to *in*-hale when her lips began to purse into that breathy *W.* She turned any further mention of his name into a deep breath and exhaled it in a long sigh, slumping back in her chair. For all her supposed hard-nosed common sense, when Agnes spoke again her voice was wistful and musing. "Robert Butler is stationed in France, you know. So I didn't meet him. But I think Lily Butler must be the most interesting woman I've ever met," she said, with tactless admiration.

"That's just silly," Lucille said at once. "It's just her looks. She's very stylish. It's just that she seems sophisticated to you, Agnes. It's just because she went east to college."

"No, it's not, Lucille. She's interested in everything. And she's so . . . *enthusiastic*. There's nothing ordinary about her."

"Well, she's beautiful in an *unusual* sort of way, I guess," Lucille said, but Agnes listened carefully, because she was miserably jealous of Lily Scofield Butler and Lucille seemed censorious. "I've heard about Lily Butler my whole life, because *everybody* likes her. All those men in love with her. But I truly don't think she's nearly as pretty as any of my sisters."

But Agnes didn't appear to be considering the comparison. She didn't comment, and Lucille was miffed, because she really thought she herself was much prettier than Lily Scofield Butler.

"People *do* think she's pretty, though," Lucille finally acknowledged, to regain Agnes's attention. "And she's an awfully good sport, Celia says. Celia's wild about the Butlers. Well, I think she's pretty crazy about Warren Scofield, too. They used to go about together pretty regularly. But Celia wouldn't ever admit it, because *that* would have been a hopeless cause. The Butlers have wonderful parties at Scofields. They even have a special dressing room just for when they play charades. All sorts of clothes to put together for costumes. Celia helped collect them from all their friends. And my father says Lily Butler's probably the best horsewoman in Marshal County!" Lucille was less grudging now, and had warmed to her subject. "He says she has a lot of spunk. You know that after she went away to college she came home and made them put in a golf course?"

But Agnes hadn't taken up any of Lucille's enthusiasm. "People *do* think she's beautiful? There are other men in love with her?"

"Well, Agnes! Of *course!* There's Warren Scofield, for one. Everybody knows that. But they're first cousins, so that was always doomed," Lucille said, drawing out and elongating the mournful depths of that word. "And he and Robert Butler are best friends, anyway. But Celia says that before Lily Scofield decided she'd marry Robert Butler she turned down at least two other proposals. One fellow was a classmate of Warren Scofield's who wanted her to move to *Wyoming* with him! Where his family was."

Agnes didn't say anything.

"It's just silly to suppose that any of the Scofields would ever live anywhere else but Washburn," Lucille offered eventually, tired of her own indignation and thinking that this time she must have said something that offended Agnes. But still Agnes didn't reply.

Agnes had listened calmly to Lucille, but she had fallen far past any state of real serenity and found her spirits weighed down by the thought of Warren Scofield's adoration of the lovely Lily Butler. It was such a waste, and it even made Agnes a little angry and sullen. She was filled with a disappointment that left her too listless to respond, too tired to make even cursory conversation with Lucille.

The late-afternoon light slanted across the grounds of the Linus Gilchrest Institute for Girls and cast a lustrous triangle on one half of the high glass transom above the table where Agnes and Lucille sat, leaving the rest of the window dark and suddenly opaque. Agnes had tilted her head back and let her mind go blank, and for a moment her attention was caught by the phenomenon of the light falling as it did. Her interest was mildly piqued at the little puzzle of why only part of the window was illuminated. She was preoccupied for a moment with that immediate, visual absorption. And suddenly, in less than no time, all the sticky days of her life at home and all the hundreds — thousands — of comparatively clear, translucent, ordered days of school just fell away.

Just for an instant it was as though she were brand-new, and every detail of the world possessed clarity outside of its circumstance; every detail was extraordinary and exquisite. But this compelling, startlingly acute perception of her surroundings was painfully keen and weighed down with the nearly unbearable idea of her lone appreciation of it. She was mesmerized by the complex articulation of the many-legged small beetle crawling over the windowpane, the singularity of each leaf of the tree beyond it, every separate blade of grass, and she was simultaneously overcome by the high, yeasty, sour scent of chalk overriding the waxy undertone of polished floors, the school-dusty air grainy against her skin. But it was the notion of her solitary observation of it all that hit her like a bolt of lightning. It was wearisome to her in some way that she had never before experienced. It was heartbreaking to her to understand the tragedy of her loneliness, the calamity of never being able to explain herself to a single other soul who would understand what she had discovered.

Sitting in the schoolroom in that exhausted hour of the day, with the light turned syrupy and hypnotic, Agnes was caught unawares by the shattering vividness of the world. In that otherwise unremarkable moment in the stuffy, made-over storage room in the basement of the Linus Gilchrest Institute for Girls, on an autumn afternoon when she was eighteen years old, Agnes Claytor was smitten full force by the clarification of her own desires. She fell headlong into a desperate yearning toward the glimmering blond idea of Warren Scofield, whom everyone in Washburn, Ohio, knew had always been hopelessly in love with his own first cousin, Lily Butler.

Part Two

Chapter Five

THERE HAD BEEN MOMENTS very early in his life when all that defined Warren Scofield was the full sweep of his hatred of his cousin Lily. It was an awful feeling whenever it came over him — rage overlaid by self-reproach — because there were other times when there was no one else he believed he cared for more. And he had spent long, involved hours of childhood play without being conscious of the fact that his and Lily's and Robert's sensibilities were in any way separate at all. From the time he was a toddler of two and three years old until he was nearly seven, those inexplicable spells of resentment and real loathing of his cousin merely made him sulky and remote. As he got older he instinctively covered those spates of jealousy with a kind of noisy rowdiness that was put down by any adults in the vicinity as being no more than just a natural boyishness.

Sometimes at night, though, even in adolescence — even far away in New Hampshire at Norbert-Halsey Academy — he had lain in bed brooding over something or other that he held against Lily. He would lie awake in the dark, nurturing some example of an inequity he had suffered simply because of her existence, and all at once he would be miserably ashamed of himself, because it was unreasonable for him to begrudge Lily any of the pleasures of her life. It was worse than ungenerous; it was foolish. After all, there was no one else in the world, perhaps, who knew or loved him better.

Warren lived at his cousin Lily's house for almost the entire two years he was five and six years old. His aunt Audra would remind him every day as she led him across the yards of Scofields to visit his mother that he must remember to sit still and to keep his voice down. Aunt Audra instructed him to remember that her sister, Lillian, was too tired to cope with the energy of little boys. Warren didn't know why he was only allowed to *visit* his mother. He didn't know what was wrong with her, and he often worried that she might die. He also knew that it would be shameful to beg to stay with her, unthinkable to ask for information from Aunt Audra or Uncle Leo. But Warren's unrequited yearning for his mother — for her full attention, for her genuine curiosity — made him fidgety whenever he was with her. He became anxious and silly, full of chatter and a desperate, whining eagerness.

Warren and Lily and generally Robert Butler, too, spent the mornings together, usually under the supervision of the Scofields' housekeeper, Mrs. Downs. On summer days she would carry a bowl of string beans to snap, or peas to be shelled, out onto the long back porch and keep an eye on the children while she occupied herself with one thing or another. Sometimes she sat with her sewing basket and some mending to get done, and she often suggested games for the children to play. She set out an assortment of mismatched plates and cups, odds and ends of utensils and containers, so that they could play at an endless game of their own devising that they called Robinson Crusoe and that entailed having been stranded after a shipwreck.

Bernadette Downs enjoyed having the children in her care because they were nicely behaved — she was fond of each one of them — and the mornings seemed to fly by. On the rare days when they couldn't come up with anything to do, she would set them on a search for something special that Warren could take to his mother on his afternoon visit. One morning, for example, the three children discovered a patch of yard that was full of four-leaf clovers, and they gathered them in a jar of water that Mrs. Downs provided. They collected more than two dozen, and Mrs. Downs mixed in some violets and bristly stalks of asparagus fern and wrapped the canning jar in plain brown parchment paper, which she tied in place with a nice length of green grosgrain ribbon. She thought it looked very pretty and would make a nice presentation for poor Lillian Scofield.

Warren often brought his mother bouquets of flowers that Mrs. Butler or Uncle Leo offered from their gardens, or bunches of wild black-eyed Susans and Queen Anne's lace. In October he brought branches of brilliant autumn leaves and cattails that Aunt Audra arranged as artfully as she could. Warren's earnest courtship of his mother was never communally acknowledged, although Martha Butler and her husband, Daniel, and Lillian's two brothers-in-law, Leo and George Scofield, and her sister, Audra, too, all thought that it was Warren, more than anyone, whose company was likely to snap his mother out of the debilitating grief she had fallen into after the death of the baby. The death of John and Lillian Scofield's third child.

John himself was edgy in his wife's company, and his brothers thought it stemmed from his own grief. Audra Scofield and Martha Butler never said so to each other, but they thought it was more sinister, a peculiar kind of indifference. They both thought that John Scofield was disapproving of his wife's despair and held it against her. Martha and Audra had been sitting together in Audra's parlor when John had come into the front hall muttering bitterly to Leo that it was tragic — the death of her own child — but far better in the long run. "Far more merciful . . . Why, Leo! How can she mourn like this? She's thinking of a child that never *was!*"

Martha and Audra each concluded separately that John resented his wife's grief primarily because it excluded him. They each thought he was angry at his wife for her failure to love him more than she grieved for her child. They each were offended, too, to differing degrees, by John's inability to imagine his wife's despair.

Well, men don't, Martha thought.

John *can't,* thought Audra, whose own husband, Leo, was nearly as grieved as his sister-in-law.

But after overhearing that little snatch of conversation, neither of those women ever again had any pity to spare for John Scofield.

No one but her own husband questioned the legitimacy of Lillian Scofield's long, drawn-out despondency or ever held it against her — if for no other reason than the unspoken idea that to judge Lillian Scofield harshly might call down some equal misfortune upon themselves. But, also, the Marshal sisters, Lillian and Audra, had been enormously popular young girls and the daughters of a prosperous and much-respected family — the original Marshals of what had become Marshal County. Lillian, particularly, had always been a sweet, kindhearted, remarkably gentle person. Everyone liked her, even though she was so pretty — truly lovely in contrast to her sister Audra's sensible handsomeness. Her good looks might have been a liability as far as compassion toward her was concerned, but Lillian Marshal had never been a conceited girl; she had never been vain, nor had she ever possessed a particularly assertive personality. She hadn't earned anyone's envious malice, and there was no one in Washburn, Ohio, who didn't wish her well.

One morning, when she was still so unwell, Warren and Robert and Lily pulled dozens of wild green onions as a gift to make to her. They found them growing along the verge of the grassy drainage ditch where they found cattails in the fall. Mrs. Downs wrapped the white bulbs with their long wands of dark green leaves in a dampened linen napkin, and Warren presented them to his mother that afternoon when his aunt Audra took him to visit.

His mother generally sat on the settee in her big upstairs bedroom and often read him stories, and Warren was mesmerized as she read, watching her pale sleeves rustle over the paper when she turned the pages. The afternoon of the onions, however, his mother was still lying in bed, barely propped up against her pillows, and her hair was loose and untended. In fact, Mrs. Harvey had told Audra when she and Warren arrived that Mrs. Scofield had a fever and seemed to have caught a cold, so Audra meant only to stay a moment and let Warren pop in just to say hello.

But when Warren placed the damp parcel of onions on his

mother's bed, she had taken them into her hands and her whole face had drawn up in a grimace of dismay, as if someone had yanked a basting thread that puckered all her features. "Oh, no! Warren! What have you done? Oh, no! What have you done? Oh, my lilies! They would have bloomed soon. I spent so much time . . . Oh, how could you have done it? Warren? *How* could you ruin my borders? My little garden? Your father brought those bulbs all the way from Philadelphia. They remind him of me, he always says. 'The blooming of a thousand Lillians,' that's what John says every spring. Oh, Warren! Who *told* you that you could do this? You've pulled up my beautiful lilies!" Her voice was breathy, and she leaned back into her pillows away from him.

Aunt Audra took the bulbs from her and held them up to the light from the window. "No, no, Lillian," she said. "These aren't your lilies. Lillian. Lillian. Dear, these aren't your lilies. These are lovely new spring onions. They'll be so sweet. They're just lovely, Lillian. The children spent all morning collecting them down by the creek. Look here, Lillian. Look here! This one's still flowering. Flowers that I always thought were like little stars — *not* lilies, dear. Lillian, look here! These aren't the lilies John brought from Philadelphia." But Warren's mother still shrank back from her sister and her son, making an odd humming sound of dissent — a low, moaning negative against her teeth, shaking her head in despair.

Audra turned to Warren and told him to take the onions along to the kitchen and ask Mrs. Harvey if she would chop them up for him and put them on some nice buttered bread. "And a little salt and pepper. Umm. That'll be a *delicious* treat. And she can give you some lemonade, too. You go along, and I'll be down directly, Warren."

But Warren was terrified by the expression on his mother's face. For a little while he was sick to his stomach with the shock of her anger at him, and he only went downstairs and sat in the hallway, holding the bedraggled heap of onions on his lap. He slumped on a straight-backed chair next to the tall clock, and the longer he waited the more keenly he felt the unfairness of it, and the more deeply he felt the desolation of not being cherished by his own mother.

Audra Scofield had had a full plate that long year, and she simply didn't remember how fragile was the dignity of children. Warren's aunt Audra was upset by Lillian's outburst and sat on with her for some time. For at least an hour or so Audra didn't give much thought one way or another to Warren, who was just a little boy, after all, and this sort of thing rolled right off children like water off a duck's back. And besides, she assumed he was off in the kitchen visiting with Mrs. Harvey. But Warren was stranded in a state of heartsickness as he sat in the sunshine that fell through the lights above the broad front door. It shone down in elongated rectangles over the polished hall floor and glinted off the clock's glass, behind which the pendulum swung in an even tick*tock*, tick*tock*.

The sound was disheartening in the hushed foyer. It emphasized the surrounding quiet of the musty rooms, and Warren was so overwhelmed with loneliness and sorrow and the true, deep anger of grief that he simply shut away all his longing for his mother. He had a formidably flinty self-possession, and he closed off his desperate, sorrowing need for her. Warren could no longer survive the humiliating indignity — the self-inflicted insult — of his relentless yearning. It was too bad, because it was one of the few times that his mother was ever at all careless of his feelings, but the rest of her life she was unable to woo him back to her. He loved her, of course. What choice did he have? But that afternoon, when he was age five, and she shrank away from him and berated him for his careful gift, he gave her up entirely as the great romance of his early life.

Warren was silent in the terribly hot afternoon as they walked back to Uncle Leo's along the path, but Aunt Audra held his hand in a companionably firm clasp. He didn't realize that his aunt was speaking to him until she stooped down and fixed his attention on her by cupping his chin for a moment.

"Don't worry when your mama seems sad, Warren. It hasn't got anything to do with you. You know she's been so sick, and I'm afraid today we caught her when she has a bad cold. It's still going to take some time for her to get well. I expect sometimes she's so happy to see how big and healthy you are that it makes her think of your little brother. And probably of the first baby, too. Poor Harold. But at least James didn't linger.

"Oh, Warren, you were such a lively little baby!" she said, her voice warming and then floating above him as she straightened and took his hand again and they continued across the yard. "Harold was never so sturdy." Her words tumbled down on his head, trilling around his ears in combination with the rustle of his shoes through the heat-crisped grass, the buzz of insects, the fussy chittering of birds in the hedges.

"Poor Lillian," she mused on, "and that quiet, quiet baby. Harold never fussed at all. She never even knew if he was hungry. . . . Oh, why, Warren! It was such a relief when you were born. You were just full of life from the very *minute* you saw daylight. You were one of those long, *wriggly* babies. The doctor just laughed." And Aunt Audra laughed, too, in remembering, and her tone lost its rising urgency.

"When they put you down in the nursery, Dr. Peabody said you were just as mad as a March hen because your cousin Lily had gotten there first. You wanted to let her know she had company, he said. 'This one's going to cause you no end of trouble,' he said to your mother. Oh, Dr. Peabody was excited. . . . Well! He was downright *thrilled* with himself! I couldn't resist teasing him. 'Lillian and Martha Butler and I were talking just last week,' I said to him, 'and we decided you'd spent too much time over the summer going off fishing. Too much time sitting under some tree along the river trying to get out of the heat. We thought you needed something to keep you busy.'

"He laughed a little, but I tell you, he's really quite . . . oh . . . just filled up with his own importance. Well, just a *vain* man, really, I suppose. And that brought him up short. When I teased him. He *did* smile, but you could see that he truly did think he'd done it all himself. I should say! He didn't like being reminded that Martha or Lillian or I had anything to do with the three of you being born. And, oh! On the ides of the month, too. Why, when that got around it had people all amazed. Your uncle Leo had a grand time quoting Shakespeare everywhere he went." Aunt Audra laughed and continued on across the yard slowly, not hurrying Warren, and radiating a sense of satisfaction as she reminisced.

Warren lagged a little in her wake, enveloped in the tender, prickly scent of grass and the familiar, sharply sweet, medicinal smell of the sachet that perfumed Audra Scofield's clothes. He moved along at her side under the soothing sound of her voice and the heat of that day that beat right down on the top of his head. He was not quite six years old, and the quality of his listening was not yet separate from all his other senses. Later in his life he had a visceral memory of that afternoon — it remained one of those remembrances in which sound and scent are preserved, but no objective context. He could never see *himself* as the conversation wound out in his head. He had been too young to be other than receptive, too young to separate sensation from intellect.

Halfway across the yard, when his aunt came to an abrupt halt, turning and bending toward him slightly, her hand at her waist in a characteristic gesture of distress, and when her voice rose and thinned with sudden strain, his every perception was heightened as he tilted his head back once again to observe her. Even though Audra Scofield was only a little over five feet tall, and Warren eventually towered over her, he retained the image the rest of his life of her anxious face slanting down at an angle, her eyebrows slightly raised in concern as she regarded him. "But your mother can't help but think of Harold now, since the new baby . . . He wasn't even a day old, you see. Poor James."

Audra made the mistake so many people did with Warren; she really did take him at face value, and he had a precociously wise, unchildlike manner that was misleading. "I know how terrible this sounds," she went on, "and I shouldn't even think it — maybe I don't really mean it — but sometimes I think it would have been better if Harold hadn't lived so *long*. Eight months and he never even sat up. *Never* thrived. Your mother was just . . . heartbroken, *I* believe. I never even thought people could *be* heartbroken until I saw Lillian. . . ." Aunt Audra clasped her hands and pressed them to her chest, and Warren stood still and watched her cautiously.

"Finally," Aunt Audra said, "she wouldn't even speak. She would look at me as if she needed to tell me something. Had something she *might* say, but she couldn't . . . she *couldn't* . . .

force it out. Sometimes it seemed to me that anything she wanted to say — it was like the words she was trying to get at were at the bottom of a well! She was just too tired to haul them up."

The tremor of restrained tears in his aunt's voice froze Warren where he stood. "She couldn't tell me anything. Not anything! She didn't — *couldn't* — say a word for nearly three weeks. Even to me! Even to me!" His aunt closed her eyes for a moment, and then her pinched expression loosened and she slowly opened her eyes and took a little breath.

Audra glanced down at her nephew's attentive face and unclenched her hands, reaching down to take his once again, and they moved on slowly. "But she's much better now, of course. When she sees you so lively, Warren . . . Oh, Harold never, never was. . . . And, of course, James. She didn't *know* him, really. And your father is so . . . Well, I don't know. Restless? I'll tell you, sometimes it seems to me — and I can hardly stand it — it really seems to me that he's almost bored. You know how John's such a . . . *graceful* man. But it looks to me sometimes like he isn't even paying attention. Just at ease in a chair. Just . . . one arm just flung out and his eyes sort of lazy while Lillian watches him like a hawk. Oh, sometimes I'd like to *shake* him. . . ."

Audra stopped still once more and pressed her free hand over her mouth as she suddenly recalled herself and looked down to find Warren attuned to every word, so alert that his whole body keened upward to hear what she was saying. She studied his face, but he didn't appear to her to be upset or to have registered her consternation, and she moved along, leading him more briskly along the path.

"Well, don't listen to me. For goodness sake don't listen to me! All of it upsets me, and I'm not making a bit of sense. Your uncle Leo says your father can't stand to *know* a thing he can't do anything about. Just can't stand it. I suppose he didn't want to know . . . didn't want to think about it. I don't know. I don't know. I shouldn't say. What can he do about any of it, anyway? But all those ridiculous presents he brings her . . . those gaudy things from New Orleans. Those hats! As if she'd *ever* be off to any affair where she could wear them . . . That hair comb with *garnets* . . ."

Audra Scofield's deep suspicion of the nature of the remarkably handsome, silvery-seeming man who had married her sister was clear in her voice. Of course, he was her husband's brother, but he wasn't at all like Leo, she thought. Not in the least like Leo, who had such dignity — and who was nice looking, certainly, but not handsome in such an . . . overwrought way. Audra had always thought that John Scofield's good looks were somehow tasteless in their excessiveness, and as charming as he always was to her, he made her uneasy.

Her reservations about Warren's father suffused her voice, and although Warren didn't know precisely what she was talking about, he caught every nuance of condemnation and was overwhelmed by a fiercely defensive love for his father. In just such a way — just a careless shading of voice, an incautious arched brow signifying disapproval — by such subtle direction are the complex and mysterious loyalties within a family determined. Audra finally heard the accusatory note in her own voice and switched gears.

"But your father's so much better, too, of course. It was awfully hard on him, too. But he really is back to his old self. Now, there's a man who can charm the birds right out of the trees, that handsome father of yours. And aren't *you* exactly like him?" she said fondly, really meaning it, suddenly forgiving her brother-in-law for being less griefstricken than his wife, and repeating an observation that Warren had heard many times. It was a comparison that signaled a jolly, amiable, bantering sort of conversation within which Warren knew he was safe.

"And of course, my dear, you're the *apple* of their eye," she added. "It was just too silent. . . . That whole house was too quiet when Lillian lost your little brother. Oh, it was very bad . . . so bad when your mama lost James." Warren and his aunt continued across the yard between the houses, Audra preoccupied and Warren at once appallingly frightened and deeply ashamed at this confirmation of the carelessness of his mother. His mother who had so wrongly accused him and even discarded such a gift as the arduously harvested green onions he had brought her.

Lily was up from her nap, and she came darting out of the house to meet them. Aunt Audra dropped his hand and stooped to catch her daughter around the waist to stop her from hurtling headlong into them. But Lily did run headlong into her mother, briefly flinging her arms around her mother's waist just as Audra bent to catch her, and the unselfconscious affection in that brisk, laughing, spontaneous embrace, with Lily wriggling to get free, stung Warren unexpectedly. It was so ordinary, so clearly unexceptional, this easiness between his aunt Audra and Lily. He was extraordinarily tired in the blazing heat of the afternoon, as Lily jittered with energy in the sunshine.

Warren stood by, suddenly bereft and faced with the torrent of enthusiasm Lily let loose as she pulled free of Aunt Audra and flung herself toward him to tell him her plans for their afternoon. He went numb with the impossibility of uttering a single word to her ever again in his life. When he was two months shy of six years old, and in the heat of that Ohio day in the summer of 1894, Warren Scofield was momentarily crushed by a dreadful burden of secret envy and rage and genuine hatred directed solely at Lily. It was the most passionate moment of his life to that point, and he never regained a single moment of wholly simple and uncomplicated affection for her.

For most of his childhood Warren thrived on and gravitated toward the pace of the life that was led at his cousin Lily's house, where his aunt Audra's easy-natured stewardship was bent to the casual unfolding of the days, and where Uncle Leo was a thorough participant in the happily uneventful domesticity of the household. In fact, from the moment his uncle Leo took the time to explain to Warren the phenomenon of the sundial, Warren knew that it was from Uncle Leo's house, at the exact place where the sundial stood in the garden, that time itself originated.

"Now, look here," Leo said, bending forward a little so that he could illustrate his point. "From right here to here is the noon mark." Uncle Leo had hoisted him up so he could get an overall view, and Warren even remembered resting his cheek against the dense nap of his uncle's overcoat while gazing down on the sundial. Warren remembered Uncle Leo's gloved hand moving over its stone face. "Today the shadow will fall almost exactly in the middle. Right here." And he showed Warren where that would be. "There's not a cloud in the sky, so at twelve o'clock noon exactly the shadow will fall straight down the center. And it'll be just about then," Leo had said, "that old Saint Nick will be finishing up a good meal at the North Pole before he makes his rounds. He'll be having a nice piece of ham and some good buttered biscuits — light as a feather — and he'll be wondering what to put in your stocking. Might not be more than a lump of coal, you know. Although I'll bet he has at least some little surprise for you. And if you bundle up enough, why, I imagine your mama will let you watch the hour come around."

Whenever Warren recounted this tale as an older child, and even when he was fully grown, Uncle Leo and Aunt Audra and even Lily, who had no recollection of it whatsoever and was sure she would have been included, swore he couldn't possibly remember it. He would only have been four years old — the Christmas before his brother James was born. Surely it was an idea of his formed by tales someone had told him, images he had constructed from other people's remembrances. But Warren knew it was his own distinct recollection.

It was as clear as day to Warren, as he had paid careful attention to his uncle, that minute by minute time accrued against the blunt wedge of the stone gnomon until finally it spilled over to open outward across the rest of the world. And in spite of years of education, despite his travels, despite age and experience, it was a perspective he was unable to shake for the rest of his life.

From about the age of eight years old on, Lily and Warren and Robert Butler, too, if he was with them, were allowed the run of the main office of Scofields & Company, which was housed in a small two-story building where the three Scofield brothers, Leo, John, and George, had grown up. The ground floor had originally comprised the whole of the business, and the family had lived upstairs. Lily, especially, had a proprietary love of the efficient tumult of the place, with various clerks coming and going from other buildings, clattering up and down the stairs. All three of the children liked visiting the offices, but Lily was thrilled at the idea of her legitimate connection to all the brisk bustle of the place. The rooms were overcrowded, with file cabinets lining the hallways, and the offices buzzed with a cheerful air of urgency and prosperity.

The amiable young Mr. Adams, who presided over the main office, sitting at his desk, or sometimes perched on its corner, briskly sorting documents as though he were dealing cards, was a great favorite of Warren and Lily and Robert's. He kept an assortment of hard candies in his top drawer, and he always fished some out to offer the children, never failing to remember that Lily preferred butterscotch and Warren and Robert peppermint.

"Won't you have a boiled sweet?" he would ask, mimicking a high-toned accent and tipping his head back so he could look down his nose at them as though he were some sort of ludicrously refined gentleman. Each piece was wrapped in a twist of white paper that had collected traces of dust in its creases, and the candy itself always had an intriguing graininess. The three of them knew that their mothers would never have let them have any, but neither Lily nor Robert nor Warren would have refused it even if they hadn't liked it, because they were all three delighted to be so well known at the Company, which was the main employer in the town of Washburn, Ohio, when they were growing up.

The machine shops and the manufacturing plant, however, were off limits. The children had never had more than a glimpse through an open door of the buildings that housed the works themselves, or the fabricating or pattern shops, where the actual labor that necessitated so much administrative flurry was carried on. None of them had given it much thought; they hadn't been particularly curious about those tall, bleak, glass-eyed brick buildings ranged along the river with smoke billowing from their many chimneys.

It was a chilly, drizzly day when they were nine years old that the three children were first allowed to enter the newly constructed power plant, trailing across the vast floor after all three Scofield brothers, who needed to see about some problem that had come up. Tut Zeller, the chief engineer, was leaning against the railing of the catwalk outside his high office, barking out instructions over the hollow, reverberating din to the shop foreman, Henry Topp, standing just below, who had crossed his arms tightly over his chest and was stubbornly shaking his head to signify disagreement.

It seemed to Warren ever after that the interior of the building had been brighter than the world outside. The great flywheel of the two-hundred-ton Corliss engine rose more than three men high at the crest of its soaring arc, its huge pistons at least as wide as Warren was tall. The engine churned with a noise like a slowly oncoming train, gleaming dark silver in the flat light from the towering, multipaned windows and skylights, and under the yellow glow of the arched, swan-necked lamps high along the walls. The pale wood floor seemed to stretch out forever, and the various brass wheels and gauges glittered against the steel backdrop of that mammoth engine like jewelry flung out carelessly across the room. Warren's throat closed, and the roof of his mouth tingled with the sudden sweet combination of the smell of machine oil and the tang of metallic dust.

The air not only had flavor but was discernable to the eye in its slow, mote-filled turbulence, and the children lagged behind Leo and John and George Scofield as they joined Henry Topp and the group of men who moved with busy efficiency in the lee of that great, clacking engine. Warren was awestruck and overwhelmed by the beauty of the thing itself, with its heavy rope drives extending from one floor to another, its sturdy braces looking as fragile as threads. The whole effect was a peculiar one of spidery delicacy and elegant efficiency combined with the astounding, churning power of that relentlessly moving engine.

Everything about his first sight of the works was, to Warren, entirely marvelous, and he moved across the floor with an odd feeling of buoyancy, which lasted long enough that he thought he had achieved an improbable lightness — that he was floating just above the floor — impossible but real. At the same time he thought with some outrage: We never *knew* about this! No one ever *told* us about this! Although, naturally, there had been endless talk around the tables of the houses at Scofields about every aspect of the Company: all the problems at the works, the worry of unionization, the complications with the field offices in Pennsylvania and West Virginia, and even the amazing reliability of that great Corliss engine.

Warren was galvanized by the sight of Tut Zeller, his sleeves rolled up above his short forearms, hands braced on the railings of the metal stairway as he swung himself down two steps at a time, clambering from his overlook to sketch out a pattern with a stubby piece of chalk — right there on the shop floor — of the idea he had been trying to communicate to the tall, angular Mr. Topp. Anyone in the way fell back to give Tut enough room, while others came forward to take note of what he was doing.

Everyone was attentive, looking on with gravity at the fierce, stocky little man with his fiery round face, a shock of sandy hair standing straight up above his brow, his bow tie crisp but his shirt rumpled under his suspenders. Here were Warren's father and his uncles in their dark suits and polished shoes, and the shop foreman and a few other men, stooping a little with their hands on their knees, craning forward to watch Tut Zeller diagram an innovation that he clearly thought was so obvious an improvement he could scarcely contain his impatience while he labored to translate it.

And, all the while, the business of tending that great engine went on around them. Several men moved among the wheels and gauges without urgency but with enviable authority. Two rangy boys, a good deal older than Warren and Robert, swarmed up three stacks of ladders that zigzagged along an interior wall to the window hatch. Each boy slung his bucket over his shoulder before scrambling out onto the roof, where the two of them set to work washing the skylights. Warren stood on the floor below, watching as the boys methodically polished the broad glass panes with slow, circular sweeps of their cleaning cloths.

Rivulets of soapy water trickled through the grime before the rags swiped through them, and Warren suddenly had the sensation of having the same overview of the shop floor that those two boys with their buckets and cakes of Bon Ami were privilege to — an airy glimpse of those men made small. And here — Warren discovered so young, mesmerized in that flat, bright light, in that muscular air — was the answer to the question he had always known existed but that no one had ever set out for him. Here was the answer to the question of what *happened* in the world. Warren had stumbled into the passionate opposite of romantic love or sexual longing. He had discovered a great cerebral enchantment, a deep fascination, an intellectual intrigue.

He looked to Lily and Robert to confirm the wonderment of it all, but for the first time in his life his glance wasn't met with an answering expression of acknowledgment — of recognition of a shared idea. Neither of his friends turned Warren's way in their usual conspiracy. Lily's face was cast over with that glazed expression of courteous interest that meant her mind was a million miles away, and Robert was placidly looking on while Tut Zeller sketched quick, long lines and rough boxes in crude representations of machinery onto the floor.

Lily was all pulled together and poised in her disinterested tidiness — her hands clasped in front of her, her feet neatly together — while Warren had been craning upward, with his legs braced, canted backward from the waist, gaping at the soaring heights, the scurrying boys, the exciting busy-ness all around him. But that particular morning when he observed her grave separateness from himself, her prim, clean-limbed composure, and when he recognized Robert's habitual studious absorption in whatever was going on around him, Warren was furious at the perceived rebuff.

"Why, you're thinking something completely different than me!" Warren blurted out one second before the thought clearly formed in his head. Everyone but Tut Zeller glanced toward the three children for just a moment, because Warren's voice was high pitched with outrage above the thud and gasp of the engine. But the adults turned back to the business at hand when they saw that nothing was amiss.

Robert looked at Warren for a moment, considering it. "How do you know that? What are *you* thinking?" Robert asked calmly, his hands in his pockets and his brows pulled together in a mild expression of inquiry, and Warren just gestured with a broad sweep of his arm.

"It's so big," he finally said.

"It *is* big," said Robert pleasantly, and Warren appreciated that little bit of kindly intention in the face of all he could not possibly explain — in the face of Robert's lack of wonder.

For her part, however, Lily had no idea that at age nine it was shocking to Warren to discover that they were separate enough that their thoughts diverged. To her way of thinking, it was unlikely that she and Warren would ever be considering exactly the same thing. She had been about to suggest that the three of them return to the office, which was cheerful and warm. She found the sound of the engine deafening and had no interest in the works. But she had seen Warren watching the boys scale the ladders and climb out onto the roof, and even at age nine she had felt what was almost a maternal gladness when she recognized his fascination. Lily would never interfere in a moment when Warren was wholeheartedly happy, so she stood just where she was between Robert and Warren, not minding the wait. It seemed natural to her that between Warren and herself whatever one of them might fail to notice the other would be bound to catch on to. She assumed that the two of them made up discrete parts of one whole. She would have been amazed and upset if she had known that he held against her the fact that she departed so astonishingly from his own self. She would have been desolate if she knew he held it against her as a betrayal.

After Warren and Robert graduated from Norbert-Halsey Academy in 1906, Robert went on to Harvard College, and Warren took a salaried position at the company, where he was assigned to travel with Sam Chalmers, the company's chief field erection man, or sometimes with Hugh Gehrhart, as far south as Louisiana, helping to troubleshoot any problems that arose at an installation, learning to work out details on the fly.

Scofields' blowing engines were shipped by rail and assembled on site, sometimes installed in furnaces chiseled out of solid rock and rising as high as seventy feet. Warren liked everything about this business. He would go along to watch the men inching the huge engines on skids down Grove Street to the railroad siding. And he would often take over one of the large crowbars himself, making a striking picture when he shed his coat and bent his tall, rangy frame to the effort. Sometimes the spectators who gathered to watch would shout encouragement to him, and a smattering of applause would break out.

Warren never complained about living rough at a site, pitching a tent in some muddy field or straggling woods. And, in fact, everything about the enterprise appealed to all the pent-up romance of Warren's nature. He lived in a state of suppressed elation, bowled over with the rugged fellowship, delighted with his inclusion in the whole world of what seemed to him a great endeavor. He was as happy as he had been in his life, absorbed and interested in everything he ran into, and enamored with the novel grittiness of it all.

In early spring of 1907, Warren was put in sole charge of overseeing the installation of a Scofield horizontal compressor combination at a site in West Virginia, in the middle of fields and fields of corn where oil and natural gas had been discovered. There was no town or hotel within an easy distance of the site, but Warren secured a place for himself and the engineer, Hugh Gehrhart, to get a good night's sleep, even though they had to bed down each night in the attic of a suspicious country woman who granted them access to the room only up a ladder propped against the side of her locked house.

The engine was an ugly thing, a huge, inefficient, and complicated two-cylinder, double-acting machine, and Warren ran into resistance from the workmen, who disdained the inelegance of this particular piece of machinery as much as Warren did. Warren wrote to Uncle Leo in a fit of pique that it had such a slow action it put him in mind of his uncle George leaving the plant on an errand. "The piston goes out on Monday and comes back sometime late Tuesday afternoon."

But Warren was good at his job. He managed to minimize the inevitable discord between the engineer and the labor force he'd had to hire locally by pretending to enough ignorance of how the thing should be stabilized and regulated that Hugh Gehrhart became more patient. Warren would show up at the site and come to a slow halt, gazing at the construction this way and that. Taking off his hat and slapping it against his thigh in a show of bewilderment. "Now, Mr. Gehrhart, you've got to explain this to me again," he would say. "I know you said the frame will sit straight across here, but I don't see how in the world it's going to support the bearings." And when the engineer walked it all over once again, the workmen were satisfied that this was the best design they could hope for, ungainly as the thing would be, and they were also reassured that no one was asking anything unreasonable of them.

Toward the end of the year, though, his uncle Leo pressed him to go on to college, a small school in western Massachusetts just over the mountains from Lily, who was at Mount Holyoke, in South Hadley. Warren would never in his life think of disagreeing with Uncle Leo, but he sat in his uncle's office terribly disappointed at the prospect. His own father wasn't so enthusiastic either, but Leo thought it made good sense in every way. "A man needs to take up all sorts of ideas, John. Warren's got some experience in the field now, but you know he can do more good for us in management than running all over the country. It would be a good thing for him. And now Harry Garfield's there as president, I think it wouldn't be a bad thing for the Company either."

"Ah, Leo," said his father, "I don't see that. What difference does it make that Garfield's there?"

"Well, he's a good man. A thinker. He's got in mind some good ideas. And we've got to start thinking about Europe. Garfield's talked about bringing men from all over the world to that little college. An International Institute, or something of the sort. I don't know what his aim will be exactly. And, of course, who knows? Who knows what will come of that? But we've already got an agreement with Fours-Stein of France. We need to be looking ahead. And I don't think it would be a bad idea for Warren to make some connections back east," Leo said, while Warren sat listening without comment.

"It's fine with me if Warren goes off to college, Leo, though his mother's going to hate it like the plague. But whatever you might think about how I do business . . . Well! I'll tell you, you're not the man to make a sale, Leo! It offends you altogether to try to persuade someone to buy these fine engines we build! You think some customer is just going to discover all by himself that he needs a Scofield engine — a Scofield engine *in particular!* When he's being courted every minute by Fitch? Or Westinghouse? You've got far too fine a nature for a bit of trade, Leo!"

John Scofield had risen from his chair and leaned across the desk toward his brother, his whole posture aggressive, but his tone had grown soft, nearly menacing with restrained anger.

"Let me tell you something," he went on, though in his whispery fury he was hardly asking permission, and Leo sat on impassively. "There is not a single mill, not even the smallest textile company — not a businessman, either, in any part of the northeast — in Boston and even New York — that doesn't know me by sight! Who isn't glad to see me! And that's what's selling these engines, Leo. Because everyone and his brother has his foot in this market. But I remember the names of their secretaries, Leo! I remember the names of their wives. Their children. Great God! I remember the names of their *dogs!* You don't need to worry any little bit about our *connections!*" John was so angry that he turned his back on his brother and stuffed his hands in his pockets.

Warren was astounded and embarrassed. His father had always adopted a slightly edgy jocularity toward Uncle Leo, but Leo was eight years older than his father — had essentially been his father's guardian since his father was twelve and Leo was twenty — and Warren had always thought that Uncle Leo seemed more paternal than fraternal toward his younger brother. Warren hadn't understood until that moment in Uncle Leo's office that there was a deeper resentment at the heart of his father's manner.

Neither brother spoke for a moment, then John turned back to Leo, a good bit calmer. "And what puts you in such a mind to please the Garfields one way or another?" John asked.

"You're determined to take me wrong, John!" Leo said, and he seemed vexed, although not angry. "I tell you, I'm tired of it. I'm tired of it. You're trying mighty hard to imagine I'm insulting you. There's no one better at sales than you are, and there's not anyone at the Company who'd say otherwise. It was you who told me you'd never met a man who'd been at Williams

College that you didn't like," said Leo. "Lily's just flourishing back east. And Robert Butler's off at Harvard. Maybe Warren would rather think of going there. But you know I'm serious about keeping ties with Harry Garfield. The Garfields have been good to know when we're doing business in Cleveland. He's a good man, and naturally his connections in Washington —"

"It's fine. It's fine," John interrupted, and he sat down abruptly, stretching backward, running his broad hand across his face and massaging his forehead in a gesture of weariness. "Just don't decide you think Warren ought to go off to Princeton," he added, with a conciliatory laugh. "Now *that* I really couldn't abide." Leo and John smiled at each other across the expanse of Leo's broad wooden desk. "We've got something we *do* need to sort out, though, Leo. We've got a problem in Hiram. I'm going to need Sam Chalmers or Hugh to come along out there with me." And he and Leo turned their attention to business.

Warren did go off to Williams College in September of 1908, and made quick work of the business of school, graduating in the class of 1911. He was well liked at college, although after working in the field and keeping company with the engineers it seemed to him a tame existence he led in that little valley in the Berkshires. He was a fine student, but his intellectual devotion had been secured when he was nine years old, and he was often bemused by the earnest, meandering conversations, the amiable debates of his fraternity brothers or that Robert and Lily indulged in during the long summer vacations.

Warren had been delighted to get back to work at the Company. Leo wanted him in management, and he sometimes made short business trips with his uncle or his father, but he also still traveled in the field with Sam Chalmers or Hugh Gehrhart and was often away for weeks at a time. In the summer, if he got back to Scofields in the late afternoons, he would find Robert and Lily with a group of friends — usually Celia Drummond, Ollie Powers, and Charles Eckart and his sister Estella — ranged around Uncle Leo's garden, having just returned from a spur-of-the-moment round robin of tennis or a game of golf.

Whenever Warren came upon the group they were already in animated conversation, because Robert loved a debate, loved the exercise of civilized banter. He would latch on to some amorphous idea or other and deftly delineate two points of view — even if it was quite a stretch either to broaden or narrow whatever topic was at hand. The company would generally fall into two amiably opposed camps. The impassioned fervor of their arguments — ranging from the merits of the sport of golf versus that of tennis to the possibility of an American sensibility as opposed to that of the European — was a puzzle and a fascination to Warren.

He had visited Robert in Cambridge and sat among Robert's group of friends at Harvard, where Robert brought the same sort of energy to a discussion of literature or philosophy, and what intrigued Warren was the pleasure Robert and Lily and all the rest of them took in their efforts to persuade one another. Lily and Robert inevitably took opposing points of view, and Warren was bemused by Lily's obvious delight in their sparring matches. It was almost embarrassing, now and then, to be in their company, because the two of them so relished their disagreement that their passionate discussions seemed curiously intimate.

Early in 1917, Harry Garfield, in his capacity as fuel administrator for the Wilson Administration, prevailed upon Warren Scofield to help coordinate the industrial conversion to the manufacture of munitions and other war matériel in Ohio, Pennsylvania, West Virginia, and Illinois. Harry Garfield knew the Scofield brothers were widely respected in manufacturing circles, and he had been impressed with Warren some years earlier when he was a student at Williams College.

Leo Scofield saw the request as a great compliment to Warren and a move that would be bound to benefit the Company one way or another. And in any case the request was a formality. Warren had no choice but to accept the position in the Fuel Administration, but he was disappointed. Robert Butler had already been promoted to captain in the infantry and was stationed in France, and Warren had been eager to get overseas. It seemed to him from Robert's letters that the war was a good deal like living rough in the field, using simple cunning to adjust to unexpected difficulties and not having the energy to worry over much of anything other than the job at hand:

. . . so we're up every morning at 5:15 and haven't any curiosity all day even to know what time it is. Not until taps at 10:00 P.M. do I realize another day has passed. In the way the time goes by it is much like being a child again, but not even when I was a child did I spend days and nights on end without having a single moment of reflection.

. . . and I know you wonder how I get along without a good long discussion now and then, but about the most the men talk about here at any length is how the beans should be cooked. The Southern boys want them cooked up with fatback and the Easterners want them with sugar. Either way I have to say they're better than any I ever had at home, where they mostly tasted to me just like dirt.

There was no glory in any of this, though Warren knew that Robert would have thought it indiscreet — unseemly — to describe any heroics he might have witnessed or been part of. But what Robert did reveal was exactly what Warren loved so about being in the field — the mind-filling physicality of being alive. Warren knew the invigorating pleasure of taking on whatever assortment of tasks fell one after another in rapid succession throughout a long day, and he craved the unambivalent satisfaction of doing a job all the way through, from beginning to end. Warren envied Robert Butler.

In fact, Warren Scofield hated the business of the *business* of war. He hated being bogged down in the inevitable pettiness — the niggling small-mindedness — of bureaucracy. But he had learned in the field that he had a gift for wheedling discipline from a group of men discouraged by the daily tedium of routine, and he had discovered in the oil and gas fields of Indiana and Pennsylvania that he excelled at wrenching order from chaos. He thought he would be brilliant at leading a soldier's life.

At nine years old, Warren had invested the bustling world of the Company with a spiritual dimension. Tut Zeller strutting about, Henry Topp remaining laconically coolheaded, the great harnessed power engendered by the gleaming wheel of the Corliss engine, the reams of paper passed from hand to hand to document all the intricacies, the arcane complexities, the history of progress — well, in Warren's mind it had been tantamount to a religion. He thought that he had discovered the whole point — what to shoot for, the goal toward which one's life advanced. Just as he felt sure that time marched forward from the sundial in Uncle Leo's garden, he had also concluded that when he began to lead his real life it would be as dependable, meticulous, and elegant — as satisfying — as the working of a complex machine.

But when he held Robert's letters in his hand and thought of Robert and Lily married — thought of Robert's usefulness now and the couple's life as it would sail on after the war — he fell into unhappy reflection. He wondered what he was doing and what in the world it was he wanted. He thought of girls he had courted, of Celia Drummond, for instance, and Estella Eckart, nice girls he only liked very much.

He thought of Marjorie Hockett, who was the girl Lily had picked out for him. And Lily had been right. When he finally met Marjorie, when he joined Robert and Lily in Maine, he had been drawn to her right away. She was a tall, handsome girl with very blue eyes and a pale sprinkling of freckles across the bridge of her nose. He'd been pretty quickly convinced that he was in love with her, but Marjorie had come to find him one day when he was sitting out on the rocks reading. She had sat down companionably beside him, leaning against his arm, shoulder to shoulder.

"I just realized what Lily's up to," she said. "I just realized it, and she ought to know better. I guess she just won't ever understand. And when Lily decides on something she's like a dog herding sheep. She's just determined not to have any of her flock stray. But I knew the first year at Mount Holyoke that there might not be another person in the world I'd ever be able to fall in love with." She smiled at him when he turned to look at her to see what she meant.

"There's just Lily for me, Warren. And nothing I can ever do about it. But it isn't right that I not tell you."

It was a moment when he felt unsure and especially unsophisticated. He wasn't clear what she could mean by what she said to him, and he didn't want to press her. He was grateful to her for letting him down easily, and she was still someone he liked immensely. He and Marjorie kept up a lively correspondence.

But now he wondered why he never had been in love, and he marveled at his long infatuation with the Company. It made him angry to think that he had ever been so starry-eyed, so naive. He had a vague suspicion that somehow he had been tricked, even deceived, although that feeling was just an ongoing, brooding discontent. He never thought it out carefully enough to decide just who it might have been who had led him astray.

By the time he was twenty-nine years old, Warren was weary to the point of cynicism and disappointed to the point of grief. And the Saturday afternoon in late September when he sat in Dwight Claytor's parlor, Warren found himself entirely bereft of a single passion in all the world.

As he sat trying to persuade Dwight Claytor to consider re-opening a marginal coalfield, Warren was all at once so affected with the most peculiar, flat feeling of exhaustion that his face froze in its pleasant expression; he could not speak. He looked to Lily for help, but she was chatting enthusiastically to Mrs. Claytor, and even though Warren had begged Lily to come along and be entertaining, he was filled with disgust just watching her. In that split second he transferred all his disenchantment and dissatisfaction with his own situation onto the idea of Lily — what she represented. She was the epitome of "Scofield-ness," and yet that very charm she possessed that was characteristic of them all, Warren suddenly perceived as a dire and fundamental superficiality. And if it was business that had substituted for any bit of spirituality in Warren's nature, the idea of being part of his own extended family — of being a Scofield — had defined his connection to the world.

He watched out of the corner of his eye as Lily bent forward to engage Mrs. Claytor's attention. He saw Catherine Claytor's face take on an uncertain expression and then close in upon itself as she retreated into her own thoughts, no longer trying to follow the conversation. Her large, pale eyes grew vague, and she reclined in her chair, baffled and just sunk by intimidation when confronted with all of Lily's polished edges. Warren knew what it was like to be undone by Lily's assurance in the world, by her small, crisp, blonde person, her quick blonde mind, her fair, generous, lucent thoughts. Lily was alert and shrewd and witty as she glided through her life unencumbered by self-doubt, and all at once he could hardly stand it. For a little while Warren could hardly stand his connection to all the people he had loved for his whole life.

And it was that afternoon when he and Lily were taking their leave that Warren was caught entirely off guard by Catherine Claytor's daughter, Agnes. He was standing in the Claytors' yard in the fair Ohio countryside in that time of year when the fields have gone beige, when just the outer leaves of the walnut trees gleam butter yellow while the inner branches are still green, as if the trees are struck with sunlight even on an overcast day. He was making a polite farewell to Catherine Claytor while Lily said good-bye to Mr. Claytor when he felt the blow of that apple where it struck him just between the shoulder blades. He turned in surprise and spotted Agnes, who seemed to him, just then, to embody everything that was genuine, although he had scarcely noticed her when they were sitting in the parlor. But he looked her way in surprise and realized that there was nothing about her that was artful or disingenuous.

Warren picked up the apple she had flung at him and gazed frankly at her as he polished it on the sleeve of his coat. She seemed to him to be everything sturdy and earthy that his lithe, blonde cousin Lily was not. There Agnes stood in her blue middy dress, with wispy tendrils of hair escaping from the clip at the nape of her neck into a smoky halo around her head. He bit into the sour green fruit, and she grinned at him. She was an exotic, stolid, brunette presence in the pale end of that day, and he felt a slight lessening of the odd weariness that had plagued him. Everything else that disturbed him in the world — even the uneasy, wheeling sky, the unsettling soapy fleck of the three-quarter moon as it barely crested the horizon — was temporarily resolved in the sight of her. As the tart taste of that apple prickled his mouth and Agnes stood still under the trees, Warren began to recover just a little bit of his optimism.

Chapter Six

A LL OF A SUDDEN, in the fall of 1917, almost everything
in the world made Agnes Claytor cross. She was so busy
in her own head that the slightest distraction made her snappish,
and her friends didn't know what had come over her. Her family, even Catherine, suddenly walked on eggs around her —
everyone except her father, who didn't notice. Agnes practically
bristled with irritability. At school Edith and Sally, and especially
Lucille, were hurt, and they fell back a little, waiting to see if
this was a permanent change that had come over her.

Agnes, though, didn't know she was behaving in any particular way. In the afternoons she sat with her brothers at the table
in the kitchen doing her schoolwork without worrying
whether or not her brothers got all their homework done.
When she was eighteen, Agnes rarely interfered with them one
way or another anymore, and they were less relieved than they
had imagined they'd be. Agnes wasn't so interested in whether

they got their schoolwork done, or if they remembered to take their lunches to school, and that was mostly a relief to them. On the other hand, she no longer intervened on their behalf in the stormy confrontations with their mother that each one of them happened into now and then in brief, dramatic disturbances that swept through the house unsettling everyone. Agnes found some errand away from the sudden verbal brutality inflicted on Edson or either of the other two if her mother's day took a bitter turn and her rage sought an object.

Agnes no longer allowed herself to understand — or she really didn't remember — the awful grief of being a child who continues to hope he or she might be loved. And she no longer put herself between Edson and her mother, receiving a slap in his stead, or, as had happened once when she was twelve, being yanked by the hair all the way across the room where her mother, raging after them, had caught up with them just as Agnes was lifting the four-year-old Edson over the windowsill so he could run away across the yard.

By the fall of her last year at school, Agnes sat there in the kitchen — where Mrs. Longacre presided — without a whit of her usual deferential amiability. She didn't even ask about William Dameron and if Mrs. Longacre's family had had a letter from him. Mrs. Longacre was always so grudging in giving out any little bits of cheering news to Agnes or her mother that Agnes was finally fed up. She was so put out with everything in her life that she stopped pretending to be interested in anyone else at all.

Even her father was surprised when he asked Agnes at supper one night where the Dameron boy was stationed. If his letters came through from Europe. But it was as if her father's words reached Agnes several seconds after the sound of his voice stopped, as if she heard them only after a delay. Agnes slowly turned her round, black glance at her father, her brows drawn up into imperious inverted V's in a long, serious assessment, and then she sighed. "Well, how would *I* know that, Papa? I don't have any idea. I suppose Mrs. Longacre would tell us if he'd been *killed* . . . or injured." Her father stared back at her with the idea that she had been impertinent, but he couldn't put his finger on exactly how. For a moment he looked as if he might say something to her, and she gazed straight at him with scrupulous attention, but he gave it up and went back to his dinner.

Agnes didn't ask after Mrs. Longacre's granddaughter Bernice, who had been ahead of Agnes at Linus Gilchrest and who was now in her third year at Oberlin College, and toward whom for years Agnes had politely affected an air of humble admiration. Agnes no longer made the slightest effort to seduce Mrs. Longacre into liking not only her but anyone else in her family. She didn't even think about whether any of them had Mrs. Longacre's approval.

In fact, she shot a sharp glance at Mrs. Longacre — seemingly holding her responsible — if the least bit of teasing and roughhousing broke out between Howie and Richard, or if Edson even gave a hint of some cranky complaint. Sometimes no more than the rustle of papers other than her own sent Agnes upstairs to her room in exasperation. She would spread her work on the little table by the window or on her bed and get it done with ill-natured dispatch. She needed to free up time for more urgent things.

Agnes's disaffection with ordinary life was causing quite a crisis at Linus Gilchrest Institute for Girls. "Oh, for goodness sake!" she had said, leaning her chin into her hand with her elbow propped on the table at the playwrights meeting when Edith Fisk and Lucille disagreed once more about who should be asked to play the part of Truth in the pageant. "What in the world does it matter? Don't any of you pay attention to a single thing in the world? We're in the middle of a *war!* And here we are. Doing these silly things. It's just an embarrassment to me. I don't even like to talk about it!"

The following day the faculty class book sponsor, who was also Agnes's favorite teacher, Miss McCrory, asked Agnes to stay after class, and Agnes came to her desk when the other girls had gone. "I think you should know, Agnes, that you're causing a great deal of unhappiness among your friends. You're one of the leaders of the school, and we count on you to be a good example. I don't agree at all with your ideas about the senior-year activities." She looked carefully at Agnes, trying to decide what tack to take.

"I know that you're terribly distressed about the war, Agnes. So many boys have gone. But we are *all* concerned, you know. It's unkind of you — and, Agnes, I was truly surprised to hear how you had criticized your friends. I've always thought you were a more perceptive girl than most, and I was surprised that you wouldn't realize how unkind it was to lecture Sally and Lucille. And Edith. They're doing the best they can, Agnes. I know how frustrating it is to be able to *do* so little. To know that all those socks, mittens . . . all that *knitting* . . ." Miss McCrory's voice trailed off. She sat perfectly still for a second or two before she spoke again more firmly. "If you want to do your part in the war effort, my dear, you need to help keep spirits up at home. A good many of the girls have brothers or uncles or fathers who've been sent overseas. Poor Edith Fisk was in a state this morning, you know. She has two older brothers in the army. So it's no help to anyone for you to belittle her effort to keep going along as always."

Edith Fisk's brothers were only doing basic training no farther away than Kansas, but Edith was insufferably anxious about it all. Agnes spoke before she considered what she was saying. "But Miss McCrory! Edith's brothers aren't even in France!"

"Agnes —" Miss McCrory looked away from Agnes and out her classroom window at the school grounds. "You should never make light of the reason for another person's dismay. I've always thought that was something you understood without being told." Miss McCrory spoke to the air, in a musing tone, and Agnes watched her and suddenly was deeply ashamed of herself. She was so surprised by the reprimand — and so embarrassed by its accuracy — that she couldn't think of anything to say for a moment.

"Oh, Miss McCrory, I'm very sorry." And indeed Agnes was filled with anguish. "I don't know why I didn't see that I might hurt Edith's feelings. My brothers are all too young to be in any danger. Of course I can't even *know* how Edith must feel about Burton and Donald both leaving on the same train." She was so sincere that tears came to her eyes. "I don't know what I was thinking. I didn't mean to hurt anyone's feelings. I never meant to do that at all. I'm very sorry Edith's upset." And she was *deeply* sorry while she stood talking with Miss McCrory, who advised Agnes to speak privately to Edith. Agnes eagerly agreed and was simply overcome with good intentions there in Miss McCrory's classroom.

But Agnes's belated and incessant fascination with everything about her own self overcame her sympathy and altruism even as she stepped out into the long school corridor with the big round clocks at either end. She couldn't even keep the idea of the *war* in her head for more than a bit at a time.

The only thing Agnes thought about much at all anymore was Warren Scofield. She thought about him with thrilled despair, about his beautiful head, gleaming silver yellow as he turned in the afternoon to see that she had struck him with that apple. She thought about his broad hands, large but very finely made; his long fingers, articulated with elegant precision. She dwelled on the image of her mother's transparent Spode teacup, which had glowed with a radiant creaminess when it was struck through with the light from the parlor window as Mr. Scofield raised it to his lips to sip his tea — the idea of the fragility of that bit of china in his careful grasp. She thought about Warren Scofield's wide, square shoulders, his long legs, his beautiful, straight back as he had sat his horse when he and Lily Butler had disappeared around the bend of Newark Road. She thought of his making a hold with his cupped hands and laced fingers for Lily Butler's foot so she could mount her big Appaloosa. Every thought in Agnes's head was blond and dangerous unless she forced her mind in some other direction.

Agnes had not considered the fact or even consciously formed the notion that by the time of their last year at Linus Gilchrest Institute an unspoken conspiracy is required among those eighteen- and nineteen-year-old girls to remain fully engaged in the world of school. After Miss McCrory spoke to her Agnes did try, though, not to disparage the interests of her friends. But Agnes no longer remembered how to pretend to be much interested in the senior pageant, the work on the class book, her place in the choir. Other than her academic classes, all her time at school seemed to her frivolous, and she was tactless in saying so quite bluntly to her best friend, Lucille, who slowly came to give up the idea of her own importance in the grand scheme of things.

Agnes's indifference broke through the protective chrysalis of the Linus Gilchrest Institute and exposed the girlish concerns of the reigning hierarchy of the school to comparison with the great, wide worries of the encroaching adult world. From the moment her father had made light of her work on the class book, Agnes had had to make an effort to believe in the importance of any of this last bit of her youth. Now that her mind was caught up in a whirl of blond thoughts of general and specific Scofields, her lack of interest in any daily enterprise cast a pall over the last school year of her closest friends.

Agnes lived for the evenings of the week and the days of the weekend when her father was home from Columbus, because Warren Scofield almost invariably drove out to discuss the business of the property in Zanesville and some other land Dwight Claytor owned near Coshocton, where a second coalfield might be opened.

Agnes knew, of course, that she must seem like no more than a schoolgirl to Mr. Scofield, and that, in any case, Warren would never love anyone at all but his glamorous cousin Lily. Agnes knew that she was far too young for Warren Scofield. But there was nothing she could do that could keep her mind from wandering back to thoughts of him. And although she was downright disagreeable to everyone in her family, and they wondered what in the world was wrong with her, she was actually happier in this torment of romantic misery than she had ever been before in her life. In her case, in fact, this was the first time since her infancy that she was not distracted by anything else from full-blown solipsism; it was the first time her anxiety about the workings of the household were utterly eclipsed by the luxury of self-involvement.

Agnes spent hours on end contemplating the hopelessness of her lovesick longing. It was perfectly real — this unhappiness — but it had a quality of languor and fullness that overrode the melancholy of her domestic vigilance. The best she had ever been able to do to save her family from itself — a salvation neither recognized nor sought after by them — was to offer a distraction the way the killdeer mimes an injury to draw a cat or hawk away from its nest. When her father entered a room just so — his shoulders stiffly squared, his mouth a straight, humorless line, his expression flat and with an aggressive air of deliberation — all the family but Catherine would tense in apprehension. Their mother seemed to her children hopeless at anticipating danger.

But of the four children only Agnes had learned to pretend a sweet unawareness of the threat to the whole family's tentative equanimity if any tension between her parents were to escalate. Agnes would pepper her father with bright questions about his day, about farm prices, about a bill moving through the legislature. And whatever fury had been roused against his wife would fade as at first he clipped off quick answers to his daughter and finally became interested in whatever subject she had thrown in his way. Then he would hold forth for some time, inquire about Agnes's opinion, perhaps, and explain whatever issue was under discussion in further detail. The two of them would often become quite absorbed in a little disagreement or in differing interpretations of one thing or another.

The two middle boys would look on sullenly, and Edson would offer up a comment now and then, envying Agnes's ability to earn their father's serious regard. Catherine could hardly stand it. "Oh, the two of you! I wouldn't be surprised in the dead of night to hear you trying to decide if the sun was shining. You talk and talk and talk. So self-important, Agnes! But so dreary! So dull! My father always said that politics were simply vulgar, Dwight."

Sometimes Catherine's complaints would draw her husband's fury to the fore again, and Dwight would fall into a terrifying rage toward her that would throw the household into a scramble. With luck, though, if Catherine was in a mood to disparage everything about her husband's occupation, he and Agnes would become even more deeply involved in their conversation, and Catherine would finally drift off in a sulk.

Agnes hadn't an inkling that her mother and all three of her brothers believed she was the only one among them who had earned Dwight Claytor's admiration. She had no idea that they counted it against her, too. That they believed she purposefully wooed his favoritism with unnatural — with *affected* — interest in the subtleties of setting corn prices, that she pretended to be mesmerized by the ins and outs of political intrigue. And she had no idea that lately — in the face of her cool disinterest — her father had begun to believe he had lost his primary ally within his own family.

Agnes was utterly preoccupied, and a portentous atmosphere fell over the Claytor household. Terrifying possibilities — of which she was genuinely oblivious — arose under Agnes's inattention. She had given herself over to the lovely yearning that ran beneath the surface of her everyday thoughts, and which she could tap into whenever she wanted. It didn't even occur to her to budget her luxurious despondency.

Warren Scofield and Lily Butler came out to the house together when Dwight Claytor was at home one Wednesday evening in October, and Lily invited Mr. and Mrs. Claytor and Agnes to join them for the harness races on Saturday. Dwight declined, since he had to be in Columbus, but Warren asked if the ladies might like to come along anyway. Catherine had been both panic-stricken and excited at the idea, and she lowered her great, hooded eyes and studied her hands, but Edson asked if he could go, too, and it had been settled.

Lily and Warren collected them Saturday morning, and they drove south to Judge Henry Lufton's Lakeview Farm to watch the first races at the new half-mile track the judge had built. He had constructed a little section of three-tier viewing stands where Warren and Catherine sat while Lily took Agnes and Edson off to look at the horses and see the judge's new, lighter-weight sulky. Warren sat next to Catherine in a posture of kindly attentiveness. Straight backed but turned toward her just a little bit in case she might have something to say. And for the first time in years, Catherine Edson Claytor, from Natchez, Mississippi — renowned throughout the Delta as a belle — felt utterly pleased with her plight in the world.

Warren never thought much at all about how he looked, but Catherine Claytor had thought long and hard about beauty. She understood its power and all its shades and subtleties, and she had a merciless eye. She was alert to all the vast gradations of feminine attractiveness. She could spot the traces of former beauty retained in the face of an older woman. She could distinguish mere pertness — which was really no more than an arresting manner, a self-confident briskness — from the enchantment of sheer prettiness *apart* from personality. And she was always aware and in awe of the gravity of real beauty. Her own loveliness was the only means of gaining approval and admiration she had ever understood.

All at once, as she sat next to a man whose good looks matched hers at their height, she lapsed into a deep embarrassment at no longer being the girl she once was; she was humiliated at no longer being a great beauty; she was mortified to think how tedious her company must seem to Warren Scofield. And since Catherine was not the least bit curious about anything or even anyone — was handicapped by a crippling self-absorption — she had never grasped the art or understood the pleasure of conversation.

"Do you like the races, Mrs. Claytor?" Warren asked, bending closer, and she gazed back at him in some alarm. Her poor mind was so busy with some little narrative of its own that she had fallen into the demure hesitation of a young girl. She was too flustered to answer him, and he filled in for her as the silence lengthened. "I suppose you like to ride, though. You have a nice stable. Or are you as happy as my mother is now that she doesn't ever have to depend on a horse again?" He laughed a little, trying to put Mrs. Claytor at ease by conveying an impression of fond amusement at his mother's adamant determination never again to have anything to do with horses or any other animals if she could help it.

Catherine finally glanced at him and spoke in the soft Southern accent that he admired. "Well, I don't ride very much, Mr. Scofield. Not these days. I wouldn't ride cross-saddle. But I ride out sidesaddle. . . . Oh, well, it's been months, I guess. My daughter rides . . . Agnes rides off into the hills wearing her *brother's* clothes. . . . Oh, in the summer she'll ride out into the country wearing the bloomers the girls at Linus Gilchrest wear in gymnasium class! She's just as stubborn as a mule, and *I* can't convince her. . . . She learned to ride aside. She had a sidesaddle even when she was little. She uses mine sometimes now. It's a beautiful saddle. Sometimes Agnes will take Bandit out. . . . But the girls like to ride cross-saddle . . . when Agnes and Lucille compete . . ." Her voice faded into soft incoherence so that he couldn't catch what else she said, and then she straightened and leaned toward him, opening her huge eyes wide and apparently waiting for an answer or a reply.

He blinked under her steady gaze and regarded her with caution. He wasn't sure what she was getting at, and her expression was so intense that she appeared to Warren to be slightly dazed. But Warren wasn't much fond of her husband, who was quick, who was quite intelligent, and who had been very accommodating, but who was impervious to charm, or at least to the easy bonhomie that Warren generally fell into when he was doing a bit of business. Warren was suddenly exceedingly sorry for Mrs. Claytor, and more than anything he wanted to keep her from realizing that she had not yet uttered a single complete sentence to which he could respond.

He smiled broadly, as though she had said something wonderfully entertaining. "Oh, yes. I see!" he said with enthusiasm. "Oh, now look there. Lily's looking for us, I think." The group standing against the boards *had* turned to look their way as the stands filled up. "I know she wants you to see Judge Lufton's new sulky. Lily loves the races. Of course, she's a real horsewoman. Well, Lily likes anything to do with competition. And you can't find a game she doesn't enjoy," Warren said, only because he couldn't think of anything else, and he rose from his seat and offered his arm to Catherine Claytor. Her face suddenly lit up in a smile, and she stood and hooked her hand through his elbow with a purposely exaggerated little bow of acknowledgment.

"Why, thank you, Mr. Scofield," she said. "We have a beautiful day for the races." They moved off together, and he spent a strained but fairly pleasant afternoon in her company, although he had less time alone with her daughter than he had hoped.

The next morning, when Agnes was getting dressed for church, her mother appeared wraithlike in her doorway. "I want you to take this along with you. You might see Mrs. Butler and Mr. Scofield at church." Catherine had nothing but scorn for the Episcopal church in Washburn, even though she'd been raised Episcopalian, and she wouldn't go to the Methodist church, where Reverend Butler was pastor and which her husband and children attended. When her husband was in Columbus on a Sunday, Catherine often railed at the children that the only reason her husband went to church at all was because most of the businessmen in town went to Park Street Methodist.

"He was brought up in the Episcopal Church," she would insist to Howie and Richard. "Though if you grew up here it wouldn't make a bit of difference. Why, you sit through a service and you might as well *be* a Methodist. These people don't understand the importance of ritual . . . oh, the *beauty* of the altar banked with flowers . . . the robes and the incense. When I was a little girl my mama said that she could always count on the incense to make me drowse off. . . ."

But by then her children were no longer paying any attention. Howie and Richard realized that they wouldn't be made to go to church at all that day, and they would wander away quietly, so as not to draw their mother's eye. When Edson was very young he avoided being dragooned by Agnes into going along with her by simply lying down on the floor at his mother's feet, arms and legs flung out like a gingerbread boy's — an audience of one flattened by his mother's reveries but spared the tedium of accompanying his sister and the Damerons and Mrs. Long-acre to church.

Agnes had fallen into the habit of going to church with the Damerons whether her father was in town or not. She liked the feeling of inclusion, of important seriousness as she made her way among the clusters of people greeting one another, the children in their tidy clothes and the women in their nicest hats standing on the shady sidewalks and then breaking away to hurry up the steps as the church bells pealed. And she was par-ticularly eager to go to town that Sunday after visiting Judge Lufton's farm.

Agnes had been filled with delight all through the night, waking and falling back to sleep in half-remembered, half-dreamed pleasure that wasn't specific but was thorough. It was a vast idea of alert contentment, of clever observations casually made, easy conversation that had a brisk, cheerful sophistica-tion. And the amazing, feathered sky, the bright colors worn by the sulky drivers. It was a glimpse of comfortable sociability and adult freedom, and she was hoping to see Warren Scofield and Lily Butler at church. Lily and her parents and Mrs. John Scofield were always there, and occasionally Warren Scofield came along with them, although Agnes couldn't remember ever seeing Warren's father at church.

But Sunday morning here was her mother in some sad straits once more, and Agnes simply couldn't tolerate the bitterness she felt at having to deal with her. It put an end to Agnes's entirely happy mood.

"Mr. Scofield would be interested in this, I think," her mother was saying. "He was so curious to know if I liked to ride. I never went in for it the way you do. And Lucille, too. We wouldn't have liked that sort of competition. We wouldn't have made a show of ourselves. And in those *awful* hats. He wanted to know if I liked to ride, and I expect he would like to see this picture. Oh, it's very . . . Well, it's lovely, I think. It's a lovely photograph. I've slipped it out of the frame so you can take it with you." Catherine had not slept at all. She had been awake all night, rustling through boxes of clippings and scrapbooks she had brought back from Natchez after her mother's death. She had paused for long moments whenever she looked up and caught her reflection in the mirror, and finally she had slipped softly down the stairs and extracted the photograph from its little easel frame on a table in the chilly parlor.

Catherine Claytor still had in her mind the gentle offer of Mr. Scofield's arm as she rose to move away from the viewing stands at Judge Lufton's farm; she still turned over the poignant memory of his little bit of gallantry. It wasn't that she wanted to instruct Warren Scofield about who she was as a forty-year-old woman, it was only that when she thought of walking along beside him she fell into a state of peculiar agitation at the need to have him know that she was once someone taken seriously by the world.

Agnes moved over to look down at the picture her mother held carefully in her hands, holding it just along the edges with the tips of her fingers. It was the familiar photograph of her mother when she was about Agnes's age, wearing a small, dashingly cocked hat with a long feather arching backward from the band. She was perched elegantly on her horse with the draped skirt of her habit artfully arranged, and Agnes always wondered how they had gotten the cooperation of the horse.

"Well, Mama?" Agnes took the photograph but didn't look at her mother. She tried to make her mind as flat as a sheet of shiny paper. The Damerons would be by to pick her up any minute. "Why don't you just leave it in the parlor in its frame? I'm sure Mr. Scofield and Lily Butler probably noticed it already."

It was true that the picture of the young Catherine Alcorn Edson, from Natchez, Mississippi, was a seductive portrait. Catherine's beautiful face and slightly tentative expression seemed to bode well. Every good thing in the world seemed possible for the bashfully serene young woman gazing from that photograph. Once when the whole family had been sitting in the parlor and their father had suddenly become enraged at some word of his wife's and in one swift bound had crossed the room from his chair to the little couch where Catherine sat, had seized her arms just above the elbows and given her a rough shake like a rag doll, Howie had grabbed that photograph and held it in front of his father's face — between his parents' angry heads.

"Look at her, Papa!" he had shouted. "Look at her!" And he brandished the image of his lovely mother at his father almost as a threat. *See!* the gesture said. *See who she is!*

"Don't you hurt her, Papa!" Howie had ordered. "Don't you *ever* hurt her anymore!" Howie had been a gangly twelve year old, and their father had turned ferociously toward him for a moment but then let go of Catherine and left the room without another word.

Agnes finally turned to study her mother on this particular Sunday morning, hoping to avoid a scene. "Oh, I do like that picture, Mama. Everyone always notices it. But I don't think I ought to take it to church." Confronted with Agnes's refusal, however, her mother's air of beseechment disappeared and her expression became eerily petulant.

"Oh, Agnes. You don't understand a single thing. Why just look at this! Just look at this! Have you ever seen a more beautiful girl? Have you ever — in this place — seen anyone at all who could compare? I've begun to think it's the sort of face that Yankees can just never have. Something in the breeding. Everyone up here has such . . . *pointy* faces. Don't you find it frightening, Agnes? Don't you? Why, look at Lily Butler and her *needle* chin! Mama would say she's got a face as sharp as glass. But look at this face! Look here!" And she brushed her hand over the photograph Agnes was holding.

"Mama! Mama! But that's your *own* face!" Agnes's voice had dropped almost to a whisper, and she was frightened by the numbing pity and fear that overwhelmed her as she was swept up in the crisis of her mother's unfathomable desperation.

Her mother only stepped back and squinted her eyes at her daughter in exasperation. "Well, certainly. It is! It *is* my own face!" And the two of them regarded each other with mutual bewilderment.

"I'll just slip it into my book, then, Mama," Agnes finally said, "so that it won't get creased." And her mother followed her downstairs and beamingly buttoned Agnes into her coat in an exaggerated, joking way, pretending that Agnes was about five years old. "What a *good* girl you are!" Catherine said, purposefully mocking the cadence of the doting mother of a young child. "You look all nice for church! Don't forget to wear your mittens!" Agnes smiled in acknowledgment of her mother's little effort at frivolity and went off to meet the Damerons with the photograph tucked into her Book of Common Prayer. She walked right out of the house not allowing herself to contemplate anything at all. She didn't allow herself to imagine what her mother was thinking; Agnes was determined not to care.

During the winter Agnes had the chance to chat with Lily Butler and Warren Scofield now and then, in town sometimes, and often at church. Just before Christmas she had run into Warren at Lessor Brothers, where she had gone with Lucille to see if the yarn Mrs. Drummond wanted had come in. Agnes spotted his gleam of blond hair across all the rows of goods and knew immediately from the angle of the neck and shoulder that it was Warren Scofield, although his back was to her. It was so unexpected that for a scant second she was frozen in place just inside the door, and Lucille looked around to find her. "They'll have it at the back, Agnes. This way! Mother said if it came in this morning it would be wrapped and ready for me to pick up." Agnes followed along the aisle that would lead her right past Warren, and he turned and saw her.

"Why, Agnes!" he said, but she was wretched about the fact that she was in her awful school uniform with her hair flying loose from its clip all around her head. She was too unnerved even to remember to greet him, and no one spoke for a moment. "And . . . it's Miss Drummond, I know," Warren added. "Celia's sister, but I'm not sure . . . ," he said, and Lucille smiled.

"I'm Lucille," she said. "Are you shopping for Christmas presents, Mr. Scofield?" she asked him, and Agnes was nonplussed until she realized that he had been peering over a display of linens: handkerchiefs, dresser centerpieces, cluny-edged scarves, doilies, tray covers, and the like.

"Yes, I am. I'm not much good at buying presents. When I'm traveling and I see something in a shop that seems to me to be just right for someone . . . well, then I enjoy it. Then I feel as though I was meant to be going along just that way. Walking down that street. I like finding something by accident that will be the right thing." He was speaking in a rush, and Agnes was sure they were holding him up, but she was unable to do anything about it. "You'd think," he went on, "that I'd have the willpower to hang on to it. Put it away in a drawer so I'd have it at the right time. But I never can. I get home and I've been just imagining how pleased Uncle George or Lily . . . Well!" And he laughed. "You can see I'm stumped. I guess I was hoping for a nice distraction." He looked straight at them with an expression of pleasure, and Lucille smiled back at him, but Agnes was still trying to catch up with herself and had not even said hello.

"My mother said she was surprised that Lessors *has* such nice linens still," Lucille said. "She'd been thinking she would have to go into Columbus. Or even order what she needed from New York. She wasn't sure she could find nice linens anywhere because of the falloff in shipping. But I guess the Lessor brothers saw this coming before the rest of us and stocked up. Well, they're German, of course."

Agnes was chagrined to hear Lucille go on so; she knew that this wasn't any original idea of Lucille's, that she had only heard her father say all this about German shopkeepers — that it was too bad there wasn't somewhere else to shop. "We have to buy everything from Germans in this town!" Agnes had heard Mr. Drummond go on about it herself. "Germans or Jews or Italians!" Lucille was merely repeating what he said, only more politely.

When Agnes had repeated Mr. Drummond's opinions at the dinner table one night, her father had thrown down his napkin and said the man was just a plain fool and that Agnes should never repeat *anything* Frank Drummond said because it made her sound just like a simpleminded, empty-headed little ninny of a girl. She had more sense than that, he said. "You're not some scatterbrained little parrot! Think for yourself, Agnes. You ought to use the good head you have on your shoulders!"

But facing Warren Scofield in her sensible silence, Agnes felt like a ninny anyway. She couldn't think of anything to say at all, and the longer she stood there the more impossible it seemed to her to say a single word.

"Now, who are you buying a present for? There *are* some nice things here," Lucille chattered on, moving over beside Warren and feeling the quality of a linen napkin as though she had any idea what the difference would be between good quality and bad.

"Well, I'd certainly be grateful for some advice," he said, looking at them both but settling his gaze on Agnes, although she still couldn't reply. "But I don't want to take up your time if you're in a hurry. Or if you've got something you need to do."

For a moment Agnes thought that Warren seemed disconcerted himself, but he turned to Lucille with his startling smile. When Warren smiled, his whole face broke into an expression of gladness, everything about him communicated real joy, and almost anyone looking on would smile reflexively, but Agnes always thought there was something a bit rueful, too, in his expression. A downward quirk at one corner of his mouth that seemed to acknowledge the possible foolishness of his own delight. "I'm hoping to find something for my mother. And for my cousin Lily. I thought about gloves. Some new gloves. But then I thought I didn't know if either one of them wanted any more gloves . . . so I was thinking about these handkerchiefs." He had turned to inspect the handkerchiefs again, and then he looked to the two girls.

Lucille was nodding. "You can't ever go wrong with nice handkerchiefs," she said. "Even if someone already has plenty they're bound to need more eventually."

"Do you think so?" He picked up a handkerchief and draped it over his palm, looking skeptical, and then he turned to them again, and he straightened a bit in surprise at Agnes's expression. She was thinking of opening a box from Warren Scofield that turned out to have nothing in it but handkerchiefs, and her face had taken on that wide-eyed, fierce disapproval that sent her brothers scurrying for cover. "Why, Agnes," he said, "you look like an owl about to swoop down on some specially tasty *rodent*. You don't look to me like you agree at all," he said with a little laugh, and Agnes finally spoke.

"Oh, no! I don't. I think handkerchiefs are a *horrible* present!" she blurted out, and then was appalled at herself.

"Well, *Agnes!*" said Lucille, who was really stung. She had embroidered a lovely set of handkerchiefs for her sister Celia's Christmas present, and Agnes knew all about that.

Agnes looked down at her hands and tried to pull herself together. "Well," she said more softly, and glanced an apology at Lucille, "of course I don't mean they're a horrible present, but I just mean that generally people have enough handkerchiefs . . . and gloves, too." She had no idea what had caused her to say what she had in the first place, and she turned to study the goods displayed on the counter. Remembering that Warren Scofield had said she looked like an owl and even now wondering how she could stand to think about any of this later.

Lucille offered a few other ideas. "What about a picture frame, then? I saw some pretty oval picture frames — they were silver — in the window of Buchroeder's. Oh! Or a nice powder box? Or maybe a little vanity case?"

Warren appeared to be considering these things; he put aside the scarf he had been holding and turned his whole attention to Lucille and Agnes.

"What do you think, Agnes? What about a little silver frame for Lily? Something very plain, because she doesn't care at all for a lot of decoration. Well, say, what would be something that . . . What would be something that when you opened it up on Christmas morning it just made you happy? Just happy that now you had it?"

Lucille smiled. "Oh, I'm always happy with all the things —"

"A music box," Agnes said absolutely, startling herself. But she was sure about it and so she didn't say any more. She was sure that anyone would be happy to open a wrapped package, put aside the ribbon and smooth out the paper, and then carefully take off the lid to discover a music box. How could that not be a wonderful present?

Warren settled back on his heels a little in surprise and with real satisfaction. He put his hands in his pockets and gazed off at an angle. "A music box," he said, trying out the idea. "That's exactly right," he said. "Why, that's exactly right!" And then he remembered himself and beamed at Lucille. "A picture frame for my mother and a little music box for Lily!"

And that Christmas of 1917, Lily was indeed delighted and deeply touched at the intricate and lovely inlaid marquetry box that, when opened, played "Clair de Lune," and Agnes spent most of Christmas day in a foul mood that she thought she concealed from everyone in her family. She didn't notice that each one was a little hesitant as he or she handed her a gift. She believed she was sufficiently enthusiastic as she opened linen handkerchiefs from her brothers, a box of very handsome writing paper from her father, and from her mother a beautiful carved ivory hair clip and an exquisitely beaded bag, both of which had been her grandmother's. The handkerchiefs *were* nice, as was the stationery, and the hair clip and little evening bag were extraordinary, but she thought bitterly all day of Lily Butler and her music box.

In March, when Agnes heard from Lucille by way of her sister Celia that all the Scofields and Lily Butler, too, were going to spend at least six weeks and maybe all of April and May in Florida and then travel up the East Coast, Agnes's spirits hit bottom. She was scarcely even civil to her friends at school, who worried over her among themselves and tried to come up with schemes that would amuse her. They had no idea what could be wrong; Agnes hadn't admitted even to Lucille her mortifying and hopeless infatuation with Warren Scofield. And at home it was no longer that she simply wasn't paying attention; she became petulantly disengaged.

For a little while the Claytors were in greater turmoil than usual. Agnes's indifference created a vacuum of *intention,* somehow. Her general insistence on a pretense of familial propriety no longer informed the workings of the household. Agnes didn't care what happened. She didn't even seem to notice.

Her brothers had certainly never welcomed Agnes's bossiness — her interference in their lives — but in its absence they suddenly felt insecure, worried. Their wariness was hardly an organized idea, but each one of them kept a weather eye on his mother. Not one of them could have put his finger on what had changed, but each one braced himself for the unexpected.

Catherine Claytor, too, put her head up and sensed the miasma of discontent that drifted through the rooms in Agnes's wake, that settled in the corners. Catherine was no more curious than ever, and she didn't name to herself whatever it was that focused her attention. But she recognized something new and dramatic in the air, and at first she was only seized with a disturbing agitation. She could no longer find solace in retreating to her dark bedroom, waking and dozing through the unhappy afternoons, but neither could she settle to any task. Day by day, however, her restlessness transformed itself into a frenzied sort of animation, and her mood spiraled upward into a steady, sustained gleefulness. Her family had not seen her so cheerful and involved with the everyday life of the household in years.

For a while Howie and Richard and Edson were surprised when they came home from school to discover their mother involved in some determined activity or other, although Agnes wasn't in the least impressed. The boys were accustomed to the afternoon gloom of the hushed house, the upstairs shrouded against any little bit of light, the shades pulled down and the curtains closed, because their mother was resting.

As the days lengthened, Catherine awoke buzzing with plans, dressed hurriedly, was busy all the time, and sometimes complained in aggravation that she didn't know what to do, that she scarcely had time to turn around. In fact, though, every day she was increasingly elated to find herself bound up in the passage of time along with everyone else in the house. One night at dinner she declared that the hours of a day were gone before you could say Jack Robin.

"*Cock* Robin," said Howie.

"Jack *Robinson,* Mama," said Edson.

Their father put his coffee spoon in his saucer, leaned back in his chair to catch Catherine's gaze, and a long look passed between them. "Well, isn't it a good thing, then," he said, "that there're so many extra hours in the night."

Agnes observed that long glance held between her parents, and she left the table without excusing herself, but her father didn't comment, and no one else noticed. Her brothers had fallen out of the habit of vigilance in less than three months, and they had each been dreamily sitting through dinner in luxurious contemplation of their own plans for the rest of the evening and for the next day. They were behaving as if they were just any family, and Agnes was disgusted.

Catherine Claytor seemed to draw increasing energy from her daughter's abdication of domestic responsibility, and her sons sought their mother out in the afternoons to tell her about a victory on the playground or to see if she had made cookies. Dwight Claytor began to believe that if only Agnes had not usurped so much of Catherine's domain, life at home might well have been more sanguine, and he developed a little bit of a grudge against his daughter, as did the three brothers against their sister. It took no time at all for the rest of the family to conclude that Catherine's newfound animation was proof enough that Agnes's persistent direction and interference had been unwarranted.

One afternoon Howie and Richard and Edson had come home to find their mother and Mrs. Longacre together in the kitchen companionably tending the stove. Mrs. Longacre was chopping raisins while their mother diced the figs for the middle layer of Catherine Claytor's famous ribbon cake, although it had been years since she had made it. Agnes was staying over at the Drummonds' in town, and she wasn't interested, anyway, when they told her about it.

Agnes didn't even realize that now it was *she* who the rest of the household avoided and catered to, and who they held responsible — sometimes with reason — for any domestic unpleasantness. Only Edson didn't give up on Agnes entirely. He adored his mother, but he felt loyal to his sister as well.

But sometimes even he, who had monitored his mother so diligently, forgot entirely that she had not always been who she was now. Catherine had been busily making plans for this and that, had become feverishly enthusiastic about one thing or another, but she managed to maintain a determined kind of organization; even her enthusiasm didn't fly out of control. She had achieved a delicate balance between elation and frenzy, and the household stopped holding its collective breath.

There were no more of the confrontations of strained civility between Catherine and Dwight that had always threatened to fall into full-fledged and dangerous fury — brutality — as their argument intensified into the night. Just at the precise moment that Agnes turned all her energy toward something else, Catherine had somehow struck a vein of sustained gleefulness that didn't seem to be about to give out.

One Saturday morning, Catherine had insisted that Agnes stand still while she took all Agnes's measurements, and even her brothers counted it against Agnes when she wasn't a bit gracious about it. "Oh, Mama, I don't have time for all this. What are you up to now? I don't need any new clothes," she said. But Catherine timidly persisted, although Howie and Richard and Edson saw that Agnes had hurt their mother's feelings. Catherine ducked her head, and her mouth trembled as she bent to measure the distance from Agnes's waist to the floor. The three boys were hurt on their mother's behalf when she approached

Agnes gingerly with a sheaf of pictures and drawings of some outfit or other — they weren't paying strict attention — only to have Agnes rebuff her with a claim of schoolwork to get done or some other brisk word.

As the end of school approached, Agnes often stayed overnight at Lucille Drummond's to finish up the business of the class book or for rehearsals of the senior pageant, but the boys were home in the afternoons and had seen their mother pore over pattern books and magazines and tear out pages, sketching in details here and there. They knew, though Agnes did not, that Catherine had some great plan for Agnes's birthday. She had sent all sorts of instructions to her Aunt Cettie in Natchez, and one afternoon she insisted Agnes come along to the parlor to see what had arrived. Agnes was unenthusiastic in the face of her mother's childish delight and coquettish manner. It made Agnes tired at the thought of dealing with it, though to her surprise Howie and Richard and Edson followed right along into the parlor without the slightest hesitation.

"Your birthday's this Saturday, Agnes," her mother said. "It's a milestone. A milestone. Oh, I remember when I turned eighteen." And Agnes began to feel a familiar dread at the prospect of her mother's breathless recollections. But her brothers watched their mother with genuine interest.

"I'll be *nineteen*, Mama."

"Aunt Cettie gave a supper party out at Ravenna. . . . My mother had wanted to have a dance on my *sixteenth* birthday, but Cettie said that it wasn't necessarily expected anymore, and besides I was still all bones. Aunt Cettie always made my best gowns, and she said what was the point when I still looked like a plucked chicken. 'Let's see if she turns into a swan or a goose,' she said to Mama. Of course, I was right there being pinned up.

But I might as well have been a dress form. My aunt Cettie wasn't ever . . . She used to say that in this world a woman better develop a thick skin. When I was just a little girl I always thought she said that because I'd end up in tears getting pricked with pins whenever I had to go for a fitting. But you can just imagine! You can guess how I worried about that — a swan or a goose! *Oh, my!*"

And Agnes really noticed her mother for the first time in months. Agnes followed her into the parlor and saw that her mother's hair was tidily arranged, no wisps straggling free, and she moved gracefully, with that beautiful confidence of height that Agnes had always found enviable. Her mother had about her a sort of sheen of complacency, and she was lovely to look at.

"Look here!" her mother said. "I had Aunt Cettie make this up for you. I think you ought to own one of your own. At eighteen you should have a gown and an evening coat, too. But in this place where would you wear it. . . . But I've given up worrying about it," she added, cutting off her own drift into bitterness. Agnes was surprised, but she could see her brothers no longer seemed concerned. In fact, her brothers looked on eagerly. Agnes realized with a start that this was a little conspiracy. The three of them already knew what was in the package.

Agnes unfolded the paper in the large box lying open on the table and found a beautifully made riding habit, with a gray jacket and vest and a bias-cut, six-gored skirt for riding sidesaddle. The skirt flared so extravagantly that it had been packed with the hem carefully folded in upon itself twice over in ever-lengthening triangles, each fold cushioned with crumpled tissue to guard against creasing. The whole outfit had been carefully arranged to lie in its wrappings the same way it would appear once it was put on. Beneath the vest was a high-necked white linen blouse, also stuffed with tissue to protect the fullness of the unstitched pleats of the bodice, which was tucked into the skirt band. A gray ribbon was artfully pinned and tied around the collar stay.

Catherine Claytor and her daughter leaned over the box with a similar reverence, and Catherine drew her fingertips over the sleeve of the jacket. "This is very fine, you see. This is very fine wool. Not heavy. No one can drape a jacket like Cettie. You'll see how the sleeves . . ."

"Oh, yes!" Agnes said, feeling the fabric herself and for the first time in a while not at all irritated or put off by her mother's dreamy consideration. "It *is* beautiful. It is beautifully made. I can see that."

Catherine straightened and looked at Agnes with a rapturous smile of exaltation, and Agnes smiled back. When Catherine was happy in the excited way she was that afternoon she was irresistible. "But, oh, Agnes, just wait and see what else . . . Wait here!" She left the room briefly and returned with two more boxes, in one of which Agnes found a pair of tall black boots with a tapered toe, an articulated arch, and a sloped heel, unlike her broad-footed laced Wellingtons. The second box Catherine clasped in front of her with an expression of de-lighted satisfaction.

"Now, you *know* how I feel about those hats, Agnes. You and Lucille look to me exactly like you've put buckets on your heads. But of course no one wears . . . Well," and she put the box down and carefully lifted its lid, "I thought this would do and not seem too . . . It's just that the brim only *dips* a little in the front and back instead of that awful helmetlike allover curve." She lifted out a handsome black hat with a very plain satin band and perched it on her own head to show Agnes.

Catherine only turned briefly to the mirror to set it at a proper angle and then she turned back to her daughter with a satisfied and rather hopeful expression.

"You look beautiful, Mama!" Catherine turned back to the mirror for a moment to see. She nodded at her reflection. She did look beautiful. "It's as beautiful as a *costume,*" Agnes said. "It's a wonderful birthday present. Oh, but Mama, I want to wear it this Sunday? I could ride to church, couldn't I?"

Agnes was imagining the figure she would make and how surprised Lucille and Edith would be. She knew it was possible that it would look as if she were showing off. But since the Scofields and Lily Butler were all away she didn't care, and she couldn't resist the temptation. She could ride to the Drummonds' house and walk over to church with them, in case she might look vain — in case she might look silly — riding past the groups of people congregating on the steps of the Methodist church and Saint James Episcopal across the way. "I'll give Bandit a bath Saturday if it's warm enough!"

Howie and Richard and Edson Claytor were soothed by all this happy girlishness, although they took themselves off feeling a little envious of Agnes's good luck in being the only daughter of their mother. Agnes did get so much more of their mother's attention than any one of the three of them.

Chapter Seven

ON SATURDAY, April 6, 1918, the morning of her nineteenth birthday, Agnes woke under the lingering influence of what must have been a pleasant dream. She tried to regain it for some long, drowsy minutes, but she couldn't fall back into it. Her mother always said, though, that you would have good luck during any day you woke up from a happy dream. And Agnes *felt* lucky. The idea of her day shaped itself into an orderly staircase of tasks she meant to get done, and she unbunched her pillow and stretched out flat under her quilt, looking forward to a length of time in which the hours had already taken on a safe, thick, busy quality.

She would need to check over the sidesaddle in case it needed cleaning, and she wanted to give Bandit a bath if it got warm enough, and that would take up the greater part of the late morning and early afternoon. But the job she most looked forward to, and which she ran through in her mind in great detail, was the business of pressing her new riding habit, being especially careful not to iron in a crease along the elegant roll of the lapel and not to use an iron on the skirt at all but to hang it over steam, as her mother's aunt Cettie had directed. For the first time in months, Agnes lay in bed considering her day without even a single thought of Warren Scofield entering her head.

The weather was not breezy, but the sky was bright blue with high, rushing clouds, so that when Agnes was in the barn checking over the saddle she happened to glance up long enough to get the rather pleasing but disconcerting impression that the very spot where she stood was spinning away from the sky. It was partly the effect of the distant, streaky, racing clouds and partly just the elation that follows a period of brooding. By midmorning the temperature had risen enough that she took off her old barn jacket and rolled up her sleeves. She set out buckets of water to warm in the sun, and after lunch she went about giving Bandit a bath.

Her mother joined her in the barn, bringing along a bar of her fine-milled French soap with its wonderful smell of fading roses — roses with their petals blown but that give off a heavy last perfume that's so profuse the scent lingers with sweet, round bitterness on the back of the tongue. "Can I help, Agnes? I've brought some of my scented soap out." Her mother was timid about asking, and Agnes was surprised and delighted.

"That would be wonderful, Mama." She felt shy in the face of her mother's goodwill and amiability.

"When we get done he'll smell like a garden," her mother said. And Catherine rolled up her sleeves as well, put on the cobbler's apron that always hung on the tack room door, and went to work with Agnes.

They sponged and lathered Agnes's horse, whom she'd

named Bandit because he had been an outlaw's horse her father had bought especially for her at a court sale in Coshocton. Bandit wasn't a particularly placid horse, but he was almost always accommodating, and he stood calmly enough, turning his head a little when he caught the first scent of Catherine Claytor's French soap. The surprise to Agnes, those four years ago when her father had thought of her exclusively, and the whole attendant circumstance of the horse he had bought her had been wonderfully exciting. "Why, Mrs. Longacre," she had said unwisely, "I'll be riding an *outlaw's* horse!"

"I wouldn't think that would be any story I'd *tell*," Mrs. Longacre had said. "A man poor enough to take to robbing banks, or no telling what, isn't likely to have been able to keep a very good horse." And, of course, Agnes hadn't thought of that, but it proved not to be true. It was generally Bandit that Agnes rode at show, although sometimes she rode Buckeye, who was smaller and on the whole had a better disposition. But she loved Bandit more, and in that early afternoon she curried him and carefully worked soapy water through his mane, stopping to address any tangles that met her comb.

Agnes was a fairly accomplished rider; she and Lucille often rode in local shows and at the Marshal County Fair. When Agnes had fallen during last year's competition, the *Washburn Observer* had mixed up the girls' names and reported that Lucille Drummond had fallen from her horse, Cash, when taking the second jump of the course. Lucille was so offended that she would scarcely speak to Agnes for several weeks.

"You aren't even being sensible, Lucille!" Agnes had finally said. "For goodness sake! It isn't *my* fault that the *Observer* got the names wrong."

That had been one Saturday when Agnes and Sally Trenholm were at Lucille's house, and Lucille's sister Celia was showing them a new way to do their hair, although she'd given up on Agnes's. "That's true," Celia said to her sister, whose hair she was pinning carefully, so that the eyes of everyone in the room were on Lucille's reflection in the mirror — their attention caught by the transformation of Lucille's sweet, long girl's face into that of an attractive but surprisingly stern-looking grown woman. "You're just being silly, Lucille," Celia said.

"Oh, *well!* How can you say that? I've *never* fallen on a jump in a show! To see my name in the paper like that was the most embarrassing thing that's ever happened in my life! But it isn't even that. Agnes, it just makes me so *mad!* Because I *know* you're glad . . . not that they got my name wrong! But you're awfully glad that your name *wasn't* in that paper! That it didn't say that *you'd* taken a fall." Agnes hadn't replied, because that was true enough.

Agnes could hardly wait to show Lucille her riding habit. On Sundays there were always so many of Lucille's sisters and brothers-in-law and nephews and nieces coming and going at the big house on the square, and Agnes knew that for a few minutes she would be the center of all that hectic commotion as one after another Mrs. Drummond and Celia and Lucille called to the others to come see Agnes's new outfit.

And it still thrilled Agnes that her mother had gone to such trouble to contrive the surprise of it. Agnes lingered over the thought of explaining to the assorted Drummonds how her mother had been dissatisfied with any pattern she had found and so had designed the skirt of Agnes's habit herself. She knew that Mrs. Drummond would exclaim over the remarkable workmanship, the beautifully bound buttonholes, the impeccably turned, notched collar. She knew Celia would admire her hat.

As Agnes worked carefully through the tangles of Bandit's mane she was caught up in the idea of herself riding regally through the square — riding through the square not seeming a bit foolish. She would sit erect and graceful, a sight to behold, a person other people would surreptitiously turn to see and whose image would haunt them later. Who was that *girl?* They would wonder about that, not recognizing the Agnes of every day, the Agnes of the navy-and-white middy blouse, of the dreary school uniform and flyaway hair. Sunday morning she would be another person altogether.

Agnes was standing on a stool to work her fingers through the crest of Bandit's mane. Catherine stood on the ground with one hand on the bridge of Bandit's nose to remind him to keep his head down, and she was using a damp cloth to clean the horse's ear. She began singing very softly, as if she meant to soothe Bandit. It was a song she had sung to her children when they were young, but she was making up new words as she went along, to tease Agnes.

> When once I was living on Newcastle Street,
> I knew a young girl, oh so pure and so sweet.
> Though she was a young lady who could not resist
> When handsome young William did beg for a kiss.

Agnes felt a smile take over her face; her expression went rubbery with pleasure, and she ducked her head to the side so she wouldn't be caught out. "Mama, that's just silly," Agnes tried to object, but Catherine continued:

> Oh Agnes, I pledge you I cannot abide
> To live my life through without you at my side

> If you'll come to Washburn to make a new life,
> It shall do me great honor to make you my wife.
> Oh hey, away awa-ay . . .

Agnes couldn't control her tone of voice either, which had the loose, chuckling quality of a repressed giggle. "Oh, Mama! For goodness sake! William might just as well be my *brother* —"

> They cro-ossed the wi-ide blue ocean,
> They sa-ailed the mi-ighty sea,
> And never more did I happen to meet
> That young girl of Newcastle Street.
>
> When once I was living down Devonshire way,
> I knew a young lady as fair as the day.
> Sweet Agnes Claytor with hair bright as gold,
> Who never was brazen, who never was bold.
> Then a young soldier came seeking the lass.
> Right by her window brave William did pass . . .

"Mama, stop it!" Agnes pleaded, but she was beaming with absurd pleasure, like a little girl. "I've only had one *letter* from William. All about learning to fly. And, Mama, those words hardly work, anyway. Hair bright as *gold* . . . ?" She looked over to see that her mother's face had an eager expression. Her mother looked pleased and light-hearted in a way Agnes had not seen her for such a long time, and Agnes couldn't help but continue to grin at her.

"I know," Catherine said, "I know . . . but what about . . ."

> Sweet Agnes Claytor with hair black as night,
> Who never did argue, who never did fight . . .

"Uhmm, that's not very good . . ."

Sweet Agnes Claytor with hair black as slate
Was never unhappy, was never irate. . . .
Sweet Agnes Claytor with hair black as coal
La da da, la da da, la da la da stole . . . ?

"Umm . . . something better to work with that . . ."

Always was happy and always was droll . . .

Agnes's spirits soared. Who in the world was ever more fun than her own mother? Who among any of her friends had such a sense of nonsense, knew the pleasure of falling into plain silliness? Agnes hadn't mentioned her interest in Warren Scofield to anyone, but she looked at her mother, who radiated delight just now. "Well, Mama, it might not be William Dameron at all that I have any interest in," she said, and Catherine turned sideways to Bandit so that she and Agnes were less than a foot apart, their eyes level since Agnes was on a step stool.

Catherine's expression widened, and she smiled with excitement. "Oh, Agnes! You can tell me! I've seen the two of you . . . since you were children. And it's just right, I think. A handsome hero! Gone off to war. Well, he'll be a nice-looking man when he fills out. A pilot!" Her voice was infused with the anticipated pleasure of learning a secret. "You can't keep *every-thing* from me! But I won't say anything, you know. I wouldn't do that. *Unmerciful* teasing. I know how your brothers . . . You're safe telling me. I always thought it must be William."

But they were interrupted just then by the sight of Mr. Evans coming across the field from the direction of the Damerons', carrying an assortment of long-handled tools — a rake and spade and two shovels — and glaring their way in obvious disapproval. Catherine waved happily at him. He had worked for Agnes's grandfather and did a little bit of everything around the property, keeping a special eye on the horses. He had known Agnes since she was a little girl, but he was a wiry, tall, dour-seeming man who suffered from terrible shyness. He never could speak for any length of time while looking a person straight in the eye; his gaze inevitably slipped sideways, giving the impression of a sort of evasive displeasure.

"Agnes, what're you putting on that horse?" he said when he got nearer. "Bandit's patient, but he's not liking that a bit."

"Oh, no. It's all right, Mr. Evans. It's Mama's soap. It smells exactly like roses. Bandit won't smell so much like a stable."

"That's where he lives, isn't it? I don't expect he minds the smell at all."

"Oh, you're probably right, Mack," Catherine answered in Agnes's stead. "But he needs some feminine attention, poor old boy," she added disarmingly. Mack Evans thought highly of all the horses in his charge, but he liked Mrs. Claytor best of the various people he had to deal with. The two of them were surprisingly at ease around each other. In the company of horses Catherine lost her self-absorption and became genuinely inquisitive, involved, and never even thought of the impression she made one way or another.

"It's Agnes's birthday, Mr. Evans." Catherine addressed him formally, which seemed almost coquettish after her initial breezy familiarity. "She's eighteen today —"

"Nineteen, Mama," Agnes said.

"— and my aunt sent her a beautiful habit. You wait till you see, Mack! And a hat. She's going to ride in to church tomorrow."

Mr. Evans didn't say anything, but his whole attitude became less recalcitrant, and he began to move off around the side of the barn.

"This horse is just going to be gorgeous!" Catherine called in his direction, and he gave a brief nod and went on his way, leaving them to what he clearly thought was a frivolous bit of work. When they'd rinsed Bandit, and while Agnes was using the side of her hand to sluice water from his coat, Catherine stood back a moment, looking him over. "My, you're handsome, Bandit," she said softly to the horse, and he looked exactly like he agreed, and Agnes and Catherine laughed at him.

"Don't think we're not onto you," Catherine said to him conversationally. "You just like to stroll around the barn because it makes old Dilly and especially poor Buckeye so unhappy." Bandit was always managing to unlatch his stall, and they would find him investigating the barn with his back to the other two, and Buckeye would be whuffling and complaining at the injustice.

"How could you have gotten so dirty? I don't like the look of the white on him, Agnes," she said. "It's yellowish still. And I never like the look of white feet when a horse doesn't have stockings on all four legs." Catherine moved around to look at Bandit assessingly. "Ummm. I know what. I have an idea. Now wait here! This horse has got to do you proud. He's got to make a fine appearance. And his white stockings . . . Wait here! I'll be right back! And I want you to tell me all about this mysterious beau, Agnes. It's not fair — you can't leave me not knowing. Leave me in suspense like this. And it'll be fair. I'll tell you a secret, too. Then we'll be even. Don't you think that's fair? I'll come up with something! Oh, I'll come up with something you've never even guessed! It's the only way to have secrets."

Agnes was unthinkingly happy. Everything in the world seemed wonderful to her. There was no horse she would rather ride than Bandit, no day she would rather be in than the day of her nineteenth birthday, no place she would prefer to the farm in the middle of Ohio, no person on earth she would rather be than herself, and certainly she wanted no mother other than the enchanting Catherine Alcorn Edson Claytor.

When her mother came back she was carrying her own powder puff and her silver box of fine white dusting powder that she used occasionally, and she made ready to apply it to Bandit's blaze and the two white stockings of his hind legs.

"Mama, don't you think he should be completely dry? Won't that turn into paste? I don't think Bandit'll like that much," Agnes said, but only as an inquiry, not with the slightest tone of reproach.

Catherine was twirling the fluffy puff in the receptacle to take up the powder. "I suppose that's right," she said. "Yes, I suppose you could do that in the morning. But look here!" And she pulled a tin of boot black from the pocket of the apron she still had on. "If we do his hooves his stockings will show up so much nicer. Don't you think so? He's a beauty, isn't he? But I never do like white feet."

"Well, Mama! I hope you brought some rouge to put some color in his cheeks." Agnes laughed, and so did her mother, at their unusual giddiness, at the idea of Bandit so gussied up, at the fact that they'd gotten so carried away.

"Agnes, you *know* I never have approved of the use of rouge." The two women had fallen into precisely the same mood at precisely the same time, and it was one of those heady moments in which any two people conspire in a kind of romance. Catherine took an old rag and blackened all four hooves to an oddly unnatural-looking evenly dark shade that certainly did emphasize the whiteness of Bandit's markings, as if his hooves were the dots of exclamation points.

But their high spirits began to fade a bit as the day length-ened, and by the time Agnes had finished with his mane and gotten to the business of shaping the horse's tail — banging it straight across — Catherine sank down on a tack trunk sud-denly, seeming very tired. Agnes looked over at her, worried all at once about the mood of this day slipping away from them. She couldn't bear to let it go, this intimacy, this exceptional con-nection. At last she fastened a blanket over Bandit and tied him in the warm sun out of any draft and so that he wouldn't roll.

"I don't feel well at all," her mother said. Agnes tugged the rope's end to be sure Bandit was secured and then moved over behind her mother and began unclasping the buckle that closed the canvas apron behind her mother's neck.

"Well, you've gotten as wet as Bandit, Mama. Lift your arms and I'll undo the waist and get this heavy apron off." Catherine did as she was told, sitting slumped like a child and looking ash white.

Agnes sat down beside her and took her mother's long hand between her own, something she had seen Celia Drummond do once when Mrs. Drummond was distressed. Catherine had never been the sort of mother who liked to be touched. "No, no. Don't be so *clingy*" had been a constant admonition to her children when they were toddlers. Nevertheless, Agnes chafed her mother's hand tentatively to try to warm it, and her mother didn't object or even seem to notice. She did turn her head and look questioningly at Agnes, and Agnes offered up the little bit of information she had been longing to disclose and that was all she had, anyway, in the way of seduction.

She smiled and lowered her voice confidentially, leaning toward her mother. "It's Mr. Scofield, Mama. Warren Scofield. I know it's just silly. . . ."

But her mother arched away from Agnes in surprise, and she narrowed her eyes at her daughter in the first hint of discord in the day. "Oh, no. Don't be silly, Agnes. I won't tell anyone about William. Not even your father. You haven't the least notion . . . You don't know anything about that sort of man. Oh, no. That . . . No, no."

"He's very nice, Mama." Catherine just looked at her daughter without animation, and Agnes went on a little desperately. "But, of course, he won't ever *know* it, Mama. Everyone knows he's in love with Lily Butler." Her mother still leaned away from her, and Agnes rushed on, "But naturally that's simply doomed," she said, using a bit of Lucille's gloomy exaggeration, making the word sound very nearly like the call of a mourning dove. "They're first cousins, after all!" Finally she fell silent, looking down at her lap to avoid her mother's appalled expression.

"Warren Scofield is *not* a man," her mother said with an indrawn tone of peculiar fury, "who could ever be interested in a woman like Lily Butler, with her little *weasel* face and all her . . . talking and talking. She's a brittle, stringy little thing . . . sharp . . . *Oh*, no. Warren Scofield wouldn't even look twice!"

Agnes was stunned, and her mother didn't say anything else; she slumped back toward Agnes and withdrew her hand, tucking it into the folds of her skirt. They sat side by side on the trunk, Agnes's spirits deflated and her mother hunched and withdrawn.

They simply sat there for some time until finally Catherine spoke up. "You don't think I'll be as sick as I was when I was carrying Edson, do you?"

Agnes looked back at her, puzzled. "Of course not, Mama. You just did too much. You didn't need to help me with Bandit. I could have gotten one of the boys. Or — really — I could have managed by myself, I think, it just would have . . ." and her voice began to run down ". . . would have taken longer." She craned around just a bit to study her mother's expression.

"But I do feel like I did when I was going to have Edson," her mother said, nearly in a whisper because they were sitting with their heads so close, and this time it was Agnes who recoiled. "Those whole nine months," Catherine said, "I thought I'd *never* feel good again. I hope it's not going to be so bad this time."

Agnes stood up and began to roll down her sodden sleeves and then fixed her attention on fastening the cuffs. "Oh, no, Mama. That can't be how you feel. You can't be feeling that. You're forty years old, Mama. You're not going to have a baby?"

Her mother's head came up, and she straightened in apparent surprise, and her face was fixed in an expression of astonishment. "I *am* going to have a baby," she said, exhaling the words after taking in a long breath of discovery, as if she hadn't known it until that very minute. "Probably late in October. Isn't that amazing, Agnes? Isn't it amazing? Oh, everything will change now. This will be different than any time before. As your father said, with the four of you . . . well, there were so many babies. All at once. And not a single one of you was ever an *easy* baby. My mother always said you were a bunch of little Yankees. All born with opinions. And just all at once. Children everywhere needing something or other. But with just one it won't be the same at all.

"You know what I think, Agnes? I think it will be like it was in Natchez on Sunday. Going to church. Mama wouldn't have *heard* of missing Sunday school. I've always wished I felt, oh . . .

compelled to go to church on Sunday. If I ever could have taken that church seriously! Mr. Werlein. What kind of Episcopal minister . . . Of course, everyone around here is German. But no *ceremony* . . . Well. But do you know how it is when you feel, oh, duty *bound* to get up and dress in your nice clothes? And fresh gloves. A pretty hat. Nothing feels so crisp and . . . important, does it? To get a new hat fixed just right on your head. Fixed just so. It gives you the idea of things being a certain way. You know that you've done your best to keep up appearances. You're all set! In a beautiful new hat! And so you know just how you'll get things done in that day. And I think that with the new baby . . . And your father says there's no reason not to stay in Columbus during the session. Mr. Dameron's *more* than capable, and Mrs. Longacre's here."

Agnes had been nearly giddy all day, enveloped as she was in her mother's singular air of inclusiveness. It had been one of the happiest birthdays she could remember. One of the nicest days of her life. But at last, enclosed there in the barn with the heavy floral scent of the soap lurking beneath the ordinary smell of horse and hay and earth, Agnes stepped away from where her mother was sitting and went briskly about putting away the brushes, emptying the buckets and setting them upside down to dry thoroughly so they wouldn't hang from their hooks with a bit of water in them and rust.

Catherine Claytor was childish in her tactlessness but also childish in her keenly honed sensitivity to any change in the emotional atmosphere, and as the wave of her daughter's abrupt and icy disaffection washed over her, Catherine began to feel defensive just in general. She sensed that this imperious daughter of hers had found some fault with her once again. A familiar weariness descended on her, and she began to lose her hold on the energy and sustained gleefulness that had buoyed her for weeks and weeks now.

Catherine began to be overtaken by a cranky, buzzing sort of agitation, and it made her cross, all of a sudden, to be damp and uncomfortable. She was edgy and impatient, but she sat quite still, looking down at her hands resting in the folds of her skirt, which was wet despite the fact that she had worn the heavy apron. She held her arms out in front of her, palms down, and was disturbed by the rough look of her hands, their chapped redness, by what suddenly seemed to her their grotesquely articulated knuckles, the unsightly blue tracery of veins.

She observed the nearly smug, restrained expression on Agnes's face as she went about putting away the saddle soap and straightening everything with maddening deliberation. Why weren't she and Agnes having fun anymore? Catherine was resentful all at once, having done all this wet work and receiving so little gratitude. Agnes's small, square hands were all smooth, supple flesh, and her skin seemed infinitely elastic as she deftly put things back exactly where they belonged.

"Well, I can't stay out here all day," Catherine said, as if Agnes had implored her to. "I don't feel well at all, and I've gotten too wet. I can hardly stand it if I catch a cold on top of everything else." She and Agnes didn't exchange any look — there was no communication in their gaze — it was just that their faces were turned toward each other with a blankness that, in Agnes's case, was a perfectly accurate reflection of what she was thinking. She closed her mind to the fact of her mother's pregnancy; she simply declined to absorb it.

As for Catherine, she didn't want to know anything about

Agnes's opinion. Catherine tucked her chapped hands into the unsatisfactory shelter of the damp gathers of her skirt, and her general frame of mind, which had expanded ecstatically for weeks and weeks, stretching out light and clear, began to be shadowed at the edges. During that brief moment of encroaching despair Catherine was appalled at her helplessness against her darkening mood, but then it overcame her like a shift in the weather — it was inescapable and accompanied by an odd, briny scent in the air and a metallic taste that made her mouth water.

Catherine looked up at the sky expecting to witness some change — a closing in — of the atmosphere. But, even as she sought an external source for whatever was befalling her, a familiar and debilitating sense of suspicion and brooding restlessness overtook her completely. She simply sat for a few moments trying to warm her hands and stared up at the patches of bright blue sky revealed by the steady rush of the high-flying clouds.

The next morning Agnes woke so early that she made herself stay in bed until it would be reasonable to get up and get dressed for church. She took a good deal of time combing out her tangled hair, finger pressing as smooth a wave as she could manage over her brow and wings over her ears. She gave up on the little side curls that Celia Drummond had shown them, but she pinned the back as firmly as possible low on her neck to accommodate the hat. There was no choice but to peer closely into the mirror in order to do a good job, but she was careful to pay attention to herself only one bit at a time. She avoided taking a long look at herself as she fastened all the buttons of her blouse and did up the little hooks of her skirt. She sat turned away from the mirror to lace up her new boots, although she did sit for a moment, holding her foot out in front of her to admire the grace of the tapered toe and fitted arch.

When she put on the vest and then the closely fitted jacket she finally turned to the mirror to set her hat on just right, and she was truly startled. She was amazed at her reflection. She stood still for a long time gazing at herself, and then she put on her hat and carefully tucked her hair under the edges of its brim. She was astonished at how entirely different she looked. It was hard for her to decide if she looked wonderful or absurd, but she certainly didn't look ordinary. She could even see that she wasn't pretty at all in the way the prettiest girls at Linus Gilchrest were. She was nothing like Sally Trenholm, for example, who had long, tilted blue eyes and shiny hair, or even Lucille, who had a gentle, melancholy face.

And even as those thoughts came into her head she was abashed at the conceit of comparing herself to Sally, who was conceded to be the prettiest girl at school. Lucille the sweetest, Agnes the smartest, and Edith the best sport all around. Agnes stepped back from the mirror, striving for an objective view. She turned from one side to the other to catch her reflection at an angle; she walked away from the mirror and then strolled in front of it, only looking up just as she passed by, and then she turned and crossed in front of it once again to steal a glance at herself going in the other direction.

At last she faced the glass full-length and head-on and studied herself solemnly. Finally she broke out in a smile and pressed her hands together almost in an attitude of prayer, bringing them up against her mouth as she took a long breath. "I am so *beautiful*," she breathed out. Watching herself as her mouth formed the words to see if she believed what she was saying. And then she had a brief, stern thought about the folly of vanity while she stood earnestly studying the mirror before she turned and left the room.

She had asked Howie to saddle Bandit, and she went downstairs, savoring the swing of her new skirt and the delightful importance of her beautiful new boots clicking down the staircase, and when her mother came into the hall from the back parlor Agnes smiled almost shyly. "Oh, Mama! This was a wonderful present." Catherine gazed at Agnes distractedly, and immediately Agnes remembered how aloof — how ungenerous — she had been to her mother in the late afternoon of the day before, when they were both tired and damp and chilled. "It's a wonderful present, Mama," she said again, and took several steps forward, being silly, parodying the attitude and stride of some very fine, aristocratic lady, and then twirling twice around, holding her arms out slightly bent with her hands exaggeratedly but gracefully canted. Her skirt swung out widely in the second turn, wrapping around her legs when she stopped abruptly and then falling back into its draped flare. She laughed a little and relaxed into her natural posture. "Isn't it nice, Mama? I'll write to Aunt Cettie tonight."

But Agnes realized her mother's mind was somewhere else. "I don't feel well at all, Agnes," Catherine said with a little urgency. "I can't keep anything down. Mrs. Longacre will be off to church with the Damerons, and Edson's putting up such a fuss again. Oh, about his ear." She gestured toward the room behind her, where Edson leaned sideways against the arm of the old horsehair sofa. His eyes were closed and he appeared to be oblivious to his mother's displeasure.

"He's just going on so, and your father's worried about getting into Columbus. I'll need you here. I just can't put up with it, and you know Edson won't listen to me." She was exasperated, as she always was if any one of her children was sick. Any illness on their part seemed to Catherine to be an indictment of her and, also, an unfathomable demand, somehow, that she had no idea how to appease. Her children's illnesses made her feel inadequate and uneasy, and she was convinced it was some ruse to ask of her something more than she had the ability to provide. She was undone by their vulnerability, and any sort of ailment made her deeply suspicious and uncertain.

Even when they were very young it was their father the Claytor children learned to depend on if they got sick, if they came down with the croup, for example, as Richard often had, in the middle of the night. Dwight had been endlessly patient with the whiny plaintiveness that his wife could not abide, and he would sit holding the feverish child on his lap over a steaming pot of water on the stove with an umbrella open above their heads to catch every drop of moisture. And Richard would wake up soggy against Dwight's chest — his father's own head nodding against sleep, and the wide umbrella still in his hand but canted open on the floor — and be able to breathe easily in the moist air of the kitchen, where the light finally illuminated the windows, which ran with condensation.

"I can't keep anything down this morning," Catherine said once more. "And I just can't tolerate Edson when he thinks he's sick. If that child gets so much as a splinter . . . He's so . . . *overwrought* about everything. You'll have to stay home. Your father's got to get into Columbus, and I don't feel at all well. I'd forgotten how tired I was when I was carrying Edson." Her mother spoke with absolute confidence in the reasonableness of what she was saying, but Agnes refused to know what her mother was talking about. In fact, Agnes had to fight off a feeling of disgust, and she could scarcely bear to meet her mother's eyes.

"I have to go to church, Mama. I'm going to ride in to Lucille's to show her my beautiful new riding habit!" She infused her voice with enthusiasm. "It truly is the best present I've ever gotten, Mama! And then after church I'm going to have Sunday dinner at the Drummonds', because Lucille and her mother are making a cake to celebrate my birthday. Sally and Edith are coming over in the afternoon so we can finally finish the class book."

Catherine Claytor moved along the hall and hovered near her daughter. "I don't feel well at all, Agnes. Even the light hurts my eyes. . . . Why, even the *light* makes me feel nauseated . . . in the *condition* I'm in," she added, lowering her voice to a conspiratorial whisper. "You can wear your new habit next Sunday. Keep an eye on the boys. Could you be sure the boys have breakfast? The smell of food —"

Her mother's hand was on her arm, and Agnes was suddenly, and for the first time in her life, physically revolted by her mother's proximity. Agnes had been so pleased with her own looks that morning she hadn't taken into account until just then that her mother's hair was lank and disarranged, that her complexion was bleached of any sign of good health. She seemed unwholesome, somehow. Agnes stepped away from her touch without realizing she had done so. She didn't feel even a whit of pity. The only thought that came to Agnes as clear as a bell was that her mother was a woman who was reckless with her life.

Her mother's stubborn inability to live a seemly life, her wispy fragility and distractedness were not, this morning, in the least sympathetic. They called up not one ounce of protective loyalty from her daughter on this particular Sunday in April. Agnes was repelled by her mother's dispirited dependency, standing as she was in the drafty hall in her cotton wrapper when the morning was so chilly, imploring Agnes — *assuming* that Agnes would stay close at hand. Catherine Claytor seemed thin and slatternly; she seemed to be everything that was not ordinary or dependable.

"Oh, no, Mama. I can't stay home. I'm all dressed for church. Look at how nice my riding habit looks."

But Catherine Claytor had survived a long time on pure instinct. She moved away from her daughter, and Agnes followed her into the parlor, where her mother turned to the mirror and began tucking her hair more carefully into the knot at the nape of her neck. She fluttered her hands against her cheeks to bring up her color, and she touched a fingertip to her tongue and then smoothed her lovely, gently arched eyebrows. And as she regarded herself — leaning into the reflection in the glass with intense scrutiny — she became that woman she sometimes was who was *never* to be pitied. When she turned to face Agnes once more, Catherine's head was drawn back swanlike on her long neck, and she stood in a tall, elegant silhouette against the light.

"Yes," she said, "Cettie did such good work with that beautiful piece of wool." Her tone was detached and ominous to Agnes, and Edson, lying against the stiff arm of the sofa, opened his eyes and slid his gaze in his mother's direction. But she continued to look at Agnes straight on. Catherine pursed her mouth in concentration and then exhaled a little whispery puff of resignation. "It's too bad . . . Well, it's my fault, I suppose. I *insisted* on that fitted jacket. Cettie wrote me twice about it before she'd even make a cut. She said I was thinking of Alcorns, not Claytors. Oh, through the chest!"

And she made a little clicking noise against her teeth. "I meant for it to be . . . oh, to have a tailored cut. A *restrained* look, you see. I suppose it takes a taller girl to carry that jacket off. . . ." She gave a rueful little laugh. "And certainly there's been no restraining your figure since you were no more than twelve years old. I remember when I realized that even the farmhands turned to . . . well, to *gape* at you, and I thought, 'I won't be able to let *that* girl out of the house until she grows into her figure.' But, of course, you never did. The color's good on you, though. Your skin doesn't look so green against that gray. Oh, but your *hips* . . . in that *skirt* . . . Ah, well . . ."

Her father had come into the parlor holding his hat, ready to leave, waiting to say a word to his wife, and anxious to be on his way. But he looked carefully at his daughter in her brand-new jacket, fitted over her full breasts, her skirt flaring from her small waist, and his expression tightened down around his mouth in disapproval. "Edson's sick, Agnes. And your mother's feeling bad. But I know you want to go in to church. I'll ask Mrs. Long-acre to come over and see about Edson. Or Mack Evans can look in. Edson doesn't have a fever. But I don't want you leaving the house in that getup." He looked frankly at her. "It's far too . . . It's too old for a girl in school. It's always in bad taste to show off, Agnes. You'll make a fool of yourself. Go put on something sensible, and I'll let you off at the Damerons'."

Catherine was startled; she hadn't heard Dwight come into the room, and she turned to him in surprise. "Oh, well, Dwight, I expect she'll be fine in that. . . ." She made a vague wave in Agnes's direction. "She'll be riding sidesaddle, and the skirt's . . ."

"She won't leave this house on a Sunday showing her figure so! What were you thinking, Catherine? She's a schoolgirl of seventeen. . . ."

Agnes had aimed her gaze out the window while she endured her mother's scrutiny; she had struggled to remain as steely in her refusal to incorporate her mother's disappointment in how she looked as she had been the day before to hear about a new baby. But as her father joined in, Agnes let out an involuntary little grunt of despair and turned coldly on him. "I am *nineteen* years old, Papa! I *am* going to wear this to church. Howie's saddling Bandit with Mama's sidesaddle, and Mama gave me this habit for my birthday. I won't be . . ." Her voice started to break, but she pulled herself together. "I won't have you say such things to me. I've never done anything vulgar in my life! Aunt Cettie made this for me! I'm nineteen years old, and I *am* going to church this morning in my new dress that *Mama* gave me herself!"

"Yes, Dwight. She'll be all right. She will. She'll look just fine," her mother added, but her husband didn't pay any attention.

Agnes had never seen anyone turn pale with anger, but Dwight Claytor shuddered with rage, and every bit of color left his face. He moved squarely to face Agnes, and she saw his whole body tense. "Don't you ever speak that way to me. You seem to think you run this household. But I'll tell you . . . I've put up with a lot from you over the years. You boss everyone . . . your poor mother, Mrs. Longacre . . . your own brothers. I've never laid a hand on you in your life . . . not one of you children . . ." His voice was not loud but was slippery with menace, and he took a step toward Agnes, who would not retreat but who was filled with an awful, desperate dread as he came toward her.

She was shocked at her father's unknowableness — at his utter unfamiliarity to her. He had been annoyed, even angry, at her before, but his face, as he approached her in the parlor, had the terrifyingly pleased expression of a man whose appetite has been piqued and who sees an opportunity to sate it. She was frozen under his gaze; she was appalled. She had no ability even to object as he came nearer and grasped her upper arm, jostling her backward a step or two. She didn't even make a move to protect herself. And then all at once Edson and her mother were on him like furies — Edson launched himself off the sofa like a rocket, and the impact threw Dwight off balance, while Catherine flailed at his face with her open palms.

". . . and *kill* you *kill* you *kill* you *kill* you . . ." Edson was saying through clenched teeth, pummeling his father with one clenched fist and gripping him around the neck with his other arm. Her father's reaction was slow; for a moment the straight, satisfied line of his lips held in a near smile, and then his mouth opened as if he might object, his eyes widened, his whole face lengthened in a slack O of surprise. His wife slapped at his face and shoulders and knotted her fists, battering at him and muttering wildly. "*Don't* you touch her! *Don't* you touch her! No! No! No! No! *Don't . . . you . . . dare . . . Don't . . . you . . . ,*" and he was knocked to the floor, where he lay on his side, curled knees to chest, with his arm up to protect his face.

". . . hate you! I'll kill you *hate* you I'll kill you I *hate* you I'll kill you . . ." Edson was in a frenzy of flying feet and fists, crowding in on his father.

Agnes looked on paralyzed and finally opened her mouth as well, at first just in surprised noise, just an appalled and elongated wail that resolved itself in calling Edson's name. "Edson. Edson. Eddie. Eddie. Stop! Eddie, stop! Mama! Mama! Stop! No, stop! Stop, stop, stop, Mama. Let him up! No. Stop, Eddie!"

Edson backed away but still stood bunched and ready to leap at his father again, and Catherine backed off, too. The room was absolutely silent except for the sounds of Dwight Claytor, who remained huddled on the intricately patterned carpet for a long moment and then grunted with the effort to rise. He rolled himself to his hands and knees, his head bowed between his arms as he struggled for breath. The room was quite still, but the atmosphere was saturated with a sour, peculiar air of confounded defeat. They were stranded there together in an intolerable domestic unseemliness, and everyone in the room knew it was really Agnes's fault.

Edson had expended every ounce of energy, and he went limp with dismay, as did his mother, who sagged in fatigue against the doorway. Both of them, and Agnes, too, looked on in appalled fascination as Dwight slowly righted himself, finally managing to sit back on his haunches. His wife and two children gazed at him blankly. He was horrible to see — pitiable, almost, revealed in his essential impotence — and Agnes fled the room and the house and headed toward the stable. Not one of the four of them ever mentioned the incident to any of the other three — or to anybody else, for that matter — for the rest of their lives.

Chapter Eight

A GNES FLED THE ROOM and the house with no thought at all in her head, and as she approached the barn she branched off and slowed a bit, taking the path up the hill to the pasture. She stood leaning on the fence under the walnut trees and looked off toward the woods. She was short of breath and her mind raced, but she refused to let any image settle in her head. Eventually she heard Howie calling her and she turned and saw him crossing the barnyard in the direction of the house. She called out to him that she was coming. He swiveled around to see where her voice was coming from, peering up the hill, shading his eyes with his hand to see her in the glare.

"What are you doing, Agnes?" He came along to meet her as she started down the path. "Bandit's ready to go, and I've been waiting. . . ." Then he hesitated as he came nearer. "You look like . . . I don't know, Agnes. You look *beautiful*," he said in surprise. But she could do no more than nod her head that she had heard him. He turned and walked along beside her to make his point. "You look like someone I don't even know," he said, throwing his arms outward to indicate the many people he had seen and admired but did not know. "I can hardly believe it's just *you*, Agnes. How'd you do that? How did you?"

She had nothing to say to him, but he trailed along beside her, reining in his longer lope, frowning a bit in earnest bewilderment at what his sister had pulled off. He was genuinely curious. "What did you do, exactly? I can't tell what it is. Is it your hair? It might be that with that hat on . . ."

Finally she stopped still and turned to him, staring at him blankly for a moment. "I don't *know*, Howie. I just don't know when this happened. It's nothing I did on purpose." Howie was subdued by her odd expression, and he didn't say any more but just followed along and held Bandit while Agnes mounted and arranged her skirt and adjusted her seat.

But Agnes no longer had a vision of the day ahead one way or another. She brought to bear a single-minded concentration on the matter at hand. She hadn't ridden aside in such a long time that it required considerable attention to remember to keep her right toe pointed — which felt unnatural after riding cross-saddle. She had to remember to keep her hips forward, her knee and thigh pressed down firmly for leverage against the upright pommel of the sidesaddle. "See how I do, Howie. I don't think I've quite got my purchase." She rode out around the pasture and made a circuit of the far field.

"You look good," he called out to her as she approached. "You look really good," he said again, and she pulled Bandit around and made the loop once more. When she came around again Howie was gone, but Agnes felt fairly comfortable, even with the unaccustomed heavy drape of her beautifully made skirt.

She had to hold Bandit in check, because he was eager to go when he realized they were heading off toward town as opposed to taking the path through the fields and out into the countryside. He was so high-spirited that Agnes spoke firmly to him, trying to settle him down a little, giving a gentle pull on the reins now and then, and she tried to keep a settled purchase against the pommel. But even with all that and the morning behind her as well, a picture of herself slowly took shape in her mind's eye: a pretty girl riding a gleaming chestnut horse, progressing down the tree-lined drive of the farm, moving along with stately grace over Newark Road, her black hat and soft gray habit vivid against the gently rolling fields still winter browned.

Everyone in the Claytor family was practiced at selective recall, careful anticipation, and determined hopefulness, not unlike the members of so many other families. The whole sky lowered over her, bright platinum, overcast but glaring white, so that Agnes squinted her eyes a little bit as she held Bandit to a trot, because she could tell he wanted to break out full speed.

She was becoming a little disheveled as she struggled with Bandit, but she maintained her will over his by the sheer strength of her resolve and the peculiar sensation she had of being held safely in place on the earth by the taut membrane of the flat, silvery light of the day. Her happy reconstruction of herself, as she rode down the lane, was held fast by the strange tension of the light's inflexible sheen.

She picked cautiously through her imagination and resurrected the image of herself as a pretty girl so well turned out in her new habit on her good-looking horse that total strangers would turn to stare at the sight of her. Even though they knew it was rude to stare they would glance back involuntarily, wondering who she was. It was a romantic idea that required a good bit of concentration, though, given all the other things in her life that she didn't dare allow herself to consider just now, and Agnes had her hands full with Bandit, too, who was prancing and sidestepping in his eagerness to go.

She continued to try to settle him down, but when she had gotten no farther than two miles along Newark Road the tamped-down day broke open into heavy sun. The white light turned to a syrupy gold, and the cloud cover thinned, revealing rifts of deep blue. It was suddenly very warm. The fields stretching out on either side gave off a sour, marshy scent of new growth breaking through, and all of a sudden the morning was oppressive with a fertile, humid heat.

There was no shade for quite a while yet, and Agnes was increasingly distressed as the air grew thick all around her. She had been delighted as she had done up her hair that morning to have achieved that tension against her scalp which always assured her that every strand of her unmanageable hair was securely pinned. But as the sun blazed down she could feel sweat under the knot of heavy hair at the nape of her neck and at her temples. She could feel the carefully arranged wings of her hair — which she had smoothed so satisfactorily over her ears — springing back into damp, wiry, unrestrained curls; she could feel the heat under her handsome new hat, and her self-confidence began to evaporate.

Bandit was too warm as well and was working up a lather, and Agnes became flustered and realized too late that she had automatically pressed her heel down as if she were riding astride. This had thrown her too far back in the saddle, and her right leg had crept up Bandit's neck. She forced her toe into a point once more and pressed her foot into Bandit's shoulder, but she was slightly twisted, and she struggled to regain her seat. Bandit was rattled, too. He was full of himself this morning anyway, and he picked up on her uneasiness.

The wool of Agnes's vest and jacket was so fine that it was almost gauzy to the touch, but, lightweight as it was, it was still far too warm, and she felt perspiration trickle between her breasts and down her sides, and her boots were hot under the weight and dense weave of her loden cloth skirt. But most awful of all was that she felt tears sliding down her cheeks. And then Agnes had to wrestle with her flagging idea of herself as anyone who was at all lovely. As anyone who should even be seen in public. Perhaps she *was* no more than vulgar looking, with her frizzing hair and coarse, blatant, inelegant figure. A plain Claytor, a farmer's fool of a daughter, overhorsed on her big Kentucky saddler. What in the world did she think she was doing in this ridiculous outfit riding sidesaddle through the unassuming farmland of central Ohio?

Finally she simply could not escape the ill will her mother had revealed once more, or the disgust that had crossed her father's face when he had first caught sight of her in her closely fitted new habit. Her *father*. And Edson was so . . . And finally the awfulness of everything caught up with her. The culmination of lifelong despair cut straight through her as she looked down the road where no one traveled this Sunday morning. She made an involuntary and agonized little exclamation. Bandit's ears flattened, and he danced sideways.

But Agnes still tried her best to collect herself. She pressed her thigh hard down against the pommel: Toe *down!* Thigh *down!* Knee *down!* Hips *forward!* But she sighed with tears in spite of herself. And then she was flat on her face in the road, her cheek pressed into the sandy grit, aware of nothing at all but a wide, flat pain. She opened her mouth, desperate for breath, but nothing happened, no air moved, and she couldn't make a sound. She lay with her eyes wide open. She was stunned with light and unable to breathe, unable to make a sound. And then she could. Air rushed into her lungs, inflating her ribcage with such force that she gasped, and was relieved to gasp once more. She lay in the dust just breathing, and thinking about nothing more than breathing with each painful inhalation. And then an exhalation. It was an astonishment: inhale, exhale. She didn't consider where she was; she didn't think about time; she had no thoughts to spare for anything except finding breath.

She lay very still for only a few minutes, but — when she finally began to pull herself together, to sit up gingerly — it seemed to Agnes to have been a broad, round bit of time. Seemed to have been an hour, at least. She couldn't tell. She sat for a minute or two, taking off her gloves and brushing the gravelly dirt from her face and clothes as best she could. And then she stood up very carefully to be sure she was all in one piece, and she bent and retrieved her hat and looked up to see that Bandit had moved off a little way but was standing still, aloof and indignant.

She moved toward him, but he turned his head and caught sight of her and moved ahead a little farther and stopped once more. And so they proceeded along Newark Road on their way to church: Agnes — with steady, silent tears and shallow, ragged breath — approaching, and Bandit, keeping a suspicious eye on her, moving on just as she got near.

At the very same moment Agnes Claytor went flying off her horse and landed in the dust, Warren Scofield had his second flat tire in a mile and a half, but he didn't much mind. He'd already used his spare wheel, and he hadn't decided whether to patch the inner tube of the second flat or walk back to town for a new tire and a ride. He wasn't in any hurry to do either, since he didn't have to be anywhere. He took off his coat and rolled up his sleeves in the suddenly hot morning and studied the tire for a moment. But then he just sat down on the running board and leaned against the warm metal of the door and looked out at the fields stretching away to the distant woods. He had simply been out for a drive, very glad this morning to be all on his own.

As a child, Warren had thought that the inevitable stir of Sundays at Scofields actually centered on him. Eventually, of course, he had realized — with the muffled, resigned disappointment of childhood — that it was only that his father relished any chance to needle his brother Leo. For years and years of Warren's growing up, if his father dressed and joined the family for the short walk to church, he would proclaim when they arrived that upon reflection, he realized once again that during the preceding week he had not gotten religion.

He would adopt a tone of jocular pomposity, a little twist in his voice to indicate that he was just teasing them all. "No, no," he would say as he stood with them under the trees across the street from the church steps, "I'm afraid my soul is still unfettered. Still as free as a bird. I'll leave the salvation of it to you, Leo, and anyone else who might care for me just a little bit.

Anyone who might care enough to send up a prayer or two on my behalf. In case I've got it wrong. I'll leave it to someone who might think enough of me to attempt to save me from consignment to eternal perdition."

Warren's mother, Lillian, would turn her face away; she would concentrate on carefully smoothing the seams of the fingers of her gloves, or she would move away altogether and speak to a friend, bending toward some other churchgoer with a soft gesture of inclusion and interest. "Mrs. Rydell," she would murmur, as though the conversation among her family had long ago been dealt with by her, "I'm awfully glad to see you out this morning. You must be feeling a good deal better." She could not betray embarrassment or anger because in the face of her husband's good-natured teasing she would appear either foolishly sensitive or would seem to be carping. And besides, John would do exactly as he wanted in any case.

He would cock his head at Warren with a wink, and Warren would be thrilled at being singled out. "Lillian, I'll leave this boy in your hands until he's twelve years old," he would say, and Warren's mother would turn toward him with a beatific smile, as if she were delighted to participate in this little joke. She would place her hand on the arm of whomever she had been speaking to, indicating that she intended to return to their conversation in only a moment. "Oh, yes, John. Yes, yes. Well, I'll do my best, you know," she'd say airily, as if it were of little consequence, and then she would direct her attention elsewhere while her husband carried on.

"And you, too, Leo. Exert whatever persuasion you like, but after that he can decide for himself. He can decide whether Dan Butler is offering superstition or salvation. Warren here can decide it for himself soon enough. But I'll be down at the Company, ensuring the stability of our *earthly* kingdom."

Warren was delighted to be treated so seriously by his father, but he was also unnerved by the anxiety the whole thing caused his mother, who sometimes spoke to him with soft intensity as they walked home from church, the two of them some distance from the others, or when she came up to tell him good night. "Warren, I don't think it would be bearable to . . . well, to *live* life without knowing that God watches over you. I don't think I could ever be happy for a second of my life if I didn't know there was heaven where there's eternal peace. I'm certain you understand that. *No one* could be happy without believing that. You know your father believes the same thing. Why, Warren, I know he does."

On those Sunday mornings, too, Warren was dismayed by the detached but stern look of disapproval leveled in his father's direction by his uncle Leo as his father engaged once more in this customary banter. Uncle Leo didn't bother even to respond, and Warren worried over this, because so very young he had transferred the majority of his familial loyalty from his mother and even his aunt Audra to that brisk world of the two elder Scofield brothers. Any disagreement between them threw Warren into a dilemma of allegiance.

Each Sunday the playing out of this little production was unsettling until he was old enough to anticipate the repetition of the scene from week to week. But when he was very young — even in the face of his deep belief that Uncle Leo was in every respect beyond reproach — Warren always experienced a brief stab of triumphant pride as John Scofield, tall and curiously loose-limbed and graceful, hat at a slight tilt, moved briskly away from the group of Scofields as they crossed the street and made their way up the steps of Park Street Methodist.

When Warren was only nine or ten years old and repeated to his father what his mother had said — that no one could be happy who didn't believe that God watched over him — his father's face had taken on a rare expression of serious consideration. He had looked solemnly at Warren for some little while, and finally he had said, with no hint of any other meaning under the surface, "Your mother is a good person. She's certainly a finer person than I am. She's a Marshal, and her family are strong believers. But she's not given to questioning much of anything, Warren. She's one of those women who believe whatever's easiest. She was a beautiful girl. . . . She's a very handsome woman who's never *had* to think for herself, you see. That happens to pretty women, you know. She's a fine person. She's a very fine woman, but, I think, Warren, that she has little more than a very ordinary mind."

Whenever Warren remembered that conversation he winced with a pang of disloyalty, because he hadn't disagreed with his father; he hadn't even thought to protest on behalf of his mother. When his father declared that his wife was a finer person than he, Warren had thought his father believed it himself, and therefore Warren had been certain that just the opposite was true. What a fine person it must be who could declare his own inferiority! John Scofield had been the romantic ideal of his son's childhood, while Leo had served as a safe harbor.

But there was little work for John Scofield to do at the Company with the war on, since the rail crisis had made delivery of parts and small engines virtually impossible to guarantee for the Company's commercial customers. In fact, though, Warren knew that his father had been disgruntled by Leo and

George's decision, as far back as 1914, to delay conversion from steam engines to the sole production of steam turbine and gas engines. John Scofield thought — and said — that the reciprocating steam engines would, and *should,* in his opinion, soon be obsolete, and when Leo disagreed, John was furious. He thought he wasn't being taken seriously.

His resentment had begun to show itself even then, and the relations between the two older Scofield brothers became strained on both sides. One spring day in 1914, shortly after the decision had been made to continue production of those reciprocating engines, Leo Scofield had caught sight of John making his way briskly down the hallway past Leo's always open door. John had his briefcase in hand, his hat at a reckless tilt, and for some reason his general air of gladness hit Leo wrong, struck a nerve somehow.

Leo was feeling the weight of the responsibility for making a decision that he knew might well be wrong — George's opinion was uninformed and no comfort at all, and the workforce had been unenthusiastic when they got wind of the direction the company would continue to take. It irritated Leo to see John swinging along the hallway, apparently carefree and full of enthusiasm.

"Say, John!" he called to his brother, amiably enough. "Where are you off to in such a hurry?"

John had turned back and stepped just inside the door, grinning that rapturous grin that when he was a child had always given away his deep enthusiasms, his secret thoughts and plans. "I've got a good line on a prospect in Pittsburgh, Leo! And for one of your big steam engines!"

Leo looked steadily back at his brother without making any remark for a moment, and then he swiveled his chair to look out the window of his office across a weedy patch of grass at the building across the way, and slowly shook his head. "We have enough business, John," he said, tilting backward and still gazing out the window. John didn't reply, wasn't really paying attention, was eager to get going, and he shifted his stance restlessly. Leo turned to size him up once more. "Unpack your case, John. There's no *point* in it. We don't need the business. No point at all in your traipsing off to Pittsburgh."

John Scofield retreated down the hall to his own office, where he borrowed a ball of sturdy twine from his secretary, tied two lines to his heavy briefcase, and successfully lowered it out the window, sailing his hat out afterward, where a group of workmen sitting outside to eat their lunch watched it land within three feet of the briefcase. When John next passed Leo's doorway, hatless, his hands deep in his pockets and proceeding at an aimless ramble, Leo only glanced his way.

Down the stairs John went, outside and around the corner, where he snatched up his bag, adjusted his hat on his head, and gave an exaggerated salute of farewell to the laughing workmen. "Somebody's got to *sell* these behemoths," he called across to them happily, "if that's what we're determined to build, by God!"

And he was off, and the story became a legend — in no more than an hour and a half — that cast John Scofield as the champion of the workers of Scofields & Company. A man who cared nothing for himself, they said, nothing for his salary. Why, he didn't even know *what* it was he earned. No, John Scofield only cared about getting business for the men out in that plant so they wouldn't find themselves without jobs to do.

Generally, though, as the story was repeated around a dinner table, or at Harvey's Tavern, or at the Beer Garden at Kroner's Lake, someone would remember all the tales of John Scofield's long nights of card playing, or would remember seeing him making his way home just before dawn, and whoever it was would say something along the lines of Mr. Leo Scofield certainly being a good man, having a sober head for business. Nevertheless, John Scofield remained their hero.

When the United States declared war on Germany in 1917, Leo placed the Company entirely at the disposal of the government and rushed into production of high-capacity presses to forge large guns and shells. It was all necessary, and John would wander through the plant to observe the frantic pace of the work, but mostly it bored him. He was a salesman, but there was no persuasion needed these days on any front.

John easily finished up in no time whatever paperwork Leo gave him to do, although sometimes he sat regarding it and was so overcome with anger and despair that he had to get out of his office. He came to take a wicked delight in throwing a monkey wrench into the deliberate workings of the Company's daily operations. He would range along the corridors, wander through the shop floors, hunch down in a chair in the corner of Tut Zeller's office and pepper him with questions and suggestions. But Tut liked John Scofield and generally enjoyed the diversion of the long conversations about the merits of some innovation or other.

The laborers loved John Scofield as much as they respected Leo, because John would turn up at one or another of the taverns where the men often gathered after work. He would have a few drinks with them and listen with great attention to stories of the adventures of their lives. There was no one else in the world who would listen to the tale of a man's woes — or of his triumphs — with the avid attention that John Scofield brought to bear.

But toward the middle of March 1918, a little while after John and Leo and Warren Scofield had returned from Washington, having seen the rest of the family off on their trip south, John Scofield had begun to fall out of the trappings of civility. As soon as he had spent any time at all in his own house at Scofields without his wife at home, he began to fall to pieces. He and Leo had traveled with Lillian and Audra and Lily to Washington to meet Warren — who was already in the Capital for a series of conferences. The family spent a week visiting old friends, and during those few days, John had been in fine spirits. But when he and Leo and Warren boarded a train home after seeing the ladies off at Union Station, John became subdued.

After a few days at home in the absence of his gentle, sweet-natured wife, it became clear that John Scofield was in a bad state. He began to leave work early, saddle his big bay, and ride back and forth down River Road, which bisected the layout of Scofields & Company. The offices were across the road from the buildings that housed the works, which were scattered out along the river and the railroad tracks. John would get up an impromptu horse race — or insist that some hapless soul match his automobile against Soldier — or simply amuse himself riding up and down calling out to the men who were loading the boxes and boxes being shipped overland to the eastern ports and then on to Europe.

No one said aloud to Warren or Leo or even to George, who drifted around town rather aimlessly himself, but with less disruption, that early in the day John Scofield was already feeling no pain and by evening was generally drunk as a skunk. It enraged and embarrassed Leo, and it truly grieved Warren, who would look out the window and take note of his father's suddenly fragile-seeming lankiness as he sat his great, powerful mahogany-colored horse.

Leo had finally approached Warren on the first Saturday in April, the moment Warren came into the office after a quick three-day trip to Grove City, Pennsylvania. Warren hadn't even gone home to change clothes; he had come straight from the station. "Your father's been causing no end of fuss, Warren," Leo said, standing in Warren's office doorway before Warren had even sat down at his desk. "It was so bad last night they put him in a back room at the Eola Arms Hotel to sleep it off and sent a man to bring him home this morning. Art Copeland's boy, it was, who came by to tell me, so it'll be all over town. It's time you did something about your father."

"Uncle Leo, I don't know what I *can* do. I'm wondering if I should try to get my mother home."

But Leo had bristled with disapproval. "You won't involve any of the Marshal family in this business! They never did think those two girls should have anything to do with your father or me. *Certainly* didn't want them to have anything to do with two fellows who ran a foundry!" Leo Scofield was sixty-seven years old, and there were no more Marshals in Washburn. Warren's grandparents on both sides of his family were dead, and although there were a few Marshal cousins here and there in central Ohio, none of them was likely to have any objection to being connected to the most successful industry in that part of the state. Warren didn't point that out to his uncle, however, who was stiff and unkind with reproach.

"I've never said this to you before, Warren, but I tell you it's been true since you were a boy! You're the spitting image of your father!" Leo had, in fact, said exactly that many times, only it had been a fond observation. It was rare for Leo Scofield to show his anger, and Warren was taken aback. "That's just what John would do. He'd rely on your mother. But she shouldn't be here now. It's no time to have her see your father. There's John running around with all sorts. Well! You won't do it! You won't even write to your mother or your aunt Audra — not even Lily — about any of this business. I can hardly stand to see that it's true. I've about given up, Warren. I've just about given up on him." And then he sounded no more than wrung out, and without the animation of indignation his voice went flat. "I can't tell you how surprised I am to find out that your father has a *weak* character. He has no sense of propriety. *No* willpower! I don't believe I've ever been as disappointed in anyone in all my life."

So on Sunday morning of that week in early April 1918, Warren had been awake since he had heard his father come in at just past four A.M., and Warren had finally gotten up and dressed and gone out to walk off his dark brooding. For the first time in his life he had had the urge to disagree with his uncle. For the first time in his life he had understood just exactly how onerous Leo's insistence on maintaining the family's impeccable reputation must be to his own brother John, who was never so bitterly amused by anything as he was by sentimentality or any hint of pretentiousness. Warren had walked along High Street, past the Eola Arms Hotel and down School Street, where he took note of the gradual lightening of the sky, so that the branches showed up black and encouragingly flexible above the silhouettes of houses. The air was cool but springlike.

Finally he came full circle but couldn't summon up the energy to go back inside his own house. He settled on a park bench across the street, in Monument Square, throwing an arm over the slatted back, which was slightly damp with dew, and cocked his head to gaze at the Union soldier atop his column amid the budding trees. It was a handsome statue, but it was such a fixture in the square that Warren had forgotten to pay any attention to it. It was just barely light, and the inscription was hard to read, so Warren stepped with care through the masses of early daffodils planted around the statue's base to read the inscription again.

OUR COUNTRY!
BY THAT DREAD NAME . . .

Warren was truly startled, and he traced the letters with his fingers to be certain he wasn't misreading it in the dim light. But the word was *dread,* not *dear,* which is what he had thought it said for all the time he had been aware of its existence — for all of his remembered life. And every Fourth of July, at any political speech, at every bond rally, some politician standing on the bandstand would recite what he assumed was the inscription in order to stir up a greater inclination among the people in the audience to part with a vote, or a little bit of money, in the name of patriotism.

Warren stepped away from the statue and beyond the fragile circle of daffodils to contemplate the actual inscription. What could it mean? Why would anyone have chosen such a peculiar sentiment to inscribe on a war memorial? He sat down again on the bench and finally was mightily amused in spite of himself. He thought of how gleeful his father would be to discover this incontrovertible bit of evidence of the endless, sentimental foolishness of his own friends and neighbors. He thought of how delighted his father would be to point out this vinegary, bitter inscription to Leo, who had taken on the price of the up-keep of the statue some years ago when it had fallen into disrepair. And then he thought of Robert Butler, who was indeed dear to him, and from whom no letters had arrived for some time. Lily hadn't heard from Robert, nor had his mother and father.

Warren knew that Reverend and Mrs. Butler were doing their best not to imagine anything at all, and one day when he went along with Lily to collect the mail, and as they stood in the post office while she shuffled through the envelopes a second time to be sure there was no word from Robert, she had let her guard drop for just a moment. She had lost her crisp composure and drooped despondently, staring down at the clutch of envelopes, none of which offered her any consolation.

"There's no one I can think of more likely to be all right than Robert," Warren said to her. "He's levelheaded. He'll be careful. He wouldn't ever take a foolish chance. . . ."

"That won't do him a bit of good. . . . It's not a *chess* game, Warren! It won't matter. . . . I can't let myself *think* about it! I can't be upset! I can't be worried! You know it would be . . . Oh, it could be a *curse*. It would bring him bad luck if I even imagine it. I can't ever, *ever* let myself imagine the worst or it might come true. You remember that? You remember my father always said that!" And Warren did remember it, but Uncle Leo had said that when they were about five years old and learning to swim. In the echoing marble lobby, though, Lily's voice was high and thin, and she seemed as alarmed as she had been when — as an unusually nonbuoyant child — she had stood on the dock out at the lake working up the courage to dive in.

He hadn't brought it up again. He didn't interfere with how she dealt with that deep underpinning of dread that was spreading through the family. And she probably had the right idea. It never did any good at all to prepare yourself for the worst; it was just as awful whether you had imagined it ahead of time or not. He knew Lily too well to offer false cheer.

Finally, as he sat regarding the statue with less amusement, Warren felt thoroughly sad and disenchanted with everything — his father's terrible behavior and tiresome cynicism, his uncle Leo's stuffiness and his unfair criticism of Warren himself. Warren was sick of thinking about the war, tired of worrying about his family, and he leaned forward and rested his head wearily in his hands. All Warren allowed himself to think about was that he needed to be without Scofields for just a morning. Warren wanted not to be in the company of his father, or Uncle Leo — each one so certain he had the only right slant on things. Each one unshakable in his convictions, turning out opposing opinions on just about everything — notions as plentiful and absolute as a handful of silver dimes, exact and elaborate and perfectly shaped.

"I'll tell you, Warren," his father had said to him as the two of them had their supper at the hotel a few nights earlier, "I can't say a thing anymore to Leo. He's awfully righteous. Mad at me all the time. He always has been, and it's made it hard all these years to be at the Company. But now . . . he's gotten close-minded. He's gotten old and arrogant. Won't listen to a single idea."

"Oh, I don't know," Warren said. "If you're careful not to —"

"I don't want to hear it, Warren! The man's obstinate as a mule."

Warren was tired, too, of keeping tabs on his uncle George, amiable as he was, but who was also armed with that caustic Scofield wit so handy for avoiding inconvenient requests. Warren did feel a pang of remorse when he thought about his mother, to whom it meant so much that he attend church whenever he was in Washburn. On the other hand, if she had not gone off with Aunt Audra and Lily for such a long trip his father would never have fallen into this state. That particular Sunday morning he was worried about Robert Butler and thoroughly tired of his whole family, and he decided to take his car out for a spin and just see where he ended up. He wanted to get out of town into the countryside and clear his head.

But after his second flat tire he supposed that right there on Newark Road was where he was going to end up, and he sat on the running board relieved at the quiet of the morning without the turmoil of forgotten umbrellas, misplaced gloves, the hurried rush to be on time, the long negotiation of the walk to church with much pausing and chatting and then once more progressing until other friends were encountered. And he was relieved to be spared the exertion of paying attention to the meaning beneath any words exchanged between his father and Uncle Leo. He looked out at the farmland all around him and thought that it was a relief to be un-Scofielded for a little while. He braced his back against the car door and enjoyed the sudden heavy warmth of the early spring sunshine.

Warren sat there wondering about what it was — if anything — he actually believed in. To what, if anything, he could turn his devotion. And he was feeling a little pleased at the leisurely intricacy of his own clever mind. He was just leaning back pondering the idea of religion, speculating about God, and thinking that there wasn't any reason in the world for him ever to move again. That he might just sit exactly as he was night and day for the rest of his life. He was savoring this indulgent little bout of self-pitying contemplation when he looked up at the clop-clopping sound of a horse coming along the road.

A good-looking saddled but riderless horse came around the bend just down the road. Warren got up and watched for a moment, but the horse was calm enough, and Warren began to walk unhurriedly toward the animal, hoping not to spook him. He didn't speak; he only began a soft chucking call to the horse, who looked his way a little warily.

Bandit had steadily put a good distance between himself and Agnes, getting ahead and then pausing, craning his neck around, lowering and bobbing his head inquisitively. Just as she would be almost close enough to catch his reins, though, he would gather in his feet and set off a few paces at a fast walk. Agnes had fallen far behind, but she had thought for sure Bandit would stop at the bend, because that was the turnoff to the Dameron place and as far as she usually rode him in this direction. She trailed beseechingly after him, calling his name softly for a while and then just following along after him in a state of increasing misery.

She was so hot. She had shrugged out of her wool jacket, and she held it and her hat over her shoulder, suspended from one crooked finger. With her free hand she pulled the pins out of her hair, which was still caught snugly on her neck. She just let the hairpins drop along the road, and her hair fell into damp, tangled clumps around her shoulders, hanging unevenly, some of it caught up in pins she couldn't extract one-handed. She straggled along, still breathless and beginning to notice that she hurt pretty much all over. Her damp skirt wrapped around her boots, hampering her as she moved, and tears streamed down her face. She didn't know how she would ever catch up to Bandit; she hadn't even thought to put a lump of sugar in her pocket.

She continued on toward Washburn without thinking about where she was going until she came around the bend and saw that Warren Scofield had caught hold of Bandit and was coming in her direction to see what had happened. At that moment what Agnes truly believed was that nothing worse could happen to her ever again.

Warren guided Agnes along to his car, where she sank down on the running board just where he'd been sitting, and he untacked the horse, eyeing Agnes to be sure she was all right. The two of them, the horse and the girl, were in quite a spectacular lather. Warren turned the horse out into Jerome Dameron's small fenced front pasture and put the saddle and tack in the automobile. Then he came around to be sure Agnes was as fine as she said she was.

He had never in his life seen anything like the sight of her coming toward him along the road. Her face still glistened with tears; her hair sprang free in a black mass around her head, drifting around her shoulders as she moved. Her face was flushed, and she and her horse, too, gave off a musky, mysterious scent like old apples and vanilla. In the heavy air he was reminded of flinging himself down in the cool grass of Robert Butler's mother's garden at age nine or ten in the heat of late summer. All his boggy senses of that Sunday morning were jolted alert, and his weary dissatisfaction dropped away at the drama of her sudden disheveled appearance — she seemed to him just then the embodiment of all that was not a Scofield, and he looked down at her, fascinated. "I've never known a horse to smell so good," he finally said.

Agnes caught his stunned expression, and she was so mortified by her drenched skirt clinging to her boots with every
movement, the sleeves of her blouse darkened with the soapy
residue of lather that had slid off Bandit in foamy sheets, that
she could not stop her tears, which embarrassed her even more,
although she made no sound of crying. He asked if he might sit
down, as though he had ushered her into the parlor, and he
took his place next to her and gave her his handkerchief to dry
her eyes. She was so abashed that she couldn't think of a single
thing to say.

"You're sure you aren't hurt?" he asked once more.

She shook her head. "Oh, no. No. Just my pride, as my father would say," she finally mustered, with an attempt at a smile.
Then she gathered her wits a little, although she seemed to be
unaware that she was trembling all over. "I'm just . . . *surprised.*
But I think I'm fine. I was just riding in to church. But it got so
hot. . . ." They were both silent, so she went on. "And I was riding aside to Lucille's. . . ." Her tears started again, although her
expression was wide with surprise, not sorrow, and she shook
her head in embarrassment. Warren looked away, out at the
countryside, as if he hadn't noticed.

"I'm glad I was here, then. I was just sitting on the side of
the road feeling sorry for myself."

"Oh. Yes," Agnes said, with a little more attention, "you've
got a flat tire." She had just taken in the fact that the car was list-
ing toward the ditch at the right front.

"The second one in two miles. But I think it was provi-
dence," he said. He was sounding more like he always did, and
he had a quirked smile at the corner of his mouth. "I was sitting
here pondering the state of the world. Wondering where we all
fit. It's the best way I could find to put off fixing the tire. And

there you were off to church. Now, I think it was fate. Or maybe just good luck. For *me*, of course. It surely wouldn't be divine intervention that your horse would throw you." He had lapsed into a gentle jokiness.

"Oh, no," Agnes said dispiritedly. "Bandit didn't throw me. He didn't even balk. I don't know what happened. I forgot to keep my toe down. . . . I lost my purchase. I just fell off because I was so . . . I haven't ridden sidesaddle in a long time." She had thought that all the Scofields were out of town, and now that the very one of them whose good opinion she cared most about had come upon her in such a state she was numb with hopelessness. She gave up any bit of deception, any thought of making a good appearance, any pride at all.

"Well, I didn't mean that it was good luck that you took a fall." But then he paused for a minute and turned a serious expression her way. "You're sure you're all right? Can you take a deep breath? I'll get the tire patched up and take you in to see Dr. Hayes. He might be at church, but we can wait at his house." He looked at her carefully and saw that her breathing was trembly and shallow still. "Unless it hurts too much?"

She was finally getting her breath back a little and stopping her tears. She drew a long, shaky breath, and it *did* hurt, but she looked up from under her hair and saw him studying her with concern and she held up her hand to ward off his scrutiny. "Wait," she said. "Just let me . . . Wait." She straightened a little and pressed her hand tightly against her ribs as she arched backward and drew in another, longer breath, but she huffed a small exhalation of surprise at the sharp twinge that shot through her.

He stood up at once and hovered over her. "Let me get the tire changed and I'll tell Jerry Dameron your horse is in the pasture and we'll find Dr. Hayes."

But Agnes waved her hand to dismiss the idea while still clutching her side with her other hand and pressing her elbow tightly against her midsection. "No, no. It's all right. I just have a stitch in my side," she said. "It just came on. Just now. I knocked my breath out. Then I was trying to catch Bandit." She didn't speak for a moment while she took account of how she felt. "It's getting better. I'm much better," she finally said. She couldn't bear the thought of Warren Scofield delivering her to town in such a state, but the sharp pain had made tears come to her eyes again. Warren's face became grave in sympathy, and it made her smile all of a sudden while tears still washed her face in shiny rivulets, glistening above her cheeks.

"I really am all right," she said more calmly. "I've knocked my breath out before. Haven't you? When I was little. It takes a while."

He sank down gingerly beside her once more, and she turned sideways to brace her shoulder against the fender for more support. She leaned her head back to try another deep breath. "Oh, it's going away. It was following Bandit . . . then probably sitting down made it worse. It caught up with me."

Warren watched her still, though, seeing her small hand pressed against her damp blouse just above her waist. He looked at her for a bit too long, although she had closed her eyes for a moment to concentrate on breathing. He followed the line of her breasts as she inhaled, and he was mesmerized by the shadowed hollow at the base of her throat, just visible beneath the banded collar.

"Well, I'm glad I was here," he said, without teasing and in a curious, soft voice so that she opened her eyes to see him. He looked at her frankly for just a moment and then shifted his gaze to the countryside.

"Before you came along I was just thinking how disappointed my mother would be if she knew I hadn't gone to church this morning. She's off visiting every relative we have from Florida to New York. All the women have abandoned the family," he said, getting back a little of his note of teasing. Agnes didn't comment. "I was feeling ashamed of myself," he continued. "My mother once told me that she couldn't ever be happy if she didn't believe that God watches over her every minute of her life. Do you think he sees me down here playing hooky? Do you think that, too?" He asked as if he really wanted to know.

She still leaned against the car, but she was no longer so shaky. "I don't think he was paying much attention to me this *morning*," she answered with a weak attempt at a smile. Warren laughed and relaxed a little and sat on exactly where he was. She was surprised by his question, but she didn't consider it overly personal as much as she felt shy at giving any answer to it at all.

The fact was it was a question that had really and truly never crossed her mind. If Agnes had any strong beliefs at all it was an absolute faith in the happy virtue of what she imagined was the orderly running and comfortable regularity of any of her friends' households. Lucille Drummond's, for instance, or Sally Trenholm's. Agnes was convinced of the inevitable serenity of the lives within. Even more was she awed by the general impression of the intertwining lives, the complex and satisfying existence of all those many Scofields. Over her lifetime Agnes had conceived a fierce belief in the possibility of a tidily ordered existence. Days and days — years — without a single bout of drama. Her admiration for what she perceived as an ordinary life was so ardent that it rendered the idea of banality transcendent.

She sat in the warm sun next to Warren Scofield and thought briefly of her mother's idea of getting dressed up for church. "Well, I never thought about that, I guess." She looked away at the long dirt road, the long grasses barely moving in the still, hot morning. "I never thought about it at all, really."

Warren turned to catch her expression just as she turned to see if she had answered what he wanted to know, and without any thought at all he leaned forward and kissed her, and she sat very still at first. Then she leaned her head back against the door and her hair spread behind her in a spongy cushion as Warren bent to kiss her once more.

Beyond the fence Bandit stopped browsing his muzzle over the new growth struggling up through the dried grasses and lifted his head. He paced the perimeter of the pasture and then came around again and began to nibble once more at a patch of green. Occasionally he lifted his head, though, and nodded restlessly in their direction in uncertainty and unease.

Part Three

Chapter Nine

THAT SAME SUNDAY in April when Agnes took a spill from her horse and straggled after him around the bend, eventually running into Warren Scofield, Catherine Claytor developed increasingly strong cramping and light bleeding as the day wore on. Only Edson was at home with his mother, and he finally took it upon himself to telephone Dr. Hayes, who came out to the Claytor place late in the afternoon. He restricted Catherine to limited activity for the full term of her pregnancy: as much bed rest as possible, no stair climbing, and certainly no travel whatsoever.

At the time, Catherine had not minded the idea very much; it seemed to her an answer as to what would happen next, the answer to the question of what, if anything, she ought to do on the domestic front in the aftermath of that terrible morning when Agnes had rushed from the room and Dwight had left for

Columbus without another word to anyone. But as the days rolled on she grew increasingly despondent. Her bedroom was relocated downstairs to the small back parlor, and from that location Catherine had discovered fresh sources of dissatisfaction. She fell into a doleful brooding over sundry little daily concerns, convinced that nothing was being properly looked after in the household, and she said so whenever anyone was nearby, and, of course, as a result, everyone avoided her.

Only Edson escaped his mother's condemnation, which did him no good at all with the rest of the family; even Mrs. Longacre suddenly mistrusted him, and he had always been her favorite of the Claytor children. But Catherine developed a genuinely keen, if belated, maternal devotion toward her youngest child, and Edson was not yet beyond the age of reaping deep pleasure at the surprise of his mother's affection. When he appeared hesitantly in her doorway she urged him to come in, her voice persuasive, and when he settled tentatively on the chair beside her bed — literally on the edge of his seat — she did her best to entertain him.

One afternoon in early May, Catherine was propped up in bed relating to Edson the complicated story of the sad reason her aunt Cettie had never married after her fiancé died in the Civil War, and how she had used her wits to establish a remarkably successful millinery and dressmaking business. Agnes made a rare appearance in her mother's doorway; she entered the room with a sort of brisk self-importance and an air of urgency, but she settled at her mother's dressing table and became involved in the little drama her mother unraveled for them.

Finally Catherine leaned back against her pillow with a regretful shake of her head and let her eyes slowly close in resignation over Aunt Cettie's fate. Agnes sat up straight and leaned forward in her mother's direction.

"I wanted to talk to you, Mama," she said, "about Warren Scofield. I expect I'm going to become engaged to him." She spoke matter-of-factly while looking at her mother, but Catherine only opened her huge eyes and gazed slightly past Agnes out the window. Agnes thought that possibly her mother hadn't heard her, that she was still wrapped up in the lives of her family in Natchez. Catherine didn't say anything at all, but she finally turned a slight, conspiratorial smile in her daughter's direction, and Agnes smiled politely back at her, although she didn't elaborate on her news. She had merely offered the information as a fact.

Edson was thrilled. He kept quiet while he tried to gauge his mother's and his sister's moods, but after Agnes left the room he couldn't contain himself. "Oh, Mama! Howie and Richard and I'll be able to go to the Company anytime we want to. Even to the works. And maybe the races out at Judge Lufton's . . ."

"Oh, *hush, Edson!*" His mother cut him off with a wave of her hand. "That's all nonsense! Don't spread that idea around. It'll make Agnes look like a fool. It's some . . . It's just some pipe dream of hers. Agnes told me herself . . . Well, when William Dameron . . . Never mind, never mind, Edson. Now don't go talking about it and embarrass us all!" She didn't pay much heed to the whole idea. Catherine was thinking of the silly song she had made up about Agnes and William Dameron.

Edson, of course, as soon as he left his mother's company, rushed off to find his brothers, and he did tell Howie and Richard, but all three boys were wary of Agnes lately, and they certainly knew better than to press their mother about anything that was unpleasant to her.

Warren Scofield called formally when their father was home, and Dwight Claytor seemed pleased enough, but Catherine felt as though she had somehow been betrayed. She found all of it hard to think about; she found the whole stir in the household unnerving, and she was baffled by Agnes's refusal to be drawn in once more to what could have been an exclusive and feminine intrigue in the Claytor household, which was otherwise all male. "I asked Mrs. Longacre to unpack my wedding dress, Agnes," she said to her daughter one afternoon. "I wanted to do it myself, it's so fragile. But I can't go up those stairs. But I looked it over. It *is* still perfectly beautiful, and there's no damage. And even with your skin . . . The fabric's really a cream color, not a flat white. It will be *fine* with your coloring. And I'm sure we can fix the problem of the fit. It's for a different sort of figure, you know. *Taller* and . . . Taller. But of course the hem's not any problem to change. And you're . . . The bodice is . . . Well, it's narrow. A pleated dropped waist in the front, but I don't see why . . ."

"No, Mama. I'm going to wear my blue suit and hat that I can travel in. I don't want a fuss over a wedding dress. And anyway, it would be a terrible shame to alter your dress. Aunt Cettie designed it just for you. She sewed every stitch by hand! Oh, even cousin Peggy talked about your wedding when she stayed with us, and she hadn't even been *born* yet. No one had ever seen such a bride as you, Mama! And the ceremony! Four hundred guests. The azaleas in bloom. The gardenias! And under the live oaks at Dunleith. Everyone was still talking about it at Christmastime of that year. All through the delta. And you remember? It was seven *years* before Elsie Hanchett's wedding became as much talked about! But Aunt Cettie always said that was really because Elsie had those twelve attendants. And those lavender sashes they wore! You told me Aunt Cettie said it didn't have much to do with Elsie Hanchett at all."

Catherine was struck dumb with an odd combination of outrage and shame. She sat straight up against her pillows and had nothing at all to say to her daughter. Had she said all that to Agnes so often? Catherine had only ever mentioned her wedding to establish the fact — even in her own mind — that she had once been celebrated, had once been remarkably lovely. She had not always been the stringy wife of a Midwestern farmer.

Edson laughed, because he thought Agnes was doing an imitation of their mother, an imitation that was fondly meant. Agnes had softened her voice and fallen into the yielding elisions of their mother's Southern accent. Edson assumed Agnes was repeating word for word something their mother must have said some time or other.

"You might end up with a granddaughter who could do that dress justice, Mama," Agnes went on. "Or maybe one of the boys' brides, even. But I wouldn't think of having it altered on my account." Agnes and Catherine held a long look between them, and Edson saw that somehow his mother had been routed. She finally blinked slowly and looked away from her daughter, and Agnes smiled kindly in her direction. "But it's nice of you to think of it, Mama. It *is* a beautiful dress. You just know, though, there's no one who could ever really wear it well but you."

In Agnes's case being in love had proved not to be particularly ennobling. She was no longer burdened with imagining her mother's point of view; Agnes made no bones about speaking out and laying claim to her own life. Not only had she fallen into a deep, romantic reverie, she had also discovered the earthbound satisfaction of her own burgeoning eroticism. These days she scarcely imagined what *anyone* else might be thinking — apart from Warren, that is. She was nearly obsessed with the possibilities of what he might be thinking.

Agnes's mind was simply crowded with sensation. Not once since that afternoon when Warren had leaned forward and kissed her, then brushed aside her damp hair from around her face and kissed her again, had it even crossed Agnes's mind to be the least bit coy. It never occurred to her to pretend to some maidenly idea of modesty or morality that would have been entirely false once she had discovered the astonishment of her own lust.

She and Warren spent long afternoons — when no one had any idea they were even in each other's company — stretched out on a cot in a shack that was used in the fall by duck hunters out at Brewers Pond. The first time Warren had undressed her, she had reached up to stop his hand as he began unbuttoning her shirtwaist, only because she was afraid he would find her figure coarse — not for a minute because she was worried about the propriety of it. But finally she so much wanted him to touch her that she didn't bother to protest, and Warren only murmured to her that she was so beautiful. So beautiful! It was heady to ponder. Agnes was absorbed with the new and surprising delight of simply being flesh and blood.

Catherine was increasingly affronted, and when Agnes turned down Catherine's offer of her exquisite wedding dress, it was Edson who received the brunt of his mother's dismay at Agnes's ingratitude. "I'll tell you, Edson, I hope you won't ever know how hard it is to see that your own children have no idea . . . lose even their *charity* toward their own mother . . . don't even bother to pretend . . . to pretend or even care one way or another. Why, I don't believe she even remembers all the trouble I took to make her birthday a real occasion. None of the rest of the family . . . Turning eighteen is important, though. I wanted it to be one of those birthdays that a girl never forgets."

As the day of the wedding approached, Catherine became increasingly restless and querulous in Edson's company, because she had found she was met with an outright dismissal if she broached the subject of the marriage itself or even the ceremony to Agnes. Her brothers steered clear of Agnes, too, since she was unpredictably prickly these days. They never knew when something they said would cause her to fly off the handle — as much as Agnes ever *did* fly off the handle: She would fix them with her round-eyed glare, and her voice would drop into a dangerous, raspy range. Only Edson, though, was constantly a party to his mother's outraged indignation. He sat stoically alongside her while she rustled impatiently.

"Now, what do *you* think went on, Edson? When I think about it I remember that the day Dr. Hayes came out here Agnes came home looking like something the cat dragged in."

"I don't know, Mama. Well, Agnes had a bad fall from Bandit, she said, and Mr. Scofield brought her home." But his mother didn't seem to hear him. Her voice thinned out as if it were reverberating over a wire.

"Her hair flying around like it does, and her skirt just ruined," she said. "Why, she didn't get home till nearly evening. And she knew I wasn't well. And now . . . Oh, you can imagine it's not a good thing. *Marrying* Warren Scofield! Why *would* he . . . I *know* her, and I *never* thought . . . Why, she's *sly*, Edson! To tell you the truth, sometimes I just can't stand to look at her, knowing what she's been up to!" His mother went over this almost once a day, and when her voice eventually sank into a dark, furious timbre, Edson could hardly bear it. He didn't leave her, though; he sat on patiently, reassuring his mother, although he didn't know exactly why all this business disturbed her so much.

"Agnes'll be all right, Mama. They're going to New York and Boston after the wedding!"

But the one time he said that, it sent Catherine right over the top into a damaging rage. "She's a little sneak! Think how bad William Dameron's going to feel when he gets wind of this! Stringing him along . . . Oh! Your sister is . . . ! Oh, all that about her class *book!* The class *playwrights* meetings. *Oh,* yes. I guess she thinks I was born yesterday. She thinks I couldn't imagine what she's been up to. . . ."

Edson was frantically distressed every time his mother became so angry. She would practically fling herself out of bed and pace the room, and he would try to distract her from her furious muttering, from her scandalized resentment.

"Can't you just *see* her simpering along with her hand — oh, her stubby, *inelegant* little hands! Her hand just latched right through Warren Scofield's arm. . . . She'll just be trailing along beside him like a little puppy. Nothing refined about her! What can she be thinking? And I'll tell you, she doesn't care a bit what happens to any of the rest of us. She never did, you know. She never really cared about you at all, Edson. Before *you* there was Howie and Richard, but *they* knew better. The two of them were too much for her. She couldn't win *them* over!"

"Not me either, Mama. Agnes didn't win me over either!" he would finally say desperately, wanting her to admire his resistance to his sister as much as she admired his brothers', although he didn't know what being won over by Agnes entailed.

"Oh, yes, Edson. You *adored* her! When you were little . . . you trailed after Agnes like a little shadow. Well, she's so bossy.

You were thoroughly smitten with her when you were a little boy. And she can pretend — oh! to your father, too — to be just as sweet as honey. You never *can* trust that. You never *can* trust someone being that nice when they don't have any real reason for it. You were just a little pet for her until she got involved in other things. All that business about schoolwork. A *teacher's* pet. But now look . . ."

And Edson did eventually begin to see that Agnes hadn't ever cared much about her brothers, and that she had caused her mother to be astonishingly miserable. His mother's words would slow down into deliberate, careful, considered anger, and he, too, began to conceive a belated fury at Agnes, who had caused all this trouble, who moved around the house already as though she weren't part of the family.

But Agnes paid no attention to anything much that was going on in her house. When her mother made a cautious, anxious allusion to the secrets the two of them had exchanged on Agnes's birthday, Agnes deflected the subject. If Catherine tried to discuss what would look best for Agnes to wear on her wedding day, or what she might try to do with her unmanageable hair while she was traveling, Agnes turned icy and left the room.

And Agnes had yet to show a single ounce of remorse for the strain Catherine had put herself through when they bathed and groomed Bandit or even any concern for Catherine's welfare in the wake of all that overexertion. Catherine found herself frightened by her daughter's indifference. She felt unaccountably lonely and longed for Agnes to recognize her as a confidante. She had no idea why she was suddenly entirely irrelevant to her daughter's life, as though she were in some way her daughter's enemy. Catherine's feelings were as deeply hurt as they had ever been in her life, because on the day of Agnes's birthday Catherine had had a wonderful time, more fun than she had had since she was very young.

Now and then, as she lay in bed gazing out the window, a flicker of the moment in the parlor when she had flown at her own husband to protect her daughter flashed through her mind. Just a fleeting remembrance of rage, a remembrance of the surprise of a protective maternal fury shot through her otherwise bitter musings.

The whole idea would flatten her there against her pillows and also leave her baffled by Agnes's coolness. And Catherine was genuinely anxious for her daughter, making this marriage to a man so much older, so much handsomer than poor Agnes would ever be pretty. Catherine knew that nothing good would come of it, that her daughter would never be happy, and yet Agnes wouldn't tolerate any conversation on that front either. Catherine gave herself over to an exhausted and sorrowful resignation.

And, as it happened, no one in Washburn, Ohio, was much enthused about the idea of the marriage of Agnes Claytor and Warren Scofield. No one except Agnes's friend Lucille Drummond. In fact, the townspeople felt shortchanged somehow, since nobody had anticipated the match at all. Even Agnes's closest friends — except Lucille, in whom Agnes had finally confided — hadn't known she was seeing Warren Scofield. All around town people agreed that it was an odd alliance, and it was all so sudden.

The kindest idea was that Warren Scofield had finally resigned himself to the marriage of his cousin Lily, and his closest friend, Robert Butler, and had acted impulsively for one reason or another. Celia Drummond and Estella Eckart concluded that

Agnes had simply been in the right place at the moment Warren had made up his mind to try to overcome his devotion to Lily.

"Agnes is a nice girl," Celia said to Estella, "but I can't think it's going to be easy for her with all the Scofields. They're all so *attached* to one another . . . and the Butlers, too. She's too young, I think. Of course, I really hope they'll be happy, but it seems to me . . . I don't know how it can work out. She's Lucille's best friend, you know."

This fact did confer a little importance on the whole Drummond family for the few days after the announcement of the engagement, although even then Lucille didn't break Agnes's confidence. Lucille pretended to be as surprised as everyone else, and she went so far as to wonder aloud at the dinner table if Warren Scofield was good enough for her friend. "Agnes is the smartest girl in the class," she said. "I thought we would go off to school together. Bernice Dameron addressed the assembly about 'Women at Oberlin.'" But the rest of her family didn't pay much attention.

All of the Drummonds were fond of Agnes, though, and they spoke kindly of her. "Her mother is from the South, you know," Mrs. Drummond said. "No one knows very much about her. . . . Now, *Dwight* Claytor's really becoming fairly important. But I can't see Warren Scofield . . . He went east to school. Some school in Massachusetts. But it wasn't Harvard, I remember. That was Robert Butler. Let's see. Something with a *W* . . . Williams and Mary, I think. But anyway, everyone thought the Company might be planning to open an office in New York. Well, that's neither here nor there. What I mean to say is that Warren Scofield's been all over the place. He's a *sophisticated* man. I just hope Agnes Claytor isn't jumping in over her head.

Of course, it's a lucky match for her, I suppose. When you think about it."

And that was the general consensus. On the whole, everyone pretty much agreed that Warren Scofield could make a better match than a local girl just out of school, and that Agnes might be happier with someone from a less high-powered background.

Agnes Claytor and Warren Scofield were married on Friday afternoon, June 14, 1918, just a little over a month after her graduation from the Linus Gilchrest Institute for Girls, in a small ceremony in the Claytors' front parlor. The occasion was inauspicious. It rained steadily, and the guests arrived bedraggled and remained subdued in the watery gray daylight of the room. The bride and groom were off immediately after the ceremony in order to make their train connections, and the little reception at the Claytors' was not a particularly celebratory affair.

Agnes had hoped to have the service in town, either at church or outdoors in Warren's uncle's luxuriant garden, under the arbor, which was nearly obscured in June by the thick foliage of the trumpet vine. But since Agnes's mother was forbidden even to make the trip to Washburn, the wedding guests assembled in the Claytors' front parlor, and the Reverend Butler officiated.

Agnes's father gave her away, and her brothers stood by as groomsmen — Edson's expression turned bleakly on his sister; he did not want her to go, nor did he want her to stay. Whatever Agnes did would make his mother miserable. Howie and Richard, though, were pleased with the whole thing and their inclusion in it, and Dwight Claytor was formal and dignified and grave. Agnes's school friends Lucille Drummond, Sally Trenholm, and Edith Fisk were informal attendants.

But it was during the war. Lily and her mother and Lillian Scofield couldn't find reliable transportation back to Ohio at such short notice, and Robert Butler was still in Europe. A packet of letters had finally arrived that dated back over the past four months, delayed mysteriously but reporting him well and in good spirits. As a result, nothing about Warren and Agnes's wedding was elaborate. Travel in the States was so difficult now that one of the reasons Warren and Agnes had not delayed their wedding was so they could take advantage of Warren's War Department pass to go to New York, where he had some business to attend to, and then on to Boston for several days, and finally to Maine, where his mother and Aunt Audra and Lily had arranged to take the same big farmhouse for the months of July and August that Lily and Robert Butler had stayed in on their wedding trip.

The bride and groom, each separately, had been glad to depart the Claytor house and be on their way. Agnes had kept a weather eye on her mother all during the ceremony itself, and Warren had been uneasy about his father, who had turned up at Scofields staggering drunk at five o'clock in the morning. Catherine sat serenely through the ceremony, though, and John Scofield had been solemn and, in fact, fragilely dapper in the company of his brothers, Leo and George. Warren slowed the big Hudson, which Uncle Leo had lent him, in the Claytors' drive as they came in sight of the little crowd of well-wishers who stood out on the covered porch to see them off through the rain. He and Agnes waved, and then they were off.

Warren and Agnes's wedding trip had been uneventful as

well, as far as having any stories to tell upon their return. Otherwise, though, it had pretty much put Agnes in a trance. Once she was married she had been fairly crazed with the luxury of licit sex. She had awakened the morning after their night on the train to find Warren's head turned toward her on the Pullman pillow and found it nearly impossible to believe that this was allowed — to believe that this was not only perfectly legal but even expected. During their honeymoon she often caught herself eyeing other couples — or any women with children in tow — and thinking that it simply wasn't possible that they all took for granted the astonishing loss of self-consciousness, the remarkable *nakedness* of sex.

When they were in Maine, for instance, and she would see a local fisherman's haggard wife with children hanging on her skirts, Agnes would think that it just couldn't be. No telling where those children came from, but Agnes simply didn't believe that the woman with them had ever in her life done what Agnes and Warren had done, sometimes lazing about for hours in bed.

And although Agnes knew it was an absurd idea, she found it hard even to imagine Lily — so tidy, so *busy* with her clean, bright movements through the day — ever giving herself over to the inherent disorder and carelessness of sex. Well, Lily *didn't* have children, of course. . . . And then Agnes would force her thoughts elsewhere and castigate herself for dwelling on what was none of her business. But she could only occupy her mind with other concerns for very short spells at a time. She was in the throes of a nearly obsessive longing for lovemaking, for being touched, for pleasure so intensely physical that the sly observer who usually resided in some part of her mind — that censorious sensibility — was temporarily obliterated.

But that was hardly something she could later confide to Lu-cille, or sit in Leo Scofield's garden beneath the Chinese lanterns and expand upon in great detail, the way Lily Scofield Butler had entertained her friends and family with amusing details of her own wedding trip. It wasn't something Agnes even discussed with Warren himself. It was all she really brought back with her, though, from that trip: New York and Boston were just a blur of buildings and people, and Maine was fixed in her mind as green and cool, with a constant breeze ruffling the gauzy cur-tains in the dim light of their bedroom. And she recalled the scent and sound of the ocean and the unnerving squawk of gulls. She returned in late August from her wedding trip con-vinced that she had discovered something that she honestly didn't believe anyone else could possibly know.

In early October of 1918, the town of Washburn banned public meetings, including church services, and declared the schools closed because of the influenza epidemic. Athletic events were postponed indefinitely, although the Washburn High School football team did play one last game against Oxenberg, because there was no quarantine in Holmes County. Richard and Howie Claytor both played football for Washburn High. Richard was the left end on the varsity team, although Howie played half-back on the junior varsity. But since some boys' parents refused to let them go, both Claytor boys traveled with the varsity team.

It never crossed Catherine's mind that she should consider their relative safety, and Dwight Claytor was preoccupied with the business of the war. American troops were heavily engaged in France, and there were more and more constituents to visit whose sons had been killed or wounded. Those were terrible af-ternoons for Dwight Claytor. The light faded earlier and earlier as the fall progressed, and Dwight would sit in the darkening front parlor of some family's house, on their nicest furniture, and accept the offer of a cup of coffee — a piece of pie, a slice of cake — from a family clinging to courtesy in the face of shattered expectations, in the face of learning how to forgo hope. As it happened, two days before Washburn High School's last football game at Oxenburg, Mrs. Longacre had come over to tell the Claytors that her grandson William Dameron had been reported wounded in France, where he flew a Camel fighter plane in the Canadian Air Force.

"That's all the news we can expect to get for a while," Mrs. Longacre said to Dwight, who had happened to be downstairs when she came in. She was carefully withdrawing the hat pin from her hat. "I won't stay but an hour or so this morning, Mr. Claytor. We had a telegram, and when I spotted little David Wheatley on that old dray horse coming up the lane . . . Well. For a minute I felt like I might faint. That's not like me. Not at all like me." She turned and looked directly at Dwight Claytor and held his glance until it occurred to him to nod in acknowledgment. Then she looked down at her hat, which she held in her hands, and studied it carefully for a moment. "Now I can't get used to the idea that William isn't dead. That's what I thought when I saw David Wheatley."

"I can't tell you how sorry I am to hear that, Mrs. Longacre. I'm so sorry." He thought of adding some reassuring words about knowing at least that William was out of the fighting, but he looked at Mrs. Longacre's careful, rigid expression and picked up his own hat from the table. "I'm just as sorry to hear that as I can be," Dwight said. "Let me run you back home. I'd like to step in for a minute and say a word to Jerry and Louise. And if Bernice is home . . ."

"She'll be home day after tomorrow," Mrs. Longacre said. "They've closed the college because of this flu that's all around. But she doesn't know about William yet."

As he brought the car around to the front of the house, Dwight was overwhelmed with rage — an imprecise fury. At William Dameron himself, who had *chosen* to join up early. But then, Dwight was also enraged at the ruthlessness of the draft, at the boastful nonsense of his own sons, who longed to get into the war. At his fear that Richard probably *would* end up overseas. And finally he found himself maddened by what he considered the hysterical reaction to this influenza epidemic. The whole thing incensed Dwight Claytor in the face of the war casualties. Of course any untimely death was terrible. But surely death from illness fell within the realm of all the dangers of living one's life. It was not imposed on anyone. By contrast, the draft was in full swing, and Dwight was approached daily by families who shamefacedly sought his help in keeping their sons out of the war. He could do almost nothing to help them unless the family had already suffered such loss that he often wondered at their capacity for continuing to care about anything at all.

When her father came by Scofields on his way to Columbus to let Agnes know about William, so unreal to Agnes was anything in the world other than her preoccupation with her husband that for the most part what she felt was a guilty relief at not having to find some comfort to offer Bernice Dameron or Mrs. Longacre or William's parents. There was no end of things that, at nineteen, Agnes would fail to mourn satisfactorily until long after the fact.

Catherine Claytor was almost eight months pregnant by October, and she was nearly driven mad by her sons' being out of school and at loose ends all around the house. The legislature still had a good deal of business to conduct, and Dwight Claytor took Richard and Howie with him to Columbus, where they stayed in the rooms he kept at the Curtis Hotel. It would keep them busy, and Dwight thought the whole notion of trying to avoid contagion by huddling inside, not venturing beyond your own doorstep, was simply superstitious foolishness. He was certain that whether or not anyone caught this influenza was no more than good luck or bad.

Howie was fifteen and Richard was sixteen, but Edson, at age eleven, was simply too young to be at large on his own in Columbus, and besides, someone needed to be at home with Catherine. Mrs. Longacre only came over every now and then, and in the absence of any other distractions, Catherine and Edson entered a remote and intricate world of their own. Life inside the Claytor house out on Newark Road was pretty much cut asunder from the ongoing life of the world.

Edson would wake up early and go down to the kitchen and make himself a plate of three or four slices of bread and butter, slathered with Mrs. Longacre's currant jam, to take back to his bedroom. He would arrange everything carefully on his bed — his sheet and blanket neatly pulled up and tucked in so that if Mrs. Longacre happened to come by she wouldn't toss the bedding on the floor for washing. He used his pillow to hold open whatever book he was reading at the moment. He would settle cross-legged in the exact middle of the bed to read, and he would meticulously nibble off all the crusts of each piece of bread and then slowly relish the softer centers.

He moved right along from *The Lawrenceville Stories* and *Stover at Yale* to Robert Louis Stevenson, Dickens, and finally even Edith Wharton — anything he liked from the bookshelves, in fact — not caring much if he knew precisely what the author was getting at. The reading itself was the thing, all the words just rolling on page after page. Even if the morning was chilly he opened his window so he would be sure to hear the clank of the bolt on the barn door being thrown when Mr. Evans came to see about the horses. Then Edson pulled a shirt and trousers over his pajamas and went to take out old Dilly for some exercise while Mr. Evans saw to Buckeye. Bandit was stabled at Scofields now, of course.

Edson lent Mr. Evans a hand, but Mr. Evans's silence was generally complete and uninterrupted even by a greeting, so at first it seemed to Edson an awkwardly negotiated hour or so in each day. But eventually the whole interlude was oddly reassuring and peaceful, and effectively marked the middle of the day. Edson communed more with old Dilly, as he swung up on her broad back, than he did with Mack Evans, who rarely said a single word unless he felt compelled to give some brief instruction.

The abrupt peacefulness that had fallen over the Claytor place in the wake of the great stir that Agnes's engagement and wedding had caused — followed by the chaotic effort of getting Howie and Richard off to Columbus — was a surprise to Edson. He was not worried about anything at all, although he didn't realize that it was mostly the cessation of anxiety that had thrown him into the dreamy golden serenity of the glorious fall days. The sunlight illuminated the brilliant red leaves of the sugar maples and the yellow flickering of the fragile leaves of the old walnuts, and Edson enjoyed every moment without the heavy work of being alert to fluctuations of the mood of the household.

In the afternoons he would join his mother, who had taken to spending hours on end in what was also used as a sewing room. It was furnished with odds and ends of bureaus, a cot tucked against the back wall, and a long table in the center of the room. Two mirrors were arranged so that a hem could be checked simultaneously front and back, and an old sofa was pushed up against the windows.

Catherine and Edson would each curl up on opposite ends of the sofa and read their separate books. Or she might look up with pleasure at his company and tell him all about his family in Natchez, about the fact that he, Edson, was directly related to Aaron Burr, and also Jefferson Davis, through Davis's second wife, Varina Howell, and most telling, because it's where the Alcorns — she herself, in fact — came to have their fair complexions, their dark blond hair, General George Armstrong Custer.

"Of course, I never *met* him. He was my mother's first cousin. They had been so close as children that people took them for brother and sister. They looked so much alike, you see. I'll tell you, he was a handsome man! Dashing and quite a rake. But he was with the Union, and my mother had become a real Southerner. Oh, she . . . Well . . . Of course she never forgave him. But she never put away his picture either, and, you know, you *do* look very much like him when he was a boy."

Pocahontas, too, was part of his ancestry. "Which is why you'll *never* be bothered with a heavy beard. Now that's on my father's side. I'll tell you, I never thought about it before, but maybe Agnes's hair . . . It might be *that's* why her hair . . . I never thought of that. . . ." Catherine's train of thought occasionally wandered off on some trail of its own, but as soon as Edson grew restless she brought her attention back to him. He was flattered by everything she said, delighted by her interest in his company. His mother managed to convey the idea that these grand family connections were an unusual achievement of Edson's himself, and that she admired him for it.

Catherine even took to inventing long stories about Uncle Tidbit and Aunt Butterbean, and although Edson knew he was too old for them, he sat transfixed as his mother wound out those tales, falling spontaneously into each character's voice, each character's manner, just as she had when he was a small child. She was unstudied in her storytelling — she spoke with the enthusiasm of someone highly entertained herself by what she was saying — and that's what had drawn each one of her children in at some time in their lives. Any contrived effort by an adult to charm a child only confirms that child's darkest suspicions of the slippery nature of the larger world, but Catherine had no gift for artfulness; she was genuine in whatever she did, and she was a marvelous teller of stories.

"Of course, Edson, it was a beautifully warm and sunny day in Natchez. Oh, the weather there is so glorious! But Aunt Butterbean was all at sixes and sevens and wasn't enjoying it one bit because she couldn't find Uncle Tidbit anywhere. Not in any of his regular hiding places — or, as he always said whenever Aunt Butterbean discovered him, 'I was just meditating, my dear, in this little *retreat* I've found.' But on this particular day Aunt Butterbean had taken a great deal of trouble to make her wonderful coconut raisin cake. Seven layers high and chock-full of fruit and coconut, which was Uncle Tidbit's favorite flavor ever since he had come back from India.

"Finally she found him coming from the old smokehouse his great-granddaddy had built but that no one used anymore." Catherine's face became wide and curious, and her voice fell into a surprised drawl that conveyed the maddening innocence and intolerable good nature of the long-suffering Aunt Butterbean. "'Why, Tidbit,' Aunt Butterbean fairly shouted — you remember that she was very hard of hearing — 'I've been looking high and low for you. Where *have* you been off to?'

"Uncle Tidbit was awfully cross at having his new retreat found out so quickly by Miss Butterbean, but he collected himself on the spot." Catherine drew her brows together to imply the self-importance of Uncle Tidbit. She puffed out her cheeks and her voice was furry and pompous, "'Well, my dear, I've wanted to surprise you for some time. Ever since I was in India I've had a powerful interest in those fellows over there who can play a little tune and just charm a snake right out of a great, tall woven-reed basket. I said to myself that there couldn't be anything much more useful to know than a thing like that. No end of what you could do, don't you see? I've been practicing every day out in the smokehouse.'

"But of course Miss Butterbean was too vain to use her ear trumpet, and she didn't get it quite right. 'You've been smoking in the house, you say? But where? I looked in every room, Tidbit, and I didn't see you.'

"'No, no, Miss Butterbean. I say I've been practicing my new skills in the smokehouse.'

"'Oh, Tidbit, I've told you that I won't have you still smoking in the house. Cigars, I imagine. If only you'd take up a pipe. So much more distinguished, you see. And it wouldn't cause a bit of trouble, because it would just remind me of my own dear father. But cigars, Tidbit, are quite another matter. Oh, dear. You really must stop. And to think you were hiding from me. Aren't you ashamed of yourself?'" His mother's voice was that of poor Miss Butterbean, sweet and plaintive, her head cocked wistfully to one side. Then she straightened up and became the very embodiment of frustration.

"'*Miss* Butterbean! I am not in the *least* ashamed of myself! I say I've been *charming snakes!* Why, I've got quite good at it. The little critters'll do exactly as I say. I've been training them with a bit of food.'

"'Well! For goodness sake, Tidbit! If the sheiks are charming and need food, then please bring them to dinner. I've made my special seven-layer coconut raisin cake for dessert.'

"Well, I tell you, Edson! Uncle Tidbit was so vexed that he could hardly say a word, and whenever he was in *that* state of mind, as you know, he simply sputtered about helplessly. 'Bring them to dinner? Bring those snakes to dinner? Why, Miss Butterbean, I do think it would serve you right. I do indeed!'

"'Oh,' said Miss Butterbean, 'you mustn't think of it as a good deed. Why, I'm sure it will be my pleasure!'

"But at dinner that night, at the beautiful long table Miss Butterbean's mother had inherited from *her* mother, who had inherited it from her grandmother — and no one knows which side of the family had passed it on to her, but it would easily seat twenty-six people. And, oh! Edson! Miss Butterbean had set it with her great-grandmother's finest lace tablecloth, and a cut crystal bowl with gardenias, and the two great candelabras, each lit with thirty tall candles!

"But . . . Well . . . I'll tell you, Edson, things simply didn't go very well. No matter how persuasively Uncle Tidbit played his flute, the snakes would not come out of that basket — which, of course, was placed on the chair to Miss Butterbean's right, because she had insisted that Uncle Tidbit's guests be her guests of honor. She'd expected to receive a number of gentlemen in turbans, and she had been very worried about whether to offer to put the turbans in the cloakroom, as if they were hats, or if the gentlemen were in the habit of wearing them at the table. She was a little relieved when the sheiks didn't appear in time for supper. 'I suppose your sheiks will join us for dessert?' she said to Uncle Tidbit.

" 'Miss Butterbean! Surely even *you* can see I'm trying with all my might and main to get them to make an appearance! They're very sensitive creatures. Perhaps they're put off by your voice! You do sound rather like a thundering mouse! It's quite unsettling.'

"Well, Miss Butterbean *was* hard of hearing. She did rather shout when she spoke, but one of the odd characteristics of her hearing was that she was quite sensitive to the high-pitched notes of any wind instrument. And the sound of Tidbit's flute grated on her nerves so that she really was feeling that she was about to jump out of her skin. And although poor Aunt Butterbean's feelings were hurt, and she was surprised by Tidbit's bad humor and his persistence in playing the flute all during dinner, she decided it was the better part of wisdom to keep her own counsel about his behavior. He really hadn't been quite himself ever since returning from India, where he hadn't had much luck in the spice trade. But she saw neither hide nor hair of these sheiks of Tidbit's through the first course, or when Tidbit carved the roast beef.

"Of course, some guests are simply eccentric, she thought to herself, and nothing you could do about it. And she made general conversation so that Tidbit wouldn't feel he was disturbing her pleasure by playing the same dreary little tune over and over on his flute. She talked right over the music and at great length about the weather, the garden, the upcoming cotillion — until she had exhausted every topic she could think of. She really was at her wit's end by the time she cut towering slices of her beautiful coconut raisin cake.

"And only then — after Tidbit had put aside his flute — 'I think the blasted thing's not working at all!' he'd said with disgust. Only when the delicious cake was set out on Miss Butterbean's nicest silver platter did those snakes finally shoot out their hooded heads and flick their long, forked tongues to seize a slice of Miss Butterbean's famous coconut raisin cake.

"Miss Butterbean looked apologetically at Uncle Tidbit, who was just disappointed no end. She finally leaned toward him and said in the softest voice she could manage, so as not for one minute to be rude, 'Why, Tidbit, I don't think I agree with you at all. You're simply too generous by nature, and you think well of everyone. Which I've always said is a great credit to you altogether. But, dear, to tell you the truth, I don't think your snakes are a *bit* charming.'"

Later in their lives Catherine Claytor's children would tell these same tales of the adventures of Uncle Tidbit and Aunt Butterbean to their own children, but those children would gaze off politely, not paying attention, or wander away just in the middle, because the stories weren't in themselves particularly entertaining. What Catherine's children had reveled in was the evocation of the entire magical world of their mother's childhood itself — of tables that would seat twenty-six passed down from parents to children, of the tradition of observed occasions, for instance: particular meals, exquisite linens, fresh candles with the wicks always burned so as not to sputter, a fine patina on the wafer-thin silver, and always the expectation of impeccable manners. They were enchanted by their mother's remembrance of the fabulous condition of unmitigated graciousness to which they, too, were at least slightly connected. But the whole idea lost its luster when repeated secondhand, because no enthusiastic familiarity informed those stories as repeated by Catherine's children. After all, the stories weren't anything like what they remembered of their own childhoods.

And by the time he was eleven years old, it wasn't the stories that held Edson in thrall; it was his mother's telling of them that mesmerized him. She invented these little tales on the fly, eager for his company as she had never been before over such a sustained length of time. It was his mother who charmed him completely, so that he forbore her occasional furies, her incessant questions and brooding. His mother's little spells of dissatisfaction were brief and forgivable, and for the first time in his life Edson lived from moment to moment, from day to day, and finally from week to week without the burden of dread. Naturally he wasn't able to name it to himself, but he was entirely content. He drifted along through that loveliest of seasons without any consideration at all. He merely existed through one day and then another, and his relief was so acute that it was equal to joy.

Chapter Ten

WHEN THEY RETURNED from their wedding trip, Warren and Agnes took up residence at Scofields, where the third floor of Warren's parents' house was given over to them, with the idea of eventually establishing a nursery in what was now a small unused room at the top of the stairs. Agnes did the best she could not to disrupt her mother-in-law's household. She was shy around Mrs. Scofield, whom she admired, although Agnes didn't give the impression of shyness but instead seemed to Lillian Scofield to be a bit aloof. And Agnes had no way of knowing that simply because of her presence the formality of the household increased markedly. Agnes earnestly attempted to decipher and appear accustomed to each new nicety of the Scofields' habits that she discovered, and she had no idea of the strain caused by her blithe acceptance of the careful courtesy extended to her by Warren's mother.

Of course, Lillian Scofield did her best to make it appear as though her household ticked along effortlessly, and it never entered Agnes's mind to offer to take on some of the responsibility; she didn't want to overstep her position. But Lillian Scofield was exhausted by her own success. She said one day to her sister that she was beginning to feel that she ran a very high-toned tearoom. "Audra, you'd feel as if you were at the Eola Arms!"

Other than doing her best not to offend her, however, Agnes was scarcely aware of Warren's mother one way or another, and only a little more conscious of Warren's father, because he bore watching; he was less predictable in his behavior toward her. Sometimes he treated her with an overwrought but unimpeachable courtesy that put her on the alert, and other times he would speak to her with a kind of inclusive irony, as though what he was saying to her at that moment stemmed from some previous, private understanding from an earlier conversation. Agnes had no idea that generally John Scofield had had too much to drink, because his wife and his son instinctively knew not to offer him up to the judgment of a non-Scofield, the judgment of someone who might not understand the situation. And besides, he had been in much better shape since Lillian had finally returned, and since the newlyweds moved in.

But Agnes probably wouldn't even have been much interested, much less would she have been critical. She was entranced by the whole of Scofields, by the efficient running of the household, and by the reassuring pattern of each day, each week, and, apparently, each year. Meals were served at the same time every day and to everyone in the house, and each person sat in his or her accustomed place at the table. The bedclothes and towels were changed on Tuesdays, and after breakfast every morning except Sunday, Evelyn Harvey arrived, put on her long apron, and swept the house from top to bottom. Her husband, Mason, oversaw various concerns at Scofields and also at the Methodist church and the rectory and two other houses farther along on Church Street. On chilly mornings he arrived sometime between five and seven and went down-cellar to clinker the firebox and stoke the furnace, and within a half hour Agnes could stand barefoot on the grate in the upstairs hall and be warmed by the rush of heated air.

There was nothing about Lillian Scofield's house that was erratic or ever filled with urgency. But the very quality of domestic regularity and serenity that Agnes so admired made Warren impatient. One day Warren and Agnes passed by the dining room, where Evelyn Harvey was listening reluctantly to Warren's mother's idea of a new way of doing some chore.

"I'm determined about this, Evelyn," Mrs. Scofield was saying. "We're doing it differently this year. I want them all taken down in the bedrooms *this* week. Washed and ironed and put back up. *Before* we get to the spring cleaning. I want the *upstairs* done now. Then, when we have to deal with the downstairs draperies this spring . . . I just want things done more efficiently. I don't like that bare look the house takes on. . . ."

"I don't know, Mrs. Scofield. I've never heard of anyone doing that. And here it's already started to get chilly at night." Agnes noticed with surprise that her mother-in-law was near tears in the face of Evelyn Harvey's recalcitrance.

When Agnes and Warren were out of earshot, Warren gave way to exasperation. "Imagine living your life like that, Agnes! Imagine it! My own mother . . . Never *thinking.* The whole world going by! She won't even pay any attention about the war. . . . Well, of course that's not exactly right. Naturally she worries about Robert. About anyone she knows. She's a kind person. She's a *good* person. But she's only interested in such a *little bit* of the whole world. She doesn't pay any attention to anything much outside of Washburn. Or, really, outside of Scofields. Lily can't even get her interested in all the business about the women's vote. And Aunt Audra is just the same. It drives Lily wild. My mother's not a stupid woman, Agnes."

"Of *course* not, Warren!" Agnes was surprised to realize she felt insulted on her mother-in-law's account. She flinched at the underlying pity implied by Warren's complaint. Agnes hadn't thought much about the war or the women's vote, herself.

"To *care* as much as she does about such . . . *unimportant* things," Warren said. "What difference does any of it make? Whether the silver is polished the first Monday of the month? The rugs taken up for the summer? The heavy draperies cleaned for the winter! Or summer! *Whatever* she's always doing about the draperies."

But Agnes knew that it made all the difference in the world: It was a wonder, his mother's graceful ability to stave off chaos. Agnes could have told Warren that it was vitally important; she knew too well how fast the charm of spontaneity became exhausting, and she admired mightily the determination Lillian Scofield brought to bear on the organization of her large household. But Agnes didn't advise Warren of this, because — on her side — that would have entailed betraying her own family to the judgment of non-Claytors — a judgment made merely on the face of things, with no mitigating factors being taken into consideration.

And besides, Agnes was still in a fever of sensuality. She didn't even realize that Warren's mother was unnerved in her company, and even more so if Agnes and Warren were together.

It had been hard on Lillian Scofield ever since the couple had arrived at the comfortable old farmhouse in Maine.

Lillian and Audra Scofield and Lily Butler had been surprised upon their own arrival in early June to find the Maine spring so late, but it had been a leisurely treat to watch it unfold along the stony coast. The afternoon Warren and his bride disembarked from the Boston packet in Port Clyde, the lilacs all over Port Clyde and Tenants Harbor were just then bursting into flower, and their drifting, soft, peppery scent was everywhere. Just after Warren and Agnes had finally arrived at the house, had been given a late lunch, and had gone upstairs to unpack and rest a bit before dinner, Lillian had cut an armful of white lilacs from the front hedge. She arranged them with their lovely, bright green, heart-shaped leaves in a blue pitcher and was taking them up to Warren and Agnes's room, just rounding the corner of the landing, when she heard her son speaking in a peculiar voice that she had never heard before.

"I'll tell you," he was saying. "Look at *you!* There you are without even knowing . . ." And Agnes and Warren both spoke softly. Lillian didn't hear exactly what they said, she only caught jumbled phrases.

"Oh, Warren, I really . . . shouldn't be teasing . . ."

". . . and the figure of some showgirl."

Lillian stopped where she was, embarrassed, and she heard Warren give a soft, knowing sort of laugh. "You do," he said, "exactly like a showgirl."

Agnes said something — made some soft sound of demurral, and then Lillian could make out her words. ". . . where have *you* been seeing all these showgirls?" And then there was a little bustle of conspiratorial muttering and laughter, and Lillian turned right around and went downstairs, where she stood for a long moment at the window, holding the blue pitcher full of lilacs and staring out at the ocean in the distance, feeling something between embarrassment and shock. She was almost fifty-four years old, and in her day it would have been inconceivable to her to indulge in that sort of behavior in the middle of the day under anyone else's roof. She didn't know what to think about it. She felt injured and betrayed in some way that she couldn't quite pin down.

But it was Lily Butler who had been most tormented by Warren and Agnes's long stay in Maine, where they shared the upstairs with her, so that she was separated from the two of them only by a wall. She really did like Agnes Claytor. In fact, it had been she — when the wire from Warren announcing his intention to get married reached them in Charleston — who had been Agnes's great champion.

"This Claytor girl," Lily's mother said. "Now how in the world . . . Isn't she still at Linus Gilchrest?" They had been sitting at breakfast on the terrace with Amelia Marshal Robinson, who was Audra and Lillian Scofield's aunt, but who had moved to Charleston after her marriage and lived there still, in a handsome old house on Society Street. As she observed her nieces' discomfiture, however, she tactfully excused herself and left them to sort it out. And Warren's mother had turned to Lily, too.

"What can have happened?" Lily's aunt Lillian asked plaintively. "How . . . ? I always thought that Estella Eckard or one of the Drummond sisters. The older girl . . . Celeste? Cecily? Tall. A pretty girl."

But Lily had clapped her hands together as she looked over her mother's shoulder to read the telegram, and she was smiling with satisfaction and real pleasure. "Oh, no, Mama! Aunt Lillian! Agnes Claytor is an awfully sweet girl. Oh, I never thought of it either. But Agnes and Warren will be just right! I couldn't *be* more pleased!"

Lily had in mind a young girl in her navy blue middy blouse and pleated skirt, her hair scraped back and pinned and clasped in a school-regulation bow. She had imagined Agnes sitting in the garden with them — with Robert and Warren and herself. A kind of mascot, really. A thoroughly nice girl who would be pleasant company.

But Lily had been astounded when she met the packet boat and there was Agnes with her arm through Warren's — Agnes's dark, wide, round eyes, her luxuriant hair just barely restrained with soft, dark curls straying across her face in the sea breeze. Agnes laughed and tried to brush her hair out of the way and waved at Lily from the deck, but Lily was so taken aback by the sight of Warren and Agnes leaning together over the railing that she didn't realize she hadn't waved back. Warren shouted to her, and Lily finally raised her hand in greeting, but her expression was utterly blank. Because there was Agnes — not looking anything at all like a young girl just out of the schoolroom.

In the cool spring mornings Agnes and Warren and Lily — and generally Marjorie Hockett as well — fell into the habit of taking long walks along the path above the rocks. Lily would stroll along with Marjorie, just ahead of Warren and Agnes, and turn back often, reaching out fondly to rest her hand on Warren's sleeve to draw his attention. She would remind him of one thing or another, raising her voice to be heard over the waves. ". . . when Marjorie had to show us how to get in without turning the thing over! The expression on her face . . ."

"Well," Marjorie had said in her own defense, "I'd never in the world seen anyone so green!"

And Warren might laugh. "But you were downright *disgusted* with us . . . couldn't imagine how we had gotten so old not knowing anything important!"

Marjorie would laugh a little in acknowledgment, but Agnes could only smile, since these little remembrances — trickled out day after day — were never fully explained or disclosed. Agnes knew she was unreasonably resentful, and Lily, in one small corner of her mind, knew exactly how mean her behavior was. But she couldn't help herself.

In the midafternoon of the days in Maine, all the company, and any guests, gathered under the trees in back of the house, where there was a weathered table and assorted chairs set out with a fine view of the ocean and the sailing sloops and Matinicus Island in the distance. Marjorie was often there, and various other friends of Lily and Marjorie's from Mount Holyoke arrived now and then. There would be cake set out, or cookies, or some of the local yellow cheese and apples. A pitcher of milk or lemonade covered with a draped napkin to keep away gnats. Warren and Marjorie had teased Lily one afternoon about the wonderful fried chicken she had made for them on her own honeymoon. They had gone on and on about her unparalleled lemon pie.

"Marjorie, do you remember that meringue?" Warren asked, his mood exuberant. "Why, never in my life . . ."

"Of *course* I remember it! I've never seen anything like it before or since," Marjorie said. And both Warren and Marjorie aimed fondly inclusive smiles Lily's way. Lily laughed and bowed exaggeratedly to the left and right. "Thank you! Thank you all," she said, pretending to acknowledge a large crowd. "It's a talent that simply came to me the very moment I stood there in my wedding dress and opened my mouth to say 'I do.'" Marjorie and Warren laughed, but Marjorie's mother was chatting with Lillian and Audra, and the rest of the company hadn't really been paying attention.

The next day, though, Agnes decided not to join Lily and Marjorie on a long walk to the lighthouse at Marshall's Point, but she urged Warren to go with them. Lillian and Audra Scofield invited her to come along to Port Clyde to visit the Hocketts, but Agnes said that if they didn't mind she would take a short walk and then perhaps a nap. But as soon as the house was empty, she made her way to the kitchen and set about making a replica of that wondrous pie of Lily Scofield Butler's. Agnes had learned a lot about cooking from Mrs. Longacre, and she was delighted with this idea of hers.

Agnes was ashamed of being a bad sport in the company of Marjorie Hockett and Lily and Warren when they began to reminisce about the good times they had before she had even known Warren, and she did her best to conceal her feelings. She couldn't help it, though; she begrudged all of them the fun they had had without her. And to hear them talk about it made her feel embarrassingly young and unworldly — Warren had turned to her at one point and remarked that the last time he had been in Maine, Agnes must have been no more than fourteen years old. He had laughed. "You were probably one of those schoolgirls I passed every morning, all of you bobbing along in navy blue as cheerful as robins." He had smiled and shaken his head ruefully. But both Lily and Agnes had looked at him and been struck through with despair. Each woman felt that the reminder of Agnes's youth was somehow humiliating to herself.

Agnes did the best she could in the outdated farmhouse

kitchen and with the ingredients she could find. When she was finished she left the kitchen immaculate, and she stopped to admire the really beautiful meringue that topped the pie she had made. Mrs. Longacre had told her the secret was a copper bowl and cream of tartar, both of which she had no trouble finding on the open shelves. The meringue hadn't wept or cracked, it was high and lapped with glossy brown peaks. And for a little while that afternoon she was enormously gratified by the surprise of everyone who slowly gathered on the back lawn. Warren and Lily and Marjorie were suitably complimentary. Agnes's mother-in-law and Audra Scofield and Mr. and Mrs. Hockett, who had come back from Port Clyde with them, were really and truly impressed.

"Why, Agnes, I had no idea you could cook like that. And how nice of you, dear," Lillian Scofield said to her, truly proud of her son's wife. "You shouldn't have gone to such trouble. . . . Now *you* must cut it. I don't want to be the one who cuts into that beautiful meringue." Agnes had cut and served the pie, having to parcel out rather small slices since, with Mr. and Mrs. Hockett, they were eight.

"I should have made two pies, but there weren't very many eggs," she said, meaning to spare the Hocketts the possibility of feeling responsible for the portions' being so small, but by then Mr. Hockett was telling a tale of a trip to Brazil he and his wife had made. ". . . we always made a run with a cargo of ice and apples and hoped to arrive before Christmas. It's warm then in Rio, you see. . . ."

So Agnes took her own smallest piece along and sat with her husband and Marjorie and Lily on a blanket spread out on the grass. Agnes took a careful bite, and decided it was quite good and glanced up with relief, only to see that Warren and Marjorie were lost in amusement. Marjorie had flushed deep red with the effort not to laugh while trying to swallow. And Warren did laugh. "This certainly isn't anything like *your* pie, Lily," he said.

"No, no," Marjorie said, her eyes actually tearing with the effort of repressing her laughter. "You still hold the crown, Lily. Now, if Agnes wants to try her hand at fried chicken . . ."

Agnes's emotions were tender; they were right under her skin; she was supersensitive, and without remembering there were other guests present, without giving a thought to her mother-in-law or the Hocketts or Audra Scofield, Agnes rose stiffly to her feet. She loomed over Warren and Marjorie and Lily, who was smiling, too, with a little quirk of irony in her expression. But Agnes took no account of that; she was humiliated. "Well!" she said, her voice quavering a little in spite of herself. "It was just that there was only one lemon. But I think it's just as good . . ." There was sudden silence in the yard, and everyone turned to look at her, surprised. "And I don't believe it! I don't believe *anyone* can make a crust better than mine, but I had to add vinegar because there weren't . . . I didn't have . . ." She had to stop because she felt her eyes fill and she couldn't stop tears from brimming over.

Marjorie's amusement evaporated, and she spoke up right away. "Oh, no, Agnes. The pie is *delicious!* It's just that Lily . . . She never did . . ."

But Agnes had turned and headed toward the house, mortified, wiping her eyes as furtively as possible when she turned away. Warren jumped to his feet. "Ah, God! I can be the greatest fool," he said, suddenly tense with regret and hurrying after his wife up the incline to the doorway. All of Lily's gentle, self-deprecating smile vanished. She turned to look after Warren bounding up the hill, and her expression was transparently bleak. Lily felt at that moment — with Robert off in a dangerous place where there was nothing she could do to protect him, and with Warren moving away from her without a second thought — more heartsick than she had ever felt in her life. Marjorie leaned over and tucked her arm through her friend's.

"I think that was my fault," she said to Lily. "I thought she knew that silly story." She watched Lily make the effort to hide real grief as Warren disappeared into the house. Lily tried earnestly to assume an expression of fond indulgence. Marjorie smiled at Lily with a rueful look of her own, catching Lily's eye and shaking her head gently to signify the futility of Lily's forlorn yearning, and poor Lily bent her head forward and put her hands briefly to her temples.

"I don't know if I can stand it," Lily said so softly that Marjorie gently leaned her head against Lily's to hear what she was saying. "I just don't know if I can. And I don't want to envy her. I don't know how I can manage it, though. I don't think I can stand it."

"Oh, then you should pity me! Robert will be back, Lily. I'm sure of that. I'm sure he'll be all right. Just hang on. You'll find it's not so bad after a while. I've watched you now for years, and I'm bearing up pretty well. I know there's no chance of your loving me, Lily, but I'm glad just to be where you are. You're going to feel that way, someday, about Warren. But until Robert *does* get back . . . And, you know, you might be confusing such an intense shared history with romance, with the *emotion* of romantic . . ."

But Lily raised her head and shook it slowly to signify the impossibility of what Marjorie was suggesting, finally closing her eyes and moving her head back and forth in despairing resignation.

"Well," Marjorie said, "I have to say that Warren is great fun. He's one of my favorite people in the world. And I do like Agnes, too, Lily. But I can understand . . . And even *I* can't find a way not to love Robert!"

"I want so *much* to be fond of Agnes! And I miss Robert. . . ." She was quiet for a moment, fighting back tears. "But Warren! Warren's part of my . . . Well, Marjorie! It's true. *Both* of them and you, too! You're the only other one, and the two of them. . . . Robert and Warren and you are part of my *soul!*" But she finally laughed when Marjorie fixed her with a look of blatant skepticism.

"Oh, please, Lily. Let's don't discuss your soul ever, ever again. At least not while we're eating. I've had my fill of drama for today."

Agnes had rushed up the stairs and sat huddled on the edge of the bed, miserably embarrassed and astonished at herself. She had never before in her life let her guard down in public. But Warren sat beside her and gathered her next to him with his arm around her. "Agnes, it wasn't anything to do with your pie. It was delicious. Marjorie and I were laughing . . . It was because Lily never even *made* any pie! She never in her life made a pie. She got the whole spread done up by Mrs. Rupert, who cooked for us sometimes. And Robert and I always pretended we believed Lily had done it herself. But, Agnes! Lily couldn't boil laundry! None of us were laughing at you. . . ." Agnes and Warren didn't come down for supper that evening.

Warren did come downstairs to make their apologies, explaining that Agnes wasn't feeling very well. But by then the Hocketts had gone home, and Lily and his mother and Aunt Audra were playing cards. He didn't even notice that Lily was utterly silent and her face was blank. His mother said to thank Agnes for the lovely pie and went back to studying her cards. But Lily didn't say a word. She was still shocked with distress. For all intents and purposes, Lily Scofield Butler had been deserted by a man who didn't understand that he should always be hers alone.

And during Agnes and Warren's entire stay it never occurred to Agnes — or to Warren either, for that matter — that night after night in the bedroom just beneath hers and Warren's, Lillian Scofield lay awake nearly driven to distraction by the unequivocal sounds above her head. Neither did either one of them ever think about the fact that just on the other side of the bedroom wall, Lily Butler lay with her pillow over her ears until finally she pushed her bed to the other side of the room, the headboard against an outside wall, even though with this new arrangement the doorway was partially blocked and she had to edge her way in and out of her bedroom. She lay night after night all by herself, trying to think of nothing at all, but generally she only slept fitfully in her solitary, lumpy feather bed.

Warren's mother had assumed that in her own house in Washburn the two would be less giddy, less delighted with each other, at least in the company of the rest of the family. But when they all got settled back at Scofields there was no change at all. In fact, the familiarity of her own house somehow increased Lillian's discomfort, and she began to feel affronted. Agnes should know better. Any well-bred girl should certainly know better.

When Lillian went next door each afternoon to visit her sister, Audra, she would spin out her woes obliquely as the two of them settled in Audra's little sitting room off the parlor. "I don't *begrudge* them. . . . It isn't that there's anything wrong about it.

Oh, I know that, Audra. I don't want to sound as if I don't approve . . . or that I *do* . . . Well, I just don't know! It makes me so uncomfortable. It's more than I should know . . . more than is any of my business about Warren's marriage."

Audra laughed, and Lillian was irritated. Her sister couldn't know the strained atmosphere of the household. Every encounter with any other person was peculiarly fraught with self-consciousness in the face of the heavy atmosphere of sexuality that lurked throughout the rooms, almost as though it were corporeal, murkily drifting like ground fog in the stairwells and through the shadowy hallways.

"But think about it, Lillian." Audra infused her voice with enthusiasm in an effort to invoke the same emotion in her sister. "They must be happy together. And it seems likely to me you'll have a grandchild pretty soon. I wish I could say the same for myself. I think it's been hard on Lily and Robert. And, Lillian," she said, her voice less bright, "when you remember losing Harold and poor James . . . Warren and Agnes have plenty ahead of them they'll have to get through. If they're being foolish now . . . Oh, and I remember how much Leo and I longed for children." She smiled at her sister, and the inflection of her voice lightened. "I have to say I think it's much easier to be hoping for grandchildren!"

But Lillian snapped at her. "Oh, well!" she said. "If I were you I'd be careful what you wish for!" Lillian didn't consider herself straitlaced, but there seemed to her something unnerving and overcharged about the playing out of Warren and Agnes's intense early lust. And, too, inevitably the unbridled sensuality at loose in her household seemed to her somehow to be an indictment of herself. She had seen her husband glance after Agnes whenever she came or went, and Lillian wanted to shake him, to say to him that the girl transgressed decorum, to tell him that Agnes should be more discreet, that in some way his daughter-in-law was flaunting herself. But even as Lillian thought it she knew it wasn't true; Agnes was unaware of anything amiss in her new household. And then Lillian would be embarrassed on her husband's behalf and worried that Warren might also have noticed his father's unbecoming interest in the nineteen-year-old girl among them.

Lillian Scofield was convinced, as well, that Warren and Agnes's ardor was defined by such obvious physical urgency that surely it was a barrier to genuine affection, was an obstacle to an *emotional* connection. She didn't dislike Agnes: Lillian assured herself of that very fact several times a day. After all, she hardly knew her daughter-in-law. But her son's marriage seemed to her an oddly shaky affair. She didn't say so, though, even to her sister, because she knew that even the thought was a kind of disloyalty. It wasn't something she could speak of even with Audra. And besides, it was an unorganized idea that she didn't hold and examine. It was just that she felt strangely defensive through all the day except the hour or so she spent in the tranquil air of her sister's house. Then, with a dreary sense of resignation, Lillian would head back slowly across the lawns of Scofields to take up the task of overseeing dinner and the long evening ahead.

By mid-October, Agnes was certain she was pregnant, and Warren was delighted. Agnes's mother-in-law had urged her — as soon as Warren and Agnes announced the news — to stay at home, not to be out and about. At Fort Sherman, near Chillicothe, hundreds of troops were stricken with the flu, and the camp was quarantined. The *Washburn Observer* reported ten to twenty new cases in Marshal County every day. Celia Drummond had come down with a case that turned out to be relatively mild, but in October, when the schools were closed and public meetings canceled, it was Lily Butler who first urged Agnes to remove herself from danger.

Even Warren wanted her to go, and so by the last week in October, Agnes was installed once more in her old bedroom in the quiet countryside with only her mother and Edson for company. But Agnes wasn't happy about it, and neither was her mother, nor was Edson, who knew his mother felt slighted by his sister.

Since her marriage, whenever Agnes had visited her family out on Newark Road she had been full of news of the Scofield household and all its refinements, its exotic regulation. Catherine was convinced that in Agnes's praise of her mother-in-law's efficient management there was an indictment of her own housekeeping. Following any visit from her daughter Catherine would turn over in her mind all of her own failings that she felt Agnes had categorized simply by naming Lillian Scofield's numerous virtues, then Agnes would be off. She would blithely and unintentionally leave her mother sunk in an even deeper melancholy and filled with shame. Nothing in Catherine's life changed, of course, because she was helpless against the chaos that enveloped her, given her particular misunderstanding of the world. And, naturally, any sense of her own failure eventually turned to a deep resentment of Agnes, who — she declared to Edson — had conveniently forgotten that she had any connection to the Claytor family whatsoever.

But there Agnes was, suddenly, a permanent presence, bustling about with a sense of familiarity that her mother, in particular, truly begrudged her. Howie and Richard were with their father in Columbus, and Catherine Claytor felt unusually intruded upon, with Agnes bringing to bear on their fragile realm the sensibility of all the rest of the world. Agnes had always been so bossy!

Agnes, though, was still absorbed with the whole amazement of her marriage and the idea of a baby. She didn't sense the umbrage Edson and her mother took as she organized regular meals and expressed dismay at Edson's habit of spending the mornings in bed. "For goodness sake, Eddie, you ought to be outside. The Dameron boys are home, and even though they're older than you . . ." But Edson would make himself scarce, and Agnes's mother was downright bitter.

"I don't know why in the world you've come back, Agnes. You ought to be in town with your husband. This whole business about the flu has gotten out of hand. Your father certainly thinks so, and I do, too. I really can't think why in the world you've decided to stay here."

"Mama! Don't say that, Mama." Agnes was in her mother's room; she had been furtively glancing at her profile in her mother's vanity mirror to see if there was any sign of the baby when she stood sideways. She was amazed that her mother would be so blatantly cruel. She turned to look at Catherine, and Agnes felt her eyes begin to tear, and her voice was soft with entreaty. "Oh, Mama! How can you say that to me? I can't stand to hear you say that. You make me feel terrible when you say that." Agnes was not only anguished, she was genuinely shocked.

"Yes. Well, goodness knows your feelings are more delicate that any of ours — as your father says, you're one of the most high-strung girls there ever was. But Edson and I were just fine by ourselves. We hardly need your criticism all the time. Why in the world did you come back here if you don't approve of anything at all?"

Agnes couldn't answer easily. It was true that she *didn't* approve of anything in her mother's household after her exposure to so many better ways to lead a life, but it was also true that she loved her mother — Agnes had been surprised by her deep yearning for her mother's particular charm, her mother's sense of the ridiculous. And she had also been surprised to find that she sometimes moved about the rooms of her mother-in-law's house thinking that nothing ever happened; she sometimes found herself edgy with the *lack* of drama. She couldn't give her mother any answer at all. Agnes just replied that no matter what they might think out in the country, everyone in Washburn — and in Columbus and Cleveland, and Washington, D.C. — was taking the influenza epidemic quite seriously. After all, Agnes said, it was Dr. Hayes who had finally insisted that she leave Scofields.

But on that front Agnes felt uncertain as well. Lillian Scofield had bustled Agnes into Warren's automobile with a kiss and many packages and gifts for the Claytors, but also with apparent relief. Agnes assured herself that her mother-in-law was only worried about her and the baby's health. But Lillian Scofield had been much less convincing than she meant to be. Certainly she *was* concerned for Agnes's health, especially since she was pregnant, but it was also true that her nerves were frayed to the breaking point and she needed a rest. And Dr. Hayes, at Lily's behest, had insisted she see to it that Agnes get out of town in her condition, when two lives were at risk, after all.

Bernice Dameron and her father had been in Washburn on Friday, November 8, when false word of an armistice had been received at the newspaper office and excitement had broken out all over town. "Oh, it was nothing that was organized. Mostly just groups of rowdy men making an awful lot of noise," Bernice had told Agnes. But on Monday the eleventh, the word was official, and Agnes — and especially Edson — had been disappointed not to be able to go into town to take part in the celebrations. But the influenza epidemic had not abated, and there were still restrictions on public meetings.

Catherine Claytor went into labor late in the evening of November 14. All day everyone in the household had been out of sorts. Catherine hadn't felt well, and Edson and Agnes were restless knowing that they were missing a grand celebration that was bound to be going on in town despite the health regulations. There was sure to have been a parade at least, and probably a band concert.

After supper Agnes grew tired of reading and had gone searching through the house for Edson, to see if she could persuade him to play a game of cards or even Parcheesi or chess, neither of which Agnes much liked, but it had been a bleak, gray day, and she wanted company. He was in their mother's room, where Catherine was sitting up, braced against her pillows and telling some story or other. Edson was stretched out flat on the carpet next to the bed.

"For goodness sake, Edson," Agnes said. "What are you doing? You look like you're about five years old." But he just shifted his eyes in her direction and didn't answer.

"Oh, leave him alone, Agnes. He's not worth anything today." But her mother's voice was fond, not vexed. Agnes settled at her mother's dressing table. "Mack sent him in and wouldn't let him help with Dilly and Buckeye. So he's been lazing about feeling sorry for himself. Moping because he can't go into town." But even then it was clear she was teasing him. Edson didn't say anything.

"I know just how he feels! I know they'll have a party at Scofields. And I'm not feeling so well myself, Mama . . . ," she said incautiously. "But at least I know why I'm a little nauseated. Oh, before I knew what was the *matter* with me! Well, for a while I couldn't eat at all. I could hardly keep *water* down, and there I was —"

"I can tell you," her mother interrupted, lifting her hand, palm flat, in a signal to stop. "One of the things I've learned in this lifetime is that there may not be anything more *tedious* than hearing some woman talking about being pregnant. What on earth did she *expect,* after all? Do you know those people who as soon as you're alone with them . . . Why, the first time I even met Louise Dameron . . . I had scarcely said hello before she launched into details of Bernice being born. I'll tell you, that was the first inkling that I was going to have to accustom myself to an entirely different idea of good manners than what I was used to in Natchez. Who in the world would want to hear about it?" She gazed distractedly at Agnes, seemingly having forgotten why she was launched on such a subject in the first place. She shook her head gently and rested her hand on her own stomach with a sudden attitude of concentration. But after a moment she leaned her head back and resumed her story.

"Anyway, what Uncle Tidbit didn't understand . . ."

Agnes settled back in her chair and directed a disapproving glare at Edson, but he wasn't looking her way. It hurt her feelings more than she could account for that Edson didn't remember that the two of them had been locked in solidarity within the family for as long as he had been alive. And she was deeply injured still by her mother's lack of interest in the child that would be her first grandchild. Agnes herself, of course, was equally uninterested in — had scarcely spared a single thought for — the child who would very soon be her youngest sibling.

" 'I've never heard anything so foolish, Tidbit,' " her mother was saying in a trilling, timid sort of voice. " 'To say that Albertine is doing all the screaming . . .' " Her mother put her hands on her hips and drew her head up, arching her neck in a posture of condescension so that she almost created a double chin, and her voice dropped into a gruff, low register. " 'Blast it, Miss Butterbean! Screening! Fresh *screen,* because the flies are so bad in the dairy.' "

But then Catherine slumped back into Miss Butterbean's apologetic fluttering and gave a delighted, fluting laugh. " 'Oh, Tidbit, if it's just fresh cream she wants, then there's certainly no need to raise her voice. Why, there ought to be plenty of cream for anything at all she could want to do.' . . ." There was a long pause, but Agnes was irresistibly drawn to her own reflection in the canted mirror, and she didn't notice. "I'm feeling a little strange," her mother finally said.

Agnes wasn't paying attention to her mother's words, but when Catherine's voice dropped into its own register, Agnes turned to see what had happened. Her mother was looking back at her as though she had been startled. "What's the matter, Mama?" Agnes was alarmed, and she stood up, but she wasn't sure what to do. Edson remained exactly where he was.

"I'm not sure. I don't remember this, exactly." Her mother's hand once again rested tentatively on her stomach, just her fingertips moving lightly across the blanket. Then her face suddenly closed down in concentration, and she was only looking straight ahead. She was a little breathless when she looked Agnes's way once again.

"I expect you'd better see if you can reach Dr. Hayes, Agnes.

Leave word for him, anyway. But I don't like to . . . With Howie it was off and on for days. But I just don't quite remember this. See if Louise Dameron or Mrs. Longacre could come."

Dr. Hayes didn't get word, since he was on his way home from Chillicothe. But when he approached the Claytor place a little before midnight he saw not only the Claytor house still lit upstairs and down but also the Damerons' house, farther along the way. He was weary, but he turned into the Claytor drive to see if the baby was coming, and Dr. Hayes arrived a scant half hour before the baby was born. A big, handsome baby, vigorously healthy, but Catherine was spent, although the delivery had gone smoothly.

Mrs. Dameron had whisked the baby off to the warm kitchen, cleaned him up, swaddled him in a beautifully crocheted blue blanket, and brought him back into Catherine's room, smiling with deep pleasure when she bent to give him to his mother. "Look here! Here's this beautiful boy you have. Catherine, just look at him! You'd think he'd been born a week ago!" Catherine let her eye graze the bundled infant, the unusually smooth-featured face, the beautifully shaped head.

But Catherine had made a listless gesture to wave Louise away. "No, no. Not right now. Not right now." And she had fallen into an absolute sleep almost as she was speaking. Mrs. Dameron handed the baby to Agnes and began to straighten Catherine's bedding while Agnes held the baby cautiously, waiting to give him back to Mrs. Dameron. But Mrs. Dameron turned and smiled at her. "You see. You can get some practice. He *is* a lovely baby, isn't he?"

Agnes smiled and nodded and realized that Mrs. Dameron meant to leave this infant with her while Catherine slept. When Mrs. Dameron had first arrived, she had hustled Edson up to bed, but she hadn't said anything to Agnes, who would have welcomed being sent off with Edson. She hadn't wanted to stay at all, especially by the time Dr. Hayes arrived and the whole thing seemed to be getting out of hand. But she realized her help was expected, and besides, her mother had grasped hold of Agnes's skirt, and Agnes couldn't possibly have disengaged herself. She had leaned over and self-consciously smoothed her mother's hair, which her mother never would have stood for if she had been aware of it.

No one else had seemed in the least dismayed, though. In fact, Dr. Hayes and Mrs. Dameron had talked softly about the health conditions at Camp Sherman even as the baby's head crowned, and Agnes wanted to shout at them both to pay attention. She thought her mother might die of this, although Catherine herself complained very little. But no more than forty-five minutes after the baby was born, it was as though nothing at all had happened. The room was calm and quiet, and her mother lay in bed covered modestly by fresh sheets.

So when Catherine waved away the baby, Louise Dameron had turned and smiled at Agnes, and Agnes had had no choice but to gingerly accept him, although Mrs. Dameron seemed to Agnes to give him to her as casually as Howie and Richard handed off a football. She had held him while Dr. Hayes went to the kitchen to wash up and while Mrs. Dameron expertly changed the sheets without dislodging Catherine. When Dr. Hayes came back into the room, Agnes was aching from the tension of not dropping this child.

"I think I might as well stay the night, Agnes," he said. "Your mother and the baby are fine, but I'd just be coming right back out here in the morning. Do you think you could find me a blanket and I'll just stretch out on the sofa in the parlor across the hall."

"Oh, yes. There's a cot in the sewing room that would probably be more comfortable. And I'll bring fresh towels, too, and I'll go tell Edson. Mrs. Dameron made coffee, Dr. Hayes. And there's cake . . . there's cream. And deviled eggs in the icebox."

Agnes put the swaddled baby in his bassinet beside his mother's bed with great relief. Holding him was filled with dangerous possibilities. She had clasped her little brother and smiled at Dr. Hayes and Mrs. Dameron with feigned knowingness, and thought that this certainly couldn't be what it would be like when she had *her* baby. Agnes tried not to seem shocked, although she *was* a little scornful — and even embarrassed on her mother's behalf — at what seemed the violent indelicacy of this baby's birth. But she did know better than to say so.

When she looked in on Edson and called his name from his doorway, he didn't answer or even move. Agnes approached his bed in the little bit of moonlight, but he seemed oddly without substance beneath his blanket. Edson usually slept in a turmoil, his mother always said. And it was true. Agnes had been amused some mornings — been annoyed on other days — when she had come to get him up and found him cocooned in sheets and blankets as though he had held one end and spun round and round, spiraling the bedclothes around him. But the sheet and blanket lay smoothly in place, the margin of the top sheet was still neatly folded over the edge of the wool blanket, and only Edson's head and shoulders were visible against the pillowcase. Agnes leaned over him, meaning to surprise him awake with the news, but she jumped when she saw that his eyes were open and he was looking directly at her as she came into his line of vision.

Edson thought he had spoken to her — thought he had explained how thirsty he was — but he didn't try to move. He felt as though each joint of his body — his elbows, his knees, his ankles, his shoulders — were pinned to the mattress by a powerful force that he could not characterize. He didn't make the effort to try to convey it, but he knew he could not move. He thought he had spoken to Agnes, who was peering down at him, but he hadn't said a word, even though his head rang with a cacophony of roaring, unspecific noise that seemed to him to be a reverberation of his own words.

"Are you all right? Edson? The baby's here. Are you all right?" She put her hand on his forehead for a moment, and then he did make a noise, although he wasn't aware of it. He made a low moan in the back of his throat when her cold hand grazed his tender flesh.

"I'll get Dr. Hayes, Edson. You stay still. I'll get Dr. Hayes." Edson found it odd to see Agnes receding, and then she seemed to tip right out of the doorway. She tipped over the very edge, and he closed his eyes and gave himself over to the sensation of drifting downward, slowly drifting through water in which small, surprising flecks of light and clear, pale blue and green asterisklike creatures blossomed forth and floated upward, slowly streaming by him.

Dr. Hayes came downstairs after looking in on Edson and had a brief, hushed conversation with Louise Dameron. ". . . certainly not much choice . . ." was all Agnes heard Mrs. Dameron say. And then Agnes once again found herself in charge of the baby, and she was caught up in preparations for the two of them to go to the Damerons' for the night.

"Oh, yes, Agnes," Mrs. Dameron said to her in a tired effort at heartiness, "it's always bad luck for a pregnant woman to stay in a house where a baby's just been born. It may be an old wives' tale, but it's better to be safe than sorry. And if Edson is sick . . ."

"But I'm sure he only has the same thing I got just before graduation, Mrs. Dameron. And Howie and Richard. Even my father got sick. The baby and I'll be just fine here," Agnes objected. "It only lasts about three days. . . ."

"Well, that's a good thing. But we don't want to take the chance that the baby might catch it. And you'll have him all to yourself for a day or so. I'll tell you, Bernice will be as jealous as she can be."

Agnes was swept off to the Damerons' house, where Mrs. Dameron settled her into William's empty bedroom with the bassinet beside her bed. Mrs. Longacre and Bernice had been downstairs to greet them when Jerome Dameron finally got them home, and Agnes didn't think Bernice seemed jealous in the slightest.

William's room was right across the hall from Bernice's, and Agnes was miserable all the rest of the night whenever the baby fussed. She gave him sugar water just as Mrs. Dameron had instructed her, but she found herself overwhelmed and frantic whenever he refused the bottle and continued to cry. She was desperate not to be held accountable for failing to see to him properly.

In the morning, when Catherine was finally and fully awake and learned that Edson was very sick, she began to gather herself up and untangle herself from the blankets, swinging her legs over the side of the bed.

The doctor and Louise Dameron, who had come straight over as soon as it was light, both reached out to detain her, but Catherine became truly determined — alarming both the doctor and Mrs. Dameron. Catherine was washed over full force by a powerful need to see and to protect her own child. She was overcome with a prickling sort of energy bordering on rage, and she wouldn't pay attention to what Louise Dameron and Dr. Hayes were trying to impress upon her.

"Just let me be! Just let me be! Of course I understand how bad this flu is! Of course I do! And that's why I've got to go up and see Edson. You don't understand what I'm saying. . . . You don't seem to understand a thing in the world!" She declared this with such contemptuous finality that Louise Dameron and Dr. Hayes were taken aback, and they stepped aside to let her pass.

Catherine sat beside Edson, lifting him to prop his pillows so that he could breathe more easily. She did heed Dr. Hayes by trying to ease Edson's breathing with short, periodic applications of a bit of cotton soaked in chloroform between his teeth. Every fifteen minutes she would administer the chloroform for no more than one minute. And it did ease Edson considerably. He wasn't frightened by the dreamy, floating descent through blue green water with the fantastic colored shapes squirming upward in brief bursts of varicolored light. And he was soothed when he came back to himself and felt the unusual comfort of his mother's hand holding his or heard her voice.

Mrs. Dameron went home and went to bed, only telling Agnes that Edson was very sick and that she would have to wait until later to see him. Dr. Hayes was so tired that he was nearly asleep on his feet, and he retreated to the bed in Agnes's room across from Edson's and slept in brief spells. And Catherine sat leaning over her son for hours, speaking softly in the quiet house as she told meandering stories, sang any song she could remember, told Edson once again the history of all his family, naming relatives finally in a kind of cadence, as though she were muttering through a rosary. Catherine didn't want her son to be stranded alone in the spells of delirium that overtook him off and on during the day. She looked at his face gone oddly brown against his fair hair, and at his eyes seeming huge and sunken, and she was certain that this was the one person she needed more than any other in her life.

She thought her voice would hold him in the room, and she couldn't stop speaking without hearing the terrible struggle of his breathing, and so she talked on and on. When Dr. Hayes came out of a brief, deep sleep he crossed the hall and simply stood leaning against the doorframe.

Catherine's words dropped away for minutes at a time and finally stopped altogether when she leaned her head against the wall and fell into a deep spell of sleep herself. Dr. Hayes disengaged Catherine's hand and held the boy's hand himself; Edson didn't open his eyes. He didn't know that Dr. Hayes was in the room. Edson died in the early evening and was never aware that it was anyone but his mother with him as he drifted on and on, tumbling slowly through the translucent green water until at last he was too tired to struggle for another breath.

Chapter Eleven

WITHIN TEN DAYS Catherine Claytor, too, had died of complications of the flu, and Agnes was overwhelmed with an agitation she couldn't accommodate. She mourned in dreams. Time and again she would wake up with the panicky sensation of being unable to find her mother and her brother. It seemed to her that all night she trailed along hallways and through rooms that in her dreams were familiar but which didn't exist in the actual world. There was some bit of information she intended to tell them, some little thing she had forgotten. But her mother and her brother eluded her — not purposefully, but Agnes just missed them every time. Her mother and Edson would have just vacated a room she entered, just retreated down a staircase she approached, and, as she failed to find them, the urgency of her message increased and made her frantic. She invariably awoke, however, to the crying of the baby, and she had no time to indulge in her particular anguish or even to name it.

Louise Dameron and Lillian Scofield and Lily and her parents were — each one privately — a bit taken aback by what they collectively admired as Agnes's remarkable fortitude. It left them uncertain what to say to her. There was no clear etiquette to cover this situation. Any sign of grief on Agnes's part would have been clarifying. Warren had been unable to return from Washington, and as it was, no one knew how to approach Agnes. No one knew what might be unbearable to her, what she might be relieved to talk about, and so no one ever referred to her mother or Edson, leaving it for her to initiate any conversation about them. Growing up in the Claytor household, however, what Agnes had learned best was never to reveal how she felt or what she thought to anyone outside her family.

Agnes remained at the Damerons' during her mother's illness, but after the funeral she and the baby were settled at Scofields. Certainly Agnes — newly married and expecting her first child fairly soon — couldn't stay out in the country by herself. Couldn't possibly take care of an infant all alone in her condition. It was agreed all around — among the Damerons and Scofields as well as the Butlers and Dr. Hayes, too, who had been consulted — that Mr. Claytor was in no state to arrange for the care of his youngest son right now, in the wake of the loss of his wife and little boy.

Dwight Claytor had been urged to keep his older sons in Columbus in the aftermath of Edson's death and during their mother's illness because of the risk of contagion. But he brought Howie and Richard home for their mother's funeral and the belated service held for their brother. There was some discussion of Mrs. Longacre setting the nursery up once more out at the Claytor place, and possibly overseeing the baby's care until Howie and Richard were back in Washburn and permanent arrangements could be made. Dwight Claytor agreed to whatever idea was put forward. He seemed dazed and oddly passive, incurious about the baby. But in the circumstances, no one was surprised, and Dr. Hayes felt quite certain that it would simply take him a little time to absorb his loss.

Only John Scofield broached the subject of Dwight's wife's death and the death of his son. It never occurred to John that he didn't have the skill to make a person feel better about whatever might be troubling him, and he was right. Even at his worst John was a talented listener, and all sorts of people sought him out as a confidant, although Dwight Claytor had never been one of them. Dwight Claytor had never seemed to be a man in need of a confidant.

December 3, the day after Catherine Claytor's funeral, Louise Dameron and her husband, Jerome; Leo and Audra Scofield; Lily Butler and her in-laws, the Reverend Daniel and Martha Butler; Agnes and Warren; and Dwight Claytor and his children all gathered at John and Lillian's house at Scofields. Warren had arrived from Washington that morning and could only stay until late that night. He was exhausted from having had to stand much of the way on the crowded train, and he was anxious to be alone with Agnes. He hadn't even been able to get home for the services for her mother and brother.

Everyone concerned was on hand to make arrangements about overseeing the Claytor property and various other issues. Mrs. Longacre had not come with them, and neither had Bernice, because they had both come down with colds and didn't want to risk infecting the baby. Dwight Claytor had to return to

Columbus the next day to chair a legislative committee, and the two older boys would stay with him at the Curtis Hotel for the rest of the school year, since Dwight had enrolled Howie and Richard in the Sperry School, which had resumed classes, unlike the city schools, which remained closed.

"This is surely a terrible time for you, Mr. Claytor," John said, with real interest, not with any bit of cloying sympathy, although he clearly was commiserating. "It always seemed to me that your wife was a gentle person. I didn't know her very well, I'm sorry to say. I remember when she first arrived in Washburn, though. I admired her accent, I remember. She certainly was a lovely woman. And, of course, I know about losing a son. I've been through that twice, although they were just babies. Just babies. But there's no describing it. It's a sorrow not like anything else I can think of," John Scofield said, with inclusive and unnerving sympathy, and Dwight Claytor immediately offered a word of reassurance.

"Well, you see, Edson was his mother's son. He was devoted to her, I think, beyond anything else. He was Catherine's child. It's hard to know how he would have turned out. He was mighty bright. Good in school. But he never . . . He wasn't like the other two, you know. I think he was too sensitive for his own good. I don't know what he would've made of his life. Of my boys, I always thought he wouldn't be the one who'd be much of a success."

John had tipped his head forward in an attitude of contemplative listening. "He was *soft* natured, you mean? Edson, that is?" John Scofield asked, wanting to make certain he understood. His curiosity was genuine; all the people who had ever confided in him were invariably pleased at his interest in them, and the interest was real but fleeting. "Or was it that he wouldn't have been able to make his own life? Away from his mother? Off on his own? Needed more . . . umh . . . *ambition.* Or a sense of competition? Needed to be more out*going?*"

Agnes was holding the baby and sitting with Lily and Warren a few feet away, and she turned and gazed at her father, not registering any particular emotion but waiting to hear what her father would answer, and Lily and Warren turned, too, to see what had drawn Agnes's attention. Dwight caught himself up short and spoke succinctly. "He was a fine boy, Mr. Scofield," Dwight said. "He was a fine boy. We'll miss him."

John straightened up, seeming slightly startled. "Well, certainly you will. Certainly you will."

Agnes was taken aback to have heard her father's version of Edson's life summed up so neatly. She was filled with objections. She wanted to explain the complications of her brother's life, and she tried not to give in to a sudden resentment of Howie and Richard. Her father didn't seem to understand that there was no need to disparage Edson in order to compliment the other two. But she turned her attention back to the baby and didn't allow any thought at all to settle in her mind. She didn't want to know if her father had meant that if he had to lose a child, it was just as well that it was Edson. She could scarcely stand to consider what her own role might be in that situation, so she simply tucked the whole conversation away to consider some other time.

It had been left to Louise Dameron to bring up the subject of the naming and christening of the baby. She approached it as delicately as she could manage. "It seems to me that the first thing to do is to name that little boy," she said, trying for a cheerful tone. "We can't always be talking about him as 'the baby.' He's liable to grow up thinking that's his name." But there was only a worried expression exchanged between Howie and Richard. Their father didn't appear to realize that he should weigh in with an opinion; he merely looked on passively. Agnes was holding her little brother and jostling him gently in an effort to soothe him. She didn't seem even to have heard Mrs. Dameron.

Mrs. Dameron and Lillian and Audra Scofield and Lily Butler had worried over the name. They had been concerned that the suggestion might be made to name the baby after Edson, and they felt certain that in the long run it would be more painful than comforting. "Don't you imagine his mother would have wanted him named after his father?" Audra Scofield finally said to the room in general, uncertain to whom she should direct this idea.

"Oh," said Agnes, coming to attention when she realized that everyone was looking to her for a response, not to her father. "Well, Mama talked about calling him Armstrong if he was a boy. Because of her uncle — or maybe he wasn't her uncle, I'm not sure. He may have been her cousin . . . General George Armstrong Custer . . ."

"Oh, Agnes. *Surely* not!" Lily Butler said before she caught herself. "Of course, I know he must have been a fine *man*. A brave man. And I don't mean — what I meant was — given how things turned out for General Custer! Don't you think it might be bad luck —"

". . . or for her *mother's* cousin, Aaron Burr," Agnes went on. "I think that's right. I think that's how they were connected. I think his second wife was my grandmother's first cousin. She was from Jackson. . . . But I might have her mixed up with . . ."

"But, Agnes, there again . . ." Lily's mother spoke up this time, so that Agnes realized the women in the room must have

discussed this dilemma. "That might not be such a happy association, either. I hope you'll forgive me, Agnes, but don't you
think that given all that's happened . . . and since Howard and
Richard are each named for a grandfather . . . and Dwight's a
good name. It doesn't pin a child down, don't you know what I
mean? Aaron would be a limiting kind of name, I believe, don't
you?" The women had indeed discussed it and now they felt
protective of the name they had concluded would be most appropriate.

When they managed to put forth the idea, though, there was
awkwardness all around, although no real disagreement. Mr.
Claytor gave no sign one way or another; he was uncomfortable
and didn't make any comment. He didn't meet his daughter's
eye, but Agnes intercepted the look Mrs. Dameron sent in her
direction — a glance of entreaty — and Agnes realized it certainly wasn't for her to say, in any case, and she let it drop. The
baby born November 15, 1918, to Catherine Alcorn Edson
Claytor, was christened Dwight Burr Armstrong Claytor that
very afternoon, eighteen days after his birth, in a short, solemn
ceremony performed by Reverend Butler, before he and his
wife took their leave.

Agnes took her newly named little brother off to the bedroom she and Warren shared to feed and quiet him. All the attention had left him overexcited and arching rigidly in her arms
with incipient complaints. Agnes was glad to have an excuse to
escape to the privacy of the upstairs. She sat in a rocking chair
her mother-in-law had provided and fed the baby, and when
he'd had enough of his bottle Agnes held him up against her
blanket-covered shoulder and patted his back in circles, just as
Louise Dameron had shown her how to do, and he finally

burped and snuggled in, and Agnes closed her eyes for a moment, just resting.

Warren disengaged himself from the company in the front parlor as soon as he could and followed Agnes upstairs. He was exhausted from lack of sleep on the train, which had run so late that he hadn't gotten in until midmorning. He hadn't had any time alone with his wife. But she seemed to have fallen asleep, and he stood at the threshold, not knowing if he should disturb her. He had no choice but to take the evening train back to Washington, where bureaucratic chaos reigned. The logistics of the demobilization were going to be nightmarish. Already there were plots and conflicts brewing among the various war agencies, and Warren thought that down the road there was bound to be a problem with the railroads. He wanted to be done with it all; he wanted to be home.

He leaned against the door frame and closed his eyes briefly, not wanting to wake his wife but hoping she would stir, but he came to with a start and realized he had nearly fallen asleep himself. He straightened up and rubbed his hands over his face as though he were sluicing it with water. As he struggled into alertness, though, he experienced one of those rare moments of recognition that wasn't exactly as if he had witnessed the scene before, but was instead the certainty that the entire tableau he beheld was precisely as it should be: the alignment of the window shade, the drape of the filmy curtains, and, through the window, the outbuildings of Scofields and the woods beyond — the intricate branches of the leafless trees exposed against the flat white sky. And also just as it should be was his wife's dark hair fanned out against the red of the cherry-wood rocker, the angle at which the runner of the chair canted against the blue and white rag rug, the dull blade of shadow it cast. He felt a powerful lurch of being suspended briefly in a moment that is perfect.

He took in the scene with satisfaction, as though it were something he had known was there but had never witnessed; it was a sensation like waking after the happy but vague resolution of a dream. He forgot the reason his wife was sitting there holding an infant. He simply stood stock-still for a long moment, looking on at the baby's wispy white hair against his wife's shoulder, the baby's head turned toward Agnes's neck in a nuzzling sweetness.

"Agnes?" he finally said softly, not certain if she was awake, but Agnes turned toward the door with a relieved smile.

"Warren. I was just trying to quiet the baby. I was only resting a little."

"Well, the two of you make quite a picture," Warren said. "Everyone said he was a beautiful baby. But have you ever heard anyone say otherwise about any baby? This is the first time I've known it to turn out to be true."

Agnes laughed. "Mama said I was as plain as a mud hen when I was born."

He looked at Agnes's face carefully, although she was still genuinely smiling. He was glad but surprised that she could speak of her mother so easily. His mother and Aunt Audra had been worried about her. But for the moment Agnes was simply happy to see Warren and sheepishly relieved that she would soon be giving over the responsibility for this infant. Mrs. Dameron had spoken tentatively to her again about Mrs. Longacre readying the nursery out at the Claytor place when she was feeling better.

When Agnes had settled into her in-laws' house with the

baby, Warren's mother had been sympathetic and even helpful, but she had mostly steered clear of the whole situation. Agnes had scarcely slept in days, agonizing over the baby's habit of saving his loudest complaints for the middle of the night, when Agnes was certain it kept her mother- and father-in-law awake. There was a period between one and four in the morning when nothing Agnes could do had any effect on the baby's loud unhappiness, and she became panicky with helplessness. Occasionally she had brief periods of exhausted, desperate fury at the baby himself, at John and Lillian Scofield, whose annoyed sleeplessness Agnes assumed, and especially at her own mother for leaving her in such a fix. She was done in by her pretense of competency in caring for her mother's child.

She shifted the baby gingerly as she stood up, and for a moment Warren and the baby exchanged a glance as Agnes moved to put him down in his bassinet. The baby stared at Warren with a startled expression. He had beautiful, long-lashed, golden brown eyes, which Warren had never seen in the face of an infant.

Agnes settled the baby, who went down quietly enough, and moved toward her husband with a wistful look of longing. There was no chance at all that they would have any time alone. She put her arms around Warren's neck and leaned into him, her cheek resting on his shoulder, and Warren bent his head against her hair.

"I'm so sorry about everything, Agnes. I'm sorry you were by yourself through all this. I know nothing can ever make up for what's happened. . . ." But he stopped abruptly and made a low murmur of disapproval, moving his head from side to side and further disarranging Agnes's hair. "Well, I don't mean to say that. It's the kind of thing I hate to hear other people say. People mean well. They mean to comfort someone. But of course nothing can make up for this. Nothing will be the same. Everything I mean to say sounds simpleminded. When I came in just now I didn't know what to expect. But you looked exactly right. You and the baby facing the light from the window. Have you ever had that feeling? I knew that everything was just as it should be. That's how you looked. When I saw you in the rocking chair I thought, well, at least there's the baby. He *is* a handsome boy, Agnes. He's bound to be some comfort to you, I think. And to me, too."

Warren couldn't see his wife's face, but, in fact, with her head still resting on his shoulder, Agnes opened her eyes and blinked slowly in surprise. She didn't even like the child who had been placed in her care. She was terrified of him — of her inability to know what he wanted. And he would be brought up in the Claytor household, anyway, and she would be at Scofields, and she *would* come to like him — to love him, of course. He was her brother, after all. But Warren's admiration of her with the baby was too flattering to dispute just at the moment. "He *is* a pretty baby," she said. "He looks just like Mama, I think."

Warren leaned his head back to see her face, and he smiled indulgently. "Oh, maybe so. You might be right. But to me he looks more like a Scofield. He has such dark eyes, and your mother's were light. But you might be right. Who knows how he'll turn out? Aunt Audra always says that babies generally surprise you one way or another."

"Well, I guess that's true," Agnes said. "I guess they almost always do."

When Agnes gave birth to her first child, though, she was far more than surprised; she fell into a state of maternal devotion so at odds with her experience and expectations that she was privately a little alarmed by her own emotion. Claytor Edson Alcorn Scofield was born on April 13, 1919, five months after little Dwight's birth. Claytor Scofield was a red-faced newborn, long and thin and with all his features tightly pinched together in the middle of his face as if he were angry. And, as it happened, for the first three weeks of his life he was close to inconsolable, and Agnes was very nearly crazed with anxiety and empathic grief when she couldn't solace him.

Warren got home only twice before his son's birth, once just after Robert Butler returned in January, and again the first of February, at which point Lillian Scofield had the crib brought down from the attic and placed in the little nursery for Dwight. It was apparently going to be quite a while before the nursery out at the Claytor place could be put to rights. When Mrs. Longacre's cold had turned into pneumonia, Audra Scofield had arranged for Evelyn Harvey's niece, Evie Bowers, to come in during the week and on Saturday afternoons to look after little Dwight. And the only word that came from the Damerons' house was that Mrs. Longacre was recovering but was confined to bed. Dwight Claytor, though, was a happy baby, and he turned to the sound of Agnes's voice, he beamed when she came into sight, and generally only she or her father-in-law, John Scofield, could assuage Dwight's occasional bouts of discontent.

After Christmas, Agnes had been confined to the house when the weather got bitter, but Lucille Drummond visited often, and Sally Trenholm when she was home from school. Lily came over every afternoon, and Robert Butler often visited as well, and other than Lucille, it was Robert whom Agnes most liked to see. He was a pleasant man in every respect. He was nice looking but not dashing, interesting but not intimidating. It was clear every moment he was near her that he was devoted to Lily, and Agnes liked him very much for that. Agnes found that it was an entirely uncomplicated and happy coincidence that he and she liked each other immediately. She was surprised to be so comfortable with him as soon as they met, but she supposed that there was no more accounting for immediate friendship than there was for falling in love.

She had developed a suspicion of Robert Butler since she first began to hear his friends and family talk about him. He was so highly thought of, and not one person had even implied anything unfavorable about him. Agnes had begun to resent him and think he must not be very interesting, since he was universally and tediously described as a good and decent man. His first book of poems had been published while he was in France, and she had read it but didn't have any idea what the poems were about. Well, they were about God, but she couldn't tell exactly what he was getting at. No one had thought to tell Agnes, however, about Robert's quiet humor or his nearly eccentric courtliness.

When Claytor was born, Robert presented him with a lovely little music box he had bought in France — had bought, in fact, intending it as a gift for Lily. But when he asked Lily if she thought it might not be a more suitable gift for Agnes and her new baby, Lily had seemed enthusiastic about his idea.

"I'd forgotten that you have that handsome marquetry box, Lily," Robert had said. "This little box. It's not very fine, I know. But it does play a lullaby, and I thought . . ."

"Oh, yes. Yes, Robert. What a good idea," Lily said, with her brightest smile.

When Warren got back for a week's visit after his son's birth he brought a pretty christening dress for the baby, and for Agnes a dresser scarf of intricate cutwork, a pale rose silk bed jacket, and beautiful monogrammed linen handkerchiefs — all those things nearly impossible to come by with the ban on German imports. He was elated to be home; he was relieved more than he could ever have imagined to see Agnes so healthy. He had been quietly terrified — ever since Agnes's mother had died — that Agnes, too, would die, even though Catherine Claytor's death had been completely unrelated to having given birth.

But when Warren first looked down at his two-week-old son he was overcome with a surge of relieved glee that made him nearly giddy. He smiled broadly. "Robert, look here! Lily! Why, Agnes. Our little boy looks to me just exactly like a butternut squash! His head's so much bigger than the rest of him." He was speaking fondly. In fact, he was making an enormous effort not to reveal how shaky he felt. Warren was fearfully astonished and had the same feeling of near nausea that he had had as a child when he was excited beyond his ability to express his emotion in language. He thought he might cry. "An *exasperated* squash, though," he said, when Claytor's features drew in and he burst into a mighty complaint. Claytor was loud with distress. Warren's face drew in, too, with sympathetic misery, and he turned to look to Agnes for instruction.

But Agnes was already bending over and scooping up her son, and Warren didn't see her expression. He had no idea that she was teary eyed and deeply injured on behalf of this infant who couldn't make any case for himself, who couldn't ward off his own father's amusement. Warren assumed that he and Agnes were still in this together; it never occurred to him that she wouldn't infer the passion behind the facade of his amiable teasing. He was certain she knew how profoundly he felt his connection to this tiny living being. But, of course, Warren was entirely mistaken. It was in that exact moment that Agnes was locked into a ferocious and lifetime advocacy of Claytor Edson Alcorn Scofield against all others, although she herself wasn't aware of the long-term aspect of her immediate but unspoken indignation.

Little Dwight Claytor was five months old when the new baby entered the household, and by then no one remembered the frantic late nights of his first few weeks' dismay. At the Scofield house he had become a child adored by the whole extended Scofield family, especially Warren's father. John Scofield haunted Agnes's days and was the one obstacle to her heady amazement at the life she was living. He had set himself up as Dwight's protector in the face of what he saw as Agnes's favoritism of her own child over her helpless little brother.

Within several months of his birth Claytor Scofield was every bit as handsome a baby as Dwight Claytor had been. Claytor's dark hair had gone, and by the time he was one year old he and Dwight had the same white blond, silky hair, which Lillian Scofield called angel feathers. All the Scofield children had had hair like that, she said. And as they grew into toddlers Dwight Claytor and Claytor Scofield came to be known all over town as the little Scofield twins, which continued to perplex Agnes. She didn't think the two children looked anything at all alike, and she was puzzled and disturbed, as they reached their first and then their second birthdays, whenever she was out with the two of them for a walk and a passerby would comment on her pretty twins. "Oh, no," she said at first, "the older one's my youngest brother."

She didn't know that there were people around town who thought it terribly unkind that she and Warren had named one of the twins Dwight, for Agnes's father, but had not named the other John, for Warren's father. "John Scofield's in a bad way, too," said Evie Bowers's mother to her neighbor, whose husband was a foreman at the Company and worked under Tut Zeller. "That's what I hear. But he's just wild about those boys. Especially Dwight. You know, they aren't *identical* twins. Oh, but they do look so much alike it's hard to tell them apart. Dwight's a little bigger. He's the sturdy one. And Evie tells me John Scofield's downright foolish about him.

"Of course, those boys were born just after the death of Mr. Claytor's wife and his youngest son . . . Edward? Edwin? A nice little boy, but the flu . . . But you can see that Mr. and Mrs. Scofield might have chosen names from *her* side of the family because of that." The subject was sad and complicated, and very few people sorted it out, anyway. Now and then, even within Scofields, the two boys were casually referred to as the twins.

Only Agnes, and also Lily, didn't think of the two as brothers, but neither woman said anything, and those two children were entirely connected to each other. They measured themselves for better or worse against the other, and it never crossed their minds that they had not always been two parts of a whole. They did not know any way to consider their actions and desires except in reference to the other. They were scarcely ever apart, and as they got older nearly everyone was pleased to see them wherever they went. Two healthy, towheaded little boys with big brown eyes and those dark eyebrows that all the Scofields had. The sight of them pleased almost everyone. Only Lily sometimes felt breathless with a pang of jealousy when she saw the two, racing across the yards, or sitting quite still with their heads together considering one thing or another. It seemed to her that Agnes had everything in the world. And then she would struggle to repress that notion. She would try and try to wish Agnes well.

John Scofield was often with those little boys. And he remained certain that Agnes and Warren favored Claytor. He was fond of Claytor, too, but Dwight had about him a seriousness of purpose — a quality of earnestness — that astonished John. Claytor had a natural ease and a childish charm, and he wasn't nearly so intense as Dwight. John suspected this was the reason Agnes favored Claytor. He was convinced that she didn't fully appreciate Dwight's intelligence. He didn't hesitate to declare this notion to anyone at all. When Tut Zeller stopped by one afternoon looking for Warren, he found John Scofield and Evie Bowers out in the yard with the little boys, and he stood chatting with both of them for a bit, and said to John what fine-looking boys they were. A fine addition to the family.

"Well, they are, Tut. They certainly are. Now, their mother favors Claytor, but I think Dwight's the one to watch. I wouldn't be surprised to see him become an important man, someday. He *thinks* about things. Considers them, you see. Maybe he'll go into politics. He's not a *carefree* sort of boy. Not at all."

"He's like his father, then," said Tut.

John had been watching the little boys digging an elaborate system of tunnels with spoons Evie had given them, and he slowly turned to regard Tut. "What do you mean? Warren had his fill of politics during the war. But I don't believe Dwight is as restless." He gestured toward Dwight, who was just a little over four years old, but who was earnestly working at a rocky

patch, determined to burrow through while Claytor was digging around it. "See there. He doesn't have Warren's tempera-
ment."

"Well, now," Tut replied after a moment, "that little boy's a
Claytor, isn't he? Born out at the Claytor place just before his
mother came down with the flu?"

John drew himself up and looked at Tut in surprise. "Ah!
Well, you can put that idea right out of your mind, Tut. You
shouldn't entertain such a thought at all. Why, just because a cat
has her kittens in the oven, that doesn't make them biscuits!"

Nearly everyone in Washburn was pleased to see John
Scofield devoted to those little boys, and Agnes never said a
word about it one way or another. Her father-in-law spent
hours of his day wherever she might be if the boys were with
her. Now and then his hand would stray to her waist, if he drew
her aside to show her something or other. Or he would lean forward and brush her hair out of her face while she held one or
the other of the children so that she couldn't free her hands.
Agnes had only once been entirely alone in a room with John
Scofield, in the early days of her marriage. He had come up
quietly over the carpet behind her, reached around her waist,
and cupped her breasts in his hands. Agnes had twisted away
from him, but she didn't say a word.

Her mind went blank. She hadn't wanted to allow anything
to blot the lovely clean slate of her life at Scofields. And Agnes
continued to impute any impropriety on his part to inadver-
tence or mistake, to accident, because she didn't want to define
herself in any way that was at odds with her notion of her ordinary life. But she was very cautious in the company of her
father-in-law. Once she released a dish she was passing to War-

ren's father before he could cover her hand with his own in the act of accepting it and she spilled peas all over the table and was mortified.

Both Lily and Lillian Scofield noticed John Scofield's behavior. Lillian felt dreadful shame and real anger unfairly aimed in Agnes's direction, and Lily was peculiarly angry, too, when she remembered her uncle John teasing her, always referring to her as the runt of the litter. But Lily thought her uncle was simply falling apart.

She had heard her own father despairing of John, who didn't even go to the office anymore, who had, in fact, borrowed against his shares in the company. He had been delighted to accept a loan from Arthur Fitch, whose Fitch Enterprises in Pennsylvania was Scofields & Company's largest privately owned competitor. Lily's father couldn't stand the man, who had several times approached Scofields & Company about a merger.

"I don't know what John's thinking," Leo had said when only his wife and Lily were in the room. "Fitch'll never give up those shares. Of course, Lillian's income is separate, and Warren will be a partner soon enough. But I feel that John's got some fury . . . I would've been glad to extend a loan. He knows that. He knows I want this kept in the family. But I think it's me he's maddest at. And I don't understand it. I don't understand it. I practically raised him."

By the time Agnes was pregnant once more, she and Warren had taken up residence in the house George Scofield had built for himself but which he was happy to give over to his nephew in order to move in with John and Lillian, where the household would be looked after without any effort on his part. Robert and Lily were just next door to Warren and Agnes, where they lived with Audra and Leo Scofield.

Agnes found herself living a life that absolutely amazed her whenever she stopped to consider it. At the age of twenty-four she was in charge of a bustling household in which she had achieved a ferocious domestic order. She had paid close attention to the management of her mother-in-law's house all the while she and Warren and the babies lived there. Agnes's own household was even more organized. Any little bit of disorder made her frantic, because she had in mind an existence that would be clean and spare, that would run as efficiently as a machine. No heartbreaking disorder, no desperate sorrow, no surprises at all. She moved through the serene rooms of her house at Scofields ignoring any evidence that she hadn't achieved it.

Agnes had incorporated and improved upon all the exactitude of day-to-day arrangements her mother-in-law instituted in her own house — her careful planning, her extraordinary attention to the details of housekeeping — because Agnes would do whatever was necessary to keep her children from ever having to explain anything at all about their lives. She was determined to provide reliability of the domestic seasons. When her children raced off to Lily's, where something was always afoot — golf games, charades, partially done jigsaw puzzles to contend with, Uncle Leo's garden to investigate — Agnes knew they could leave their own household knowing exactly what they would find when they came home. It was the greatest luxury Agnes could think to give them.

During late Thursday night and early Friday morning, September 14 and 15, 1923, in Washburn, Ohio, and over much of

Marshal County, a freakish storm moved in from Canada, and over seven inches of snow accumulated. It was the heaviest snowfall ever recorded for that month in Ohio, and Lily Scofield Butler awakened on the morning of her thirty-fifth birthday a little after dawn with a sharp ache in her back more intense than it had been when she went to bed. The night before, Robert had rubbed her back and loosened the tight muscles enough so that she had fallen asleep still in some pain but much comforted. When she came awake, Robert was sound asleep and lying flat on his back with his arms and legs straight. Lily had been sleeping in her own room across the hall during the last few months of the first pregnancy she seemed likely to carry to term, and Robert seemed to have admonished himself even in his sleep not to move about and disturb her.

She turned on her side, trying to ease the tightness in her lower back, tucking her knees up and laying her head against Robert's shoulder for comfort. She lay there for long minutes waiting for the spasm to abate and fighting against panic — this didn't feel like any of the times she had miscarried, but nonetheless she was over eight months pregnant and terrified that she would lose this baby, too. Finally she got up and slipped downstairs as quietly as she could, moving with great care, as though she might break if she made any but the most cautious motion. There was only a sliver of pale gray at the curtained windows, and no one else stirred anywhere in the house.

She slipped into the dark parlor and opened the drapes and was astonished at the glistening landscape. The leaves were heavy with the burden of snow, and the branches flexed dangerously and swooped low to the ground. It was extraordinarily beautiful and exciting — the inherent tension of the early snow weighing down the full-blown trees, the hedges and blooming bushes. Snow on the honeysuckle and the trumpet vine, still lush with deep orange flowers. It was startling, the contrast. As if someone had strung Christmas decorations in her father's garden.

She stood for a long time, her sensibilities gone passive, the white, white light brightening as the sun rose. And she sat down on the window seat and felt better, her thoughts effervescing half formed, while the sky acquired a flat brightness. She was cold sitting near the glass, but the chill was distracting, and she was more comfortable sitting than she had been lying down.

Across the way Agnes emerged wearing mittens and galoshes and a scarf she must have tied on hastily, because her hair escaped in all directions. She was smiling while she helped the two little boys, who were so bundled up they couldn't flex their arms and legs. She settled Dwight and Claytor on a sled with much flailing about and jockeying for position on their part. Lily watched closely with her lips slightly pursed and her head tilted forward in concentration — as though she were studying the behavior of another species — as Agnes pulled Dwight and Claytor across the lawn, walking backward facing the little boys, with an expression as exuberant as her mass of curly, unbound hair escaping her red wool scarf.

Agnes was four months pregnant herself, but already she had had to leave her coat unbuttoned except at the neck, and Lily realized Agnes had pulled on a pair of Warren's trousers over her nightdress and turned up the cuffs in her hurry to get outside into the snow before it melted. In her wake she left a trammeled disturbance in the serene white sweep of lawn.

For just a moment Lily felt it keenly, a plummeting sense of despondency and envy. She stood watching, though, as Agnes and Dwight and Claytor crossed her line of vision, vivid and bright faced, disturbing the visual hush of the early morning, then Lily turned away and went upstairs to get dressed. She could hardly stand to witness Agnes's happiness. Lily knew it was disgraceful to give in to such envy, and on this birthday — and Robert's and Warren's — she wasn't going to allow herself any more time for loose-minded musing.

Nevertheless, the nature of her envy had evolved over the years. Lily had Robert back, and Warren was close at hand, but to her surprise it was somehow *she* who was left out. Only Lily herself perceived it — the other three would have been surprised that Lily felt in any way excluded. They would have been surprised that she pondered the thought at all. After all, it was still Lily who animated any occasion when they were together, but Agnes and Warren and Robert shared a kind of mutual regard and affection that Lily simply could not extend to Agnes. Agnes had everything in the world she wanted; there was not a single need of hers that Lily could fulfill.

But Lily tried to shake off her resentment of Agnes's unwitting rebuff — Agnes's casual independence. And, in any case, she was genuinely fond of little Dwight Claytor and also Warren's little boy, both of whom sought out and delighted in her company, and who were happy, good-natured children.

She dredged up her own vanity as a weapon against her current despondency, forcing herself out of her indulgent lapse into self-pity. Lily prided herself on being nothing if not a good sport, and she was generally disdainful of this sort of floundering about in personal reflection and maudlin regret. Nevertheless, it was terribly hard not to begrudge Agnes the children's awed faces as they looked up at her with excitement, crediting her with the world's soft, white dazzlement.

Chapter Twelve

MARTHA GERTRUDE BUTLER was born to Lily and Robert Butler the day after her parents' thirty-fifth birthday, September 16, 1923, in the middle of the most unusual spell of early snow and ice storms ever to sweep over the region. And, as it happened, five months later, February 15, 1924, Agnes gave birth to a little girl — named Catherine Elizabeth Scofield but immediately known as Betts — in the warmest February on record for Washburn, Ohio. Temperatures rose into the sixties in that usually frigid month. But there wasn't much notice paid to this small coincidence of those two girls' being born almost on the same day of separate months and each in untimely weather. There were a good many young children and new babies in Washburn by 1924, after the war, as people settled down and started families.

William Dameron and his wife, the former Sally Trenholm, had two children, and Lucille Drummond was married and living in Columbus with her husband and little boy. Agnes's father was married again, to a widow who had two children of her own who were at the Sperry School, and Howie and Richard Claytor were both attending Ohio State University. Whenever they came to Washburn they stayed with Warren and Agnes, because their father lived in Columbus, and the house out on Newark Road was rented.

By the summer of 1926, Agnes was once again pregnant, with the baby due in the late fall. Betts was two and a half years old, and she and the Butlers' daughter, Trudy, were thrown together much of the time, although theirs was a fractious alliance. One moment they were happy as clams and the next they were in tears of indignation, one at the other.

Betts was a mystery to her mother; Agnes was a little in awe of her. She was nothing at all like Agnes had been as a child. Betts didn't possess one ounce of faintheartedness or timidity or a single bit of caution. She was much admired; Warren liked the way she just dashed head-on into her life. Someone was always having to race after Betts, who popped out of her bed and down the stairs and right out into the morning and across the yards of Scofields if no one had remembered to lock the door. Even when she was sitting with her father while he read her a story she gave the impression of being ready to go someplace else — even when she had the attention of Claytor and Dwight, if they helped her, for instance, build a castle with her blocks. Betts never appeared to be concentrating on just one thing at a time.

Lily's daughter, Trudy — equally mysterious to her mother — was the older of the two girls by five months, but she was a smaller, rather delicate and more earnest little person. She was a child who was greatly absorbed by one thing at a time as the hours of the day unfolded, whereas Betts rushed through each moment hardly noticing its passage and certain that whatever would satisfy her was just about to happen. Trudy was adored by her father; he doted on her in his own way, quietly, and with a courteous restraint. But Lily was trapped in a frustrating state of maternal anxiety. With any other children she was spontaneous and daring, but she was always concerned about Trudy: Might she fall, might she catch cold, might she not thrive? Lily didn't like the sort of person she became when she was with her daughter. Lily had always disdained that very nagging sort of mother she herself turned into when Trudy was within her realm. But Trudy was a quiet, self-possessed, easy child who, even as a toddler, kept her own counsel and didn't chafe much at any restrictions Lily imposed on her.

John Scofield was sixty-seven years old in 1926, and he had made himself nearly a permanent fixture in his son's house. Almost every morning he arrived at the front door impeccably dressed, a lean, elegant, still-handsome man. He arrived ostensibly to join Warren on his way to the office, but he would sit down at the breakfast table and accept a cup of coffee. "We ought to be getting along, Warren. I'm already late, and if I'm not on my way soon I might as well give up this day and go over to the fairgrounds to see how they're getting on unloading the horses."

And Dwight and Claytor would at once begin a campaign to go along with whatever adventure John had thought up for that day. Agnes didn't like it, but Warren remained delighted by his father's interest in the little boys. "I've never seen my father sentimental about anything in his life. It's the best thing that's ever happened to him."

Warren and Leo were relieved and grateful to have John occupied. But Agnes often saw him slip into the pantry in the morning and pour a shot of whiskey from a flask into his coffee; she saw him too jovial by lunchtime, but she did realize that his affection for Dwight and Claytor was real. She had watched countless times as he sat with the two little boys and showed them over and over, with infinite patience, how to fold a hat or a sailboat out of a sheet of newspaper, or, with a piece of string, taught them the basic rudiments of making a cat's cradle, or time after time helped the boys tie and retie their shoelaces. He spent hours diligently helping them build miniature forts with glue and matchsticks. And he listened to them without any hint of adult condescension; he attended whatever they had to say with genuine gravity, and she appreciated that on their behalf. Even though John Scofield made her uneasy, she knew better than to do anything that might undermine the high esteem with which Mr. Scofield and Dwight and Claytor regarded one another.

And, too, Warren was so miserable if Agnes made known any complaint against his father that she simply kept John Scofield's sly advances — his relentless attempts to fondle or touch her — to herself. She had never said a word about it to Warren; she had only mentioned to Warren her father-in-law's occasional lapses into rough language around the children. "But Agnes, there's no protecting them from everything. When they're down at the works . . . and you know how they love to go along. But the men don't notice them. Don't change their language. And, I'll tell you, it can singe your ears. My father may lapse into the same thing now and then, but as long as they understand that they're never to repeat what they hear . . ." And John was cagey; Warren never saw any impropriety.

Agnes had long ago been unable to continue to ignore her father-in-law's advances, however, and she had once gingerly brought up the subject with Lily, who she hoped might advise her. But Lily seemed almost annoyed.

"Oh, Uncle John's always been full of trouble. I can't tell you the times he's nearly driven my father around the bend. But, you know, Agnes, I think the best thing to do is just to stay out of his way." All this business seemed to Lily to be — perversely — an odd sort of compliment to Agnes, and one more bit of proof that John Scofield still thought that Lily herself was a poor specimen. "I can't see any way to bring it up that won't hurt poor Aunt Lillian. And Warren, too. After all, it's his own father. If I were you I'd just keep out of his way." Which wasn't much help to Agnes, who was already adept at escaping any room John Scofield entered. But, although Agnes never let herself dwell on it, as John Scofield aged, Agnes thought him more and more grotesque in his lechery.

The fact was that John Scofield and Agnes simply didn't like each other, which was perfectly understandable on Agnes's part. But there wasn't any woman John held in very high regard; he viewed them with suspicion and hostility and a deep, uninvestigated resentment at the idea that they should receive societal gratitude, societal deference, merely because they gave birth, merely because every man had a mother. He was one of the few people not charmed by little Betts as she flew about Scofields, although he was astute enough to know he couldn't let all his irritation at her coalesce into apparent dislike. Nor was he particularly fond of Trudy Butler, who seemed to him a dull-natured child with no spunk.

It wasn't really any sort of lust that drew him to his daughter-in-law; it was a variation of contempt, although he was long past any chance of understanding that. He took a childish pleasure in thwarting her. She was a bossy thing, he thought as he sat at her table. In subtle ways she had taken charge of the household and brooked no interference in her agenda, even from her husband. And John could see that Warren didn't even know he was shaping his life to his wife's domestic schedule. Warren was naively happy to have the household run like clockwork.

Warren wouldn't hear a word against Agnes, but the little boys were more amenable to considering the disadvantages of Agnes's unreasonably inflexible householdery. "Now, I know this is the day your mama has the porch washed down. If it weren't, though, why, we could have a fine time with this handsome set of soldiers I came across at Flint's, downtown." Agnes would tuck in the corners of her mouth, and her eyes would widen in an owlish expression as she suppressed her annoyance when Dwight and Claytor began to implore her to let them use the porch. But Warren would grin at Agnes in amused complicity. He had no idea that there were much larger issues at stake. He had no idea that his father was attempting to undermine or make irrelevant his wife's authority.

"Oh, certainly, Mr. Scofield," Agnes would answer sweetly. "But, now, you don't mean to leave out Betts and Trudy, do you? They would just be heartbroken. Why, they worship the ground you walk on, and the boys are so patient with them. Dwight and Claytor are so grown-up for their ages that they're always sweet to the little girls." And Dwight and Claytor would be so impressed with themselves and their remarkable maturity — both seven years old in the summer of '26 — that they agreed immediately that Trudy and Betts should be included. Only Agnes and John Scofield knew that a battle had been joined. It was tiresome, though. It was she who quietly bore the brunt of John's determined self-destruction, and, in spite of his obvious loneliness and genuine affection for children she also loved, she could not muster any pity for him at all.

Audra Scofield had arranged to take the farmhouse in Maine for June, July, and August, and had persuaded her sister, Lillian, to join her. Audra was increasingly worried about her sister. Lillian showed all the signs of falling prey to another spell of the despair and lethargy that she had been prone to since she was first married. Audra privately thought that John Scofield was at the root of Lillian's despondency, and in making their plans Audra made a great fuss of her concern that John not be away from all his various business concerns. John and the rest of the family would join them for the last few weeks of August. Warren and Agnes had arranged to rent a little cottage near the farmhouse in Tenants Harbor for the month of August, and only Robert wouldn't be able to get away. The Harcourt Lees faculty convened on August 9. He hoped, though, to get some good work done without the pleasant distractions of his wife and daughter.

But, as always happened when his wife was away, John Scofield's fragile hold on some semblance of decorum shattered entirely as soon as she left. He didn't get up in the mornings; he didn't dress or shave. Finally Evelyn Harvey approached Warren and told him that she wouldn't come in anymore until Mrs. Scofield was back, but that she expected to be paid in full or she would have to give up working there altogether. Warren had been worried about his mother, too, and he certainly wasn't going to wire her for instruction, nor did he feel inclined to involve his uncle Leo, who disapproved of John as it was.

George Scofield lived in John's house, but when he wasn't at the Company he spent his time traveling — sometimes great distances — to search out relics from the Civil War. Just a week after Audra and Lillian Scofield had departed for Maine, George had returned from Pennsylvania, where he had done some business, but where he had also obtained two bullets that were said to have met midair in the battle of Gettysburg. The coincidence entranced George. "Why, right here," he had said to John, who was collapsed in a chair in the parlor, "right here's a story," he went on, holding the bullets head to head to illustrate their collision. "Right here you might have a picture of how two lives were spared. That's what it might be." He hadn't even noticed his brother's state of disarray. John was sitting unshaven in his trousers and his undershirt, with his suspenders hanging around his waist.

It was just then, while Evelyn Harvey stood in the doorway drying her hands on her apron, that she made up her mind she wasn't going to stay on in this situation. It was too upsetting. She went straight over to Warren and Agnes Scofield's house, but she waited in the kitchen with her niece Evie until Mr. Scofield got home. Even though she liked Warren Scofield's wife well enough, and as distressed as she was, she still wasn't going to say anything unfavorable about the family to someone who wasn't a Scofield.

Warren asked her to take a few days off and then give his father another chance. "I'll see if I can't get him feeling better, Mrs. Harvey. I'll have him stay with us for a few days, and I think he'll be back to himself pretty soon. You know how fond he is of the children. I think he'll want to be on his best behavior. But I thank you for all you've done, and I apologize. He has a hard time whenever my mother travels."

When John was installed in the downstairs bedroom at Agnes and Warren's, he did behave with more propriety. Warren gave over any chores that would normally fall to the head of the house to his father, and it did have the effect of sobering John Scofield up and pulling him back from the brink of dissolution. Dwight and Claytor, and even Betts, were delighted to have him in the house. He was always full of plans and ideas.

It was only Agnes who felt that to share a household with Mr. Scofield once again might tax her beyond the endurance of her courtesy. Warren had no idea that his wife didn't like his father, but the children knew it quite well. They could tell just by how she drew herself in slightly when Mr. Scofield entered a room, or how she spoke to him with frightening politeness, a chilly little formality in her voice. The two boys each thought privately that she wasn't being fair. They couldn't understand her antipathy, and in a roundabout way both felt injured that Agnes didn't like this man who loved them so much. Her unspoken dislike tarnished the wonderful fact of his affection for them. They were a little bit angry.

When Agnes roasted a nice chicken for Sunday dinner, she put it down in front of John Scofield, who had made fresh lemonade for the children that morning and still had his own glass in his hand. He placed the glass carefully on the tablecloth, with a precision that unnerved Agnes, and he took up the carving knife and fork and began ineffectively to carve the bird, managing, finally, to dislodge it from the platter, so that the chicken lay forlornly on its side, soiling the crisp tablecloth. Agnes made a breathy and irritated little exclamation of surprise, and John looked down sadly at what he had done. He put his head in his hands, and for the first time since she had known him, Agnes felt sorry for him. She had never seen him express remorse, but she found that there was nothing about his dismay that was gratifying. She started to rise from her place, "Don't bother about any of this —" she was saying, just as Claytor spoke up.

"Oh, Mama!" he said, with real sorrow in his voice. "Mama. Look! Look what happened. You must have got the wrong kind of chicken today, Mama." John Scofield had been so delighted he had fallen right out of mortification and into a state of careful charm right before their eyes. And the tale became a staple of the Scofield clan.

Warren told and retold this little vignette fondly, embellishing it as he went along, enhancing Claytor's precociousness sometimes, his wit at others. And, of course, with no culpability attributed to anyone, because Warren would never have found any of it amusing if he had understood that there was blame to be allotted. He saw it merely as one of those mishaps that are comical in retrospect, and he also thought it illustrated a hopeful kind of optimism on the part of his son, who interpreted the whole incident as the fault of the chicken and not any clumsiness of his grandfather's. Over the years other family members recounted the story — the "wrong chicken" story — at Thanksgiving or some other occasion. Agnes never held Claytor's betrayal of her against him, but she generally managed not to remain in the room whenever the story began.

Washburn, Ohio, planned to celebrate the sesquicentennial of Independence Day on July 5, 1926, since the Fourth of July fell on a Sunday. But all the Scofields & Company workers and their families were invited to a picnic at Scofields on Sunday, the afternoon of the Fourth. The Scofields & Company Band and the Silver Cornet Band would give a public concert that evening at the bandstand on Monument Square, and then the Fife and Drum Corps of the Washburn Post of the Grand Army of the Republic and the Sons of Union Veterans would perform. Following the musical performances, the entertainment committee had planned a reenactment of the dedication of the Civil War monument. It had originally been erected and given to the town under the aegis of Mrs. Marcus Dowd, whose husband, Colonel Marcus Dowd, had died at Petersburg. His daughter, Mrs. Carter Hutcheson, was coming from Philadelphia to participate in the ceremony. Mrs. Hutcheson would say a few words and read the poem from which the inscription on the monument was taken.

Leo and John and George Scofield were in rare accordance on the planning of the picnic. John had arranged for Charlie Peel at the Eola Arms Hotel to set up a bounteous buffet on long tables on the grounds and porches of Scofields, and George proposed to display an exhibit of his Civil War relics, which to his surprise was an offer matter-of-factly accepted by John and Leo.

In the absence of her mother and her aunt, all questions of logistics involving the Scofield compound were referred to Lily, and she got into the swing of things right away. She asked Dwight and Claytor to be her lieutenants — that very phrase — which they agreed to enthusiastically. Lily and the boys scouted the yards for the best place to set the stake for horseshoes and searched for level ground for the three badminton nets. They roamed the lawns, with Trudy and Betts in their wake, sorting out where to locate the children's refreshment booth, deciding where some comfortable chairs could be placed for those who might be uncomfortable on picnic blankets on the ground. The children were very nearly overwrought with anticipation for days.

Agnes did her best not to be involved. She was the only person at Scofields who was not looking forward to the occasion. It seemed to her that any sort of celebration — of anything at all — was an opportunity for the fragile order of a safely regular day to fall apart. To her mind it was only that hard-won and carefully observed routine that marked the fine line between serenity and turmoil. She alone within her family never looked forward to birthdays, or Christmas, or any holiday that was filled with the possibility of disappointment and even sorrow.

She never said aloud to her family a single word about her particular dread of any of the festivities cherished by the rest of them. She couldn't account for it herself and worried that there was something stingy in her nature. It certainly wasn't that she begrudged the pleasure of her children and Warren, Lily and Robert and little Trudy, her in-laws, or her brothers at any sort of celebration; it was just that the whole experience felt dangerous and slippery to her.

She never said anything, but the children of Scofields knew it anyway, and it made them uneasy. They sensed her reluctance to fall headlong into the fun of looking forward to all the events being planned for the Independence Day picnic and ceremony, and they wondered about it and brooded over it, each one privately. And after a while each child felt a little indignant. None of the grown-ups sensed Agnes's skepticism about the whole affair, since she pitched in to help whenever she was asked, but it was entirely apparent to the children, and it was the sole detraction from their own excitement.

When the day of the picnic finally arrived, the children were up before dawn, and Agnes and Warren were awakened by Betts's fury at Dwight and Claytor when they tried to keep her from bursting into their parents' bedroom. "You're not the boss of me, Claytor! You're not the boss of me!" And then there was a prolonged shriek as she protested when Claytor hung on to her as she lunged for the knob of the bedroom door. The boys knew they would be sent back to bed to wait until the sun was up, because that's what always happened on Christmas morning.

"Well, Miss Betts," John Scofield's voice boomed into the upstairs hallway, "*I* am the boss of you on this beautiful day. Miss Etty Betts! I'll snatch you up and stuff you full of pancakes and you won't be able to move. You'll be filled up to the very brim! You'll be sitting with your hands on your tummy to keep it from exploding! *That's* what, Miss Betts! That's what happens to little girls who don't know who's the boss of them!" And there was a joyous but alarmed squeak from Betts as John Scofield scooped her up and trundled her off downstairs, with Dwight and Claytor following fast behind.

Agnes was unhappy at all this excitement — all this dangerous spontaneity — before she even swung her feet out of bed, but Warren looked forward to the day, and he was relieved to hear his father sounding so happy. It boded well to have him teasing Betts, who so often annoyed him. "Warren, take this little whirlwind off to her mother," he would say, "so the boys and I can get our work done! Why, it's like keeping company with a tornado!" Betts was always stoic and would implore her father to give her a horsey ride on his shoulders, but Warren knew it cut her to the quick to be excluded.

John Scofield had commandeered the kitchen and was

instructing the children about the secret to good pancakes. Dwight and Claytor were lined up on either side of him as he mixed and measured, and Betts was standing on a chair on the other side of the table so she could see. "And then the buttermilk. Not from the icebox. You have to take it out the night before, but not too early. So it's a delicate business, as you can see. Out in the field you don't have the luxury of cooling the milk, so you have to take your chances. And I'll tell you, there may not be anything more unfavorable to a man's outlook on the day than forking the first bite of pancakes into his mouth only to find out the batter was made with milk gone bad." The children watched solemnly, Dwight and Claytor nodding that they understood.

It was not quite six o'clock in the morning, but John Scofield was up and alert and elegantly dressed. His shoes gleaming, his shirt crisp, and his beautifully made suit hadn't a wrinkle in it. "I'm going to drag these boys along to church with me this morning," he said to Warren, who had dressed quickly and come downstairs while Agnes was still wrestling with her hair, pinning it up as firmly as possible since the day was already hot.

"You must be looking to give the new minister a heart attack," Warren said. "I don't believe you've gone to church in over thirty years. Why, you'll give the regular churchgoers a story to tell!" But Warren was pleased at the idea, although he didn't know why, and Dwight and Claytor were delighted. Betts, though, began to protest.

"Me, too, Grandfather! Me, too, Grandfather! I have a blue dress!"

But Agnes swept into the room and caught Betts up in her arms, although Betts immediately squirmed to get down.

"Evie's coming over a little later, Betts, so that you and Trudy can meet her fiancé. And Aunt Lily wants to plait your hair with blue ribbons and Trudy's with yellow. Don't you remember when we picked out those pretty ribbons?" Betts subsided against her mother's shoulder resignedly, but she knew she was going to miss the best fun of this day. Agnes would have liked to have a reason to forbid her father-in-law from taking the boys to church. What was he thinking? Causing discontent wherever he went. Betts was too young to go to church with Dwight and Claytor, but why in the world would John Scofield have so openly excluded her when he could have been discreet?

"Well, Warren, I've decided not to let Leo corner the market on virtue," John said to his son. "I don't believe he's missed a Sunday service in his whole life. I do plan to go to church this morning! It's a grand day, after all. I don't imagine I'll even mind if the sermon's boring on the Fourth of July. Besides, I made up my mind that it was about time I became more attentive to my spiritual well-being. Why, I'm sixty-seven years old! It's about time I paid more attention to the welfare of my soul. I plan to increase my churchgoing from now on. I've made up my mind to attend at least one Sunday every fifty years or so," he said, and Warren laughed.

Agnes looked after Trudy and Betts while the rest of the family, and Mrs. Hutcheson and her oldest son, who were staying at Leo Scofield's house, went to the ten o'clock service at the Methodist church.

By eleven o'clock Agnes was at her wit's end with the two little girls already having gone through several cycles of weeping disagreements and cautious reconciliations. It was terribly hot, and Trudy's brown hair and Betts's blond hair clung in damp tendrils to their necks. Agnes decided to occupy the two girls by giving them a long bath and washing their hair before Lily braided in the ribbons that would match their new dresses. As soon as she had them settled in the tepid water in the tub their tempers improved, and Agnes had a chance to sit on the step stool and put a cold cloth to her own forehead.

She was shaky with mild queasiness in the solid, flat heat in her fifth month of her third pregnancy. She could see from the window that the crew from the Eola Arms was beginning to set up the tables, and the truck from the ice house arrived. She suddenly felt exhausted at the prospect of the long day and evening ahead. She thought she might cry, and the little girls were watching her face. Betts's face began to pucker in sympathetic unhappiness, and Agnes knelt by the tub and pulled herself together. She gave each girl a tin cup and showed them how to pour the water over their heads so that they could wash their own hair. "If you do it yourself, you know, you never, ever get soap in your eyes," she told them enthusiastically. And they began a delighted splashing of themselves and each other and inadvertently of Agnes, too, but Agnes didn't care at all; in the heat her wet clothes felt good.

Lily came dashing up the stairs; Agnes recognized the sound of her shoes clicking down the hall, and she came in looking flushed. "I slipped out early, Agnes. The church is like an oven, and Mrs. Hutcheson was surrounded by all sorts of people who remembered her parents, so I don't think the rest of the family will be back very soon. Oh, you look done in!" she said, as she took Agnes's bedraggled condition into account. But Agnes smiled.

"Well, but I've finally cooled off. Betts has got to have a nap, Lily, or she's going to —"

"No, Mama! No, Mama! I don't need a nap. I'm not sleepy! I don't —"

"Oh, Betts," Lily said over Betts's appalled grief at the injustice of this final thing, "*everyone's* going to take a nap. Trudy, too. And your mama. And me, too. Then you can stay up late and hear the band concert. After you get up, sweetheart, I'm going to fix your hair, and you can put on your new dress, and you'll be ready for anything. You can be first on the pony ride —"

Then Trudy began an objection. "But why does Betts get —"

"The *two* of you can share the first pony ride," Lily said as she lifted Trudy dripping out of the tub and wrapped her in a towel.

"Who gets to sit in front?" Betts began, and Trudy chimed in, and Lily just shook her head and met Agnes's eyes with a resigned acknowledgment. "I'll take this one home, Agnes, and leave you two to yourselves. They'll never settle down if they're in the same room." Agnes nodded; she didn't try to make herself heard over the ongoing debate between the little girls.

Agnes dried Betts off and just slipped a loose gown over her head so she wouldn't be too hot. Agnes lay down next to Betts in the big double bed in her and Warren's room, but Agnes didn't intend to fall asleep herself. There was almost nothing that made her feel worse, she'd discovered, than to sleep in the middle of the day. She knew that Betts wouldn't stay put by herself, though, so Agnes simply lay down in the damp clothes she was wearing and listened to the bustle of activity in the yard below that drifted in the second-story windows left open in case some breath of air might stir. But when Agnes woke up all of a sudden, the light had changed; the sun was no longer streaming in the bedroom window, and Betts was nowhere in the room.

Agnes rushed into the hallway and looked into the other bedrooms, feeling foolish that she hadn't remembered to close and latch the bedroom door, and then she heard her father-in-law's voice in the front hall and she began to move toward the landing.

Warren had looked in on Agnes and Betts when he got home from church and found them both asleep. He had lowered the shade to keep the sun out and quietly made his way out of the room, hurrying down the stairs to steer Dwight and Claytor over to Uncle Leo's before they burst loudly into the front hall. The picnic was getting under way, but Warren wanted to let his wife rest as much as she could; Lily could manage as hostess on her own until Agnes woke up.

It was John Scofield who, a little less than an hour later, first caught sight of Betts — without a stitch of clothing on — running sturdily across the yard toward the general company, making a gleeful yodeling sound of pure exuberance. And just then he felt truly fond of her — his determined little granddaughter with her yellow hair spiking out in all directions. He crossed the yard to intercept her, but when Betts saw her grandfather coming she swerved and headed off at a right angle with a whoop of elation. She loved the air against her skin, the attention she'd attracted, and she was purely delighted with her own speedy trajectory across the yard.

Leo and Lily had spotted her, as well, but they were walking along the drive with Agnes's father, Dwight Claytor, who was in Washburn to give a short speech the following day after the parade. They were quite a distance away, and they moved slowly in Betts's direction, since Leo didn't have his cane and was leaning against Lily's arm rather heavily. Dwight and Claytor were with Warren and Howie and Richard Claytor — who had come with their father for the Fourth of July celebration — on the far side of Leo's house, where the horseshoe tournament had begun. There was no one else to catch up to Betts but John Scofield, and he pursued her with diligence and finally caught her and boosted her up to his shoulder to deliver her back to her mother.

He was smiling as he came into the front hall and spotted Agnes at the top of the stairs. "This little lady is determined to bring scandal down on our heads, Agnes! There she was —"

"Bring her to me," Agnes said, only seeing John Scofield's grin as he approached the stairs cupping Betts's bare bottom in his large hand.

"Yes. I'll do it. I'll certainly do it. I'm —"

"Bring her to me," Agnes said again, without the slightest inflection of humor or amusement, standing like a statue on the landing where it turned. She was still disoriented from sleep.

John mounted the stairs slowly, juggling Betts from one side to another in an attempt to hold the rail, but finally giving up. "I'll certainly do it," he said, still teasingly. "I'll deliver this child before she gets away from me." He had just reached the stair two steps down from where Agnes stood when Agnes reached forward and hooked her arm around her daughter, who was doing her best to avoid the transfer. She was delighted to have her grandfather's attention. Agnes couldn't get a secure hold on Betts, who was squirming out of her reach.

Agnes leaned forward until her face almost met John Scofield's, as though she were about to kiss him. She had a sleep-induced expression of bemusement, although, in fact, she was stiff and awkward with outrage. She had turned slightly to one side, with Betts's torso clasped against the shoulder that was turning away from her father-in-law, when John Scofield released the little girl entirely, so that Agnes had to lunge forward to catch her.

John's arm flew up in the air over his head, and Agnes was momentarily baffled as his face went slack with surprise. And then he was tumbling backward. Agnes was too startled and muddleheaded even to make a sound. She just stood holding Betts, who made no sound either. And then there was Lily kneeling over her uncle for a long moment that Agnes could never afterward put into a context of chronological order.

She remembered hearing her father and Leo come in the back way as she stood looking down at her father-in-law lying flat at the foot of the stairs. He looked as if he had arranged himself there on purpose, except that one leg was bent beneath him. She remembered hearing Leo calling out to her, "Well, Agnes, John found my grandniece running around as naked as a jaybird. He's bringing her around front. . . ."

And she remembered Lily looking up at her with her face seeming more than usually pointed and pale. "He fell, Agnes. Uncle John fell down the stairs," she repeated slowly, in a cadence like a children's verse. In the determined meter of "London Bridge," as though she were instructing Agnes. "Uncle John fell down the stairs."

Lily had let her father lean on the proffered arm of Mr. Claytor, and she hurried toward Agnes and Warren's house when she saw her uncle John with Betts in hand heading up the front walk and then disappearing through the front door. She felt unreasonably alarmed as she approached the front door herself. When she entered the lower hall, the sun streamed into that shady alcove and was almost blinding. She immediately caught sight of Agnes on the upper landing, clasping Betts in one arm, her other arm extended as though she were conferring a benediction on the stilled figure of John Scofield, whom Lily finally saw lying motionless at the bottom of the stairs. Lily had gasped in surprise; she was appalled, but in spite of herself she was briefly swept over with admiration for Agnes. A single thought skittered briefly through Lily's head: I don't blame her. I don't blame her for a minute. And in that instant there was not a moment's hesitation about where her allegiance would lie.

But Agnes was in shock. Leo Scofield had come with Dwight Claytor around to the back door where the steps were shallower. He moved slowly across the threshold of the front parlor, having some difficulty navigating without his cane, and then he came to a stop. He had come into the front hall and clasped the balustrade for support and looked down with a perplexed expression of irritation at his brother John. Dwight Claytor stood off to the side, staring up at his daughter and his little granddaughter with a peculiar expression of alarmed recognition. Leo stood for a long while, gazing down at his brother, and then he spoke with a note of exasperation. "I don't like *this,* John! You come along, now. You come along. You look like a damned fool! You look like a fool, John."

And then Leo Scofield stood there without saying a thing for several minutes, finally straightening and putting his hands in his pockets. "I wish you'd get up, John," he had said in a different tone altogether, like a boy trying to persuade a friend to join some game. "I wish you'd get up. I don't think it could all just come to this."

Agnes was never able to recall much of anything else about that day. She didn't remember John being carefully moved to the parlor; she didn't remember that Warren had suggested that the family not spread this news during the picnic, nor did she know that Leo Scofield had not gone back out into the crowd, or that

Robert and Lily had overseen the festivities as best they could. She never even made the connection between this awful event and the several years that followed when she was more content than she had ever imagined in her whole life that she would be. Certainly she expressed shock and sorrow about the death of her father-in-law, but the fact is, she felt no responsibility one way or another.

Now and then, over the years, Agnes would catch Lily observing her with a speculative expression, and Agnes's own father's manner was increasingly formal in his daughter's company. But Agnes didn't associate either detail with the circumstance of that terrible Fourth of July. It never occurred to her not to agree with her children when they became sad remembering that they didn't have their grandfather Scofield among them. But she really agreed with them out of her understanding of the children's own sincere regret. Although Agnes was genuinely sorry to witness the grief of her mother-in-law and her husband and the children, of Leo Scofield, and George as well, she was never visited with the slightest disquietude about John Scofield's demise.

By the time Dwight and Claytor started back to school in September, the initial shock of John Scofield's death had abated. Audra and Lillian Scofield had returned immediately from Maine, and the rest of the family, of course, had not gone away that summer. The hottest months elapsed while the Scofields adjusted to their new circumstances, and on November 15, 1926, on the morning of little Dwight's eighth birthday, Agnes gave birth to a baby boy. He was named Warren Howard Scofield, after his father, but with a different middle name because Warren didn't want anyone to take to calling his son Junior. And, in fact, the baby was always called Howard simply to avoid confusion.

Just before Christmas, Robert Butler's second volume of poems was published, and he gained a good deal of national attention, although in Washburn, where he was so well known and liked, no one but Lily and Warren had any idea what the poems could mean. They seemed to most of his acquaintances uncharacteristically dark and severe. Agnes had not even had time to read them with the new baby in the house and the household itself to contend with.

In the summer of 1927, the whole family finally did go to Maine, although once again, Lillian and Audra Scofield went up at the beginning of June, and the rest of the family joined them in August. Warren was only able to stay for two weeks, because of various worries about the Company and some complications he was trying to sort out about his father's affairs. But a vacation in Maine became an annual event, and by the time Betts Scofield and Trudy Butler started school it seemed to all the Scofields that they had always gone away for the month of August.

Howard was the happiest of Agnes's children. Even by the time he was three years old he had unwittingly become the family conciliator. He was not as handsome a child as the twins had been at his age, but he had a rakish look, with one eyelid that was slightly "lazy." There wasn't a person in Washburn who wasn't glad to see Howard as he was taken around town on errands with his mother or with Evie McCauliff, who planned to work for Mr. and Mrs. Scofield until she had children of her own. Sometimes Dwight or Claytor would pull Howard along with them in their wagon, and usually Betts would be just behind them, sometimes with Trudy Butler tagging along as well.

As time went on, Agnes Claytor Scofield began to feel that she had managed to do the very thing that she had been sure would elude her. She had been sure of her failure to obtain it since she was a little girl. But she went about her days beginning to believe that she had managed to create a happy family. And she even believed that it would go on forever and ever.

She remained dedicated to the schedule of her days, mustering her forces against any ambush of chaos. It never crossed her mind to consider the possible untrustworthiness of the love of any of the four children of the household. And she was certain that each of those children knew that he or she was unreservedly beloved by at least one other person in the world — that not one of them could outlive her absolute devotion.

This serene elation was a constant in her life during the children's younger years. Whatever arguments or squabbles the children were involved in during any one day seemed vastly unimportant to Agnes by evening, when in the summer, for instance, she and Warren sat out on the porch after the baby was in bed. The other children were generally back at Lily's after supper, where they found a thousand things to do under Lily's guidance.

Warren always sat in the rocking chair with his long legs stretched out in front of him, crossed at the ankles, and Agnes generally settled on the swing and pulled her legs up, sitting sideways to the yard. All along the ridge beyond the verge of trees that marked the end of the property, lights began coming on in the windows of the houses in the new section of town that had gradually grown up to the north of Scofields.

Warren and Agnes sat together during that first wave of summer evening quiet that Agnes always thought of as dogs' hour. The light still sifted palely through the tops of the trees, and each household dog settled down within the boundaries of his own property and spoke across the yards in short bursts of two or three barks delivered perfunctorily, proprietarily, settling the question of territory for this night.

Agnes sat catty-cornered on the swing, swaying now and then by pushing off with her foot. But as the dogs settled in and quieted while their families ate supper, Agnes drew her feet up and lay her cheek down on her arm stretched across the back of the swing. The hour passed from dogs' hour to bird call — the day falling silent with only the chittering, cooing, and chirrups of the settling nuthatches, mourning doves, chickadees, and the occasional jarring, primeval cawing of the crows. Now and then she and Warren would talk about one thing or another, but all the urgency went out of whatever they might discuss just then.

Agnes would sit and look out at the darkening yard, thinking each moment that she ought to call the children home from Lily's, or check on the baby. But usually she stayed on, waiting for the dark to fall. And then she and Warren often sat on still, watching as the lightning bugs drifted up from the grasses, through the dark green of the trees like sparks. Eventually the fireflies no longer flickered, and the sky showed a few stars, and the night turned a pale orchid color against all the variations of green and brown vegetation and the gray white houses of Scofields. And always there was a moment when it seemed to Agnes that it wasn't the case that darkness fell; it was really that the light, all the voices, any complaints — the doings of any particular day — slowly evaporated, leaching upward into the wide, absorbent sky.